Issues of Political Marketing

Casting light on the evolution of political marketing in Central and Eastern Europe (CEE), this book delivers an intriguing snapshot into both the sophistication of campaign strategies and the triumphs and trials facing democratic progress in this increasingly complex political landscape.

Free elections, following the fall of the communist regimes in CEE, brought the need to attract voters through election campaigns and therefore, races involving political marketing began, and electoral campaigns in CEE began to resemble those of Western democracies. Most political parties operating in the region became quickly accustomed to the new approach to politics and a broad range of political marketing tools and techniques. This edited volume focuses on political campaign professionalization in general (in Lithuania) and in TV spots (in Poland), and celebritization (in Croatia). The second part of the volume focuses on struggles of opposition in authoritarian regime (in Russia), whether Facebook can serve as an effective political marketing tool in an illiberal context (in Hungary), and the communication and campaigning of authoritarian presidents in a hybrid regime (in Serbia). All of them are recent case studies.

The chapters in this volume were originally published as a special issue of the *Journal of Political Marketing*

Miloš Gregor is Assistant Professor in the Department of Political Science, Faculty of Social Studies at Masaryk University. His main research lies in political marketing, political communication, and propaganda and disinformation analysis.

Otto Eibl is the Head of the Department of Political Science at the Faculty of Social Studies and a researcher at the International Institute of Political Science, both at Masaryk University. His research focuses on political communication, branding, and political marketing.

Bruce I. Newman is Professor of marketing and Wicklander Fellow in Business Ethics in the Department of Marketing at the Kellstadt Graduate School of Business at DePaul University, Chicago, USA. Dr. Newman is the author/editor of several books and articles on political marketing, most notably, *A Reseach Agenda for Political Marketing* (2022 with Todd P. Newman), *Brand* (2018 with Todd P. Newman), *The Marketing Revolution in Politics* (2016), and *The Marketing of the President* (1994). He is the Editor-in-Chief of the *Journal of Political Marketing* and former advisor to the Clinton White House in 1995–96.

Issues of Political Marketing

East European Perspective

Edited by
Miloš Gregor, Otto Eibl and Bruce I. Newman

LONDON AND NEW YORK

First published 2025
by Routledge
4 Park Square, Milton Park, Abingdon, Oxon OX14 4RN

and by Routledge
605 Third Avenue, New York, NY 10158

Routledge is an imprint of the Taylor & Francis Group, an informa business

Introduction–Chapter 6 © 2025 Taylor & Francis
Preface © 2025 Miloš Gregor, Otto Eibl and Bruce I. Newman.

All rights reserved. No part of this book may be reprinted or reproduced or utilised in any form or by any electronic, mechanical, or other means, now known or hereafter invented, including photocopying and recording, or in any information storage or retrieval system, without permission in writing from the publishers.

Trademark notice: Product or corporate names may be trademarks or registered trademarks, and are used only for identification and explanation without intent to infringe.

British Library Cataloguing in Publication Data
A catalogue record for this book is available from the British Library

ISBN13: 978-1-032-66495-8 (hbk)
ISBN13: 978-1-032-66496-5 (pbk)
ISBN13: 978-1-032-66497-2 (ebk)

DOI: 10.4324/9781032664972

Typeset in Minion Pro
by Newgen Publishing UK

Publisher's Note
The publisher accepts responsibility for any inconsistencies that may have arisen during the conversion of this book from journal articles to book chapters, namely the inclusion of journal terminology.

Disclaimer
Every effort has been made to contact copyright holders for their permission to reprint material in this book. The publishers would be grateful to hear from any copyright holder who is not here acknowledged and will undertake to rectify any errors or omissions in future editions of this book.

Contents

Citation Information vi
Notes on Contributors viii
Preface ix

Introduction: Professionalization and Democratic Backsliding? Political Campaigning in Central and Eastern Europe 1
Miloš Gregor and Otto Eibl

1 Political Campaign Professionalization in Lithuanian Elections 8
Ingrida Unikaitė-Jakuntavičienė

2 Professionalization of Campaign Communication beyond Communication Forms. An Analysis of Poland's Political Spots 28
Mariusz Kolczyński and Marek Mazur

3 "Send in the Clowns": The Rise of Celebrity Populism in Croatia and Its Implications for Political Marketing 43
Marijana Grbeša and Berto Šalaj

4 A Rumbling from Below? Opposition Party Rebranding, Regional Elections, and Transforming the Regime in Russia 58
John Ishiyama and Mikhail Rybalko

5 Facebook as a Political Marketing Tool in an Illiberal Context. Mapping Political Advertising Activity on Facebook during the 2019 Hungarian European Parliament and Local Election Campaigns 74
Márton Bene, Márton Petrekanics and Mátyás Bene

6 Electoral Political Communication in the Post-Communist Hybrid Regime – The Case of Serbia 2020 93
Dušan Vučićević and Siniša Atlagić

Index 108

Citation Information

The chapters in this book were originally published in the *Journal of Political Marketing*, volume 22, issue 3–4 (2023). When citing this material, please use the original page numbering for each article, as follows:

Introduction
Professionalization and Democratic Backsliding? Political Campaigning in Central and Eastern Europe
Miloš Gregor and Otto Eibl
Journal of Political Marketing, volume 22, issue 3–4 (2023), pp. 175–181

Chapter 1
Political Campaign Professionalization in Lithuanian Elections Ingrida Unikaitė-Jakuntavičienė
Journal of Political Marketing, volume 22, issue 3–4 (2023), pp. 182–201

Chapter 2
Professionalization of Campaign Communication beyond Communication Forms. An Analysis of Poland's Political Spots
Mariusz Kolczyński and Marek Mazur
Journal of Political Marketing, volume 22, issue 3–4 (2023), pp. 202–216

Chapter 3
"Send in the Clowns": The Rise of Celebrity Populism in Croatia and Its Implications for Political Marketing
Marijana Grbeša and Berto Šalaj
Journal of Political Marketing, volume 22, issue 3–4 (2023), pp. 217–231

Chapter 4
A Rumbling from Below? Opposition Party Rebranding, Regional Elections, and Transforming the Regime in Russia
John Ishiyama and Mikhail Rybalko
Journal of Political Marketing, volume 22, issue 3–4 (2023), pp. 232–247

Chapter 5
Facebook as a Political Marketing Tool in an Illiberal Context. Mapping Political Advertising Activity on Facebook during the 2019 Hungarian European Parliament and Local Election Campaigns
Márton Bene, Márton Petrekanics and Mátyás Bene
Journal of Political Marketing, volume 22, issue 3–4 (2023), pp. 248–266

Chapter 6
Electoral Political Communication in the Post-Communist Hybrid Regime – The Case of Serbia 2020
Dušan Vučićević and Siniša Atlagić
Journal of Political Marketing, volume 22, issue 3–4 (2023), pp. 267–281

For any permission-related enquiries please visit:
www.tandfonline.com/page/help/permissions

Notes on Contributors

Siniša Atlagić is Professor and a Department of Journalism and Communication, Faculty of Political Sciences of the State University of Belgrade. He is a specialist in the field of theoretical and empirical research of political communication and political marketing.

Márton Bene (PhD) is a senior research fellow at the Centre for Social Sciences, Hungarian Academy of Sciences Centre of Excellence, and an assistant professor at the Faculty of Law, Eötvös Loránd University (ELTE). His research interests are in political communication, social media and politics, and political behavior.

Mátyás Bene is Researcher at the 3D Center of the University of Pécs.

Otto Eibl is Head of the Department of Political Science, Faculty of Social Studies at Masaryk University. His research focuses on political communication, branding, and political marketing.

Marijana Grbeša is Full Professor at the Faculty of Political Science, University of Zagreb. Her research interests include political communication, political marketing, populism studies, and mass media research.

Miloš Gregor is Assistant Professor in the Department of Political Science, Faculty of Social Studies at Masaryk University. His main research lies in political marketing, political communication, and propaganda and disinformation analysis.

John Ishiyama is Professor in the Department of Political Science at the University of North Texas. His research focus is on comparative politics, especially democratization and political parties in post-communist European politics.

Mariusz Kolczyński is Associate Professor at the Institute of Journalism and Media Communication at the Faculty of Social Sciences, University of Silesia.

Marek Mazur is Associate Professor at the Institute of Journalism and Media Communication at the Faculty of Social Sciences, University of Silesia.

Márton Petrekanics studies political science at the Corvinus University of Budapest.

Mikhail Rybalko is Associate Professor of history at the Irkutsk State University.

Berto Šalaj is Full Professor at the Faculty of Political Science, University of Zagreb. His research interests include populism studies, and democracy studies.

Ingrida Unikaitė-Jakuntavičienė is Associate Professor in the Department of Political Science, Faculty of Political Science and Diplomacy, Vytautas Magnus University, Lithuania.

Dušan Vučićević is Assistant Professor in the Department of Political Science, Faculty of Political Sciences of the State University of Belgrade. His research interests include elections, political marketing, and institution research.

Preface

Political marketing is an interdisciplinary field that encompasses political science, economics, sociology, psychology, media, and other related fields. Its goal is – in short and in general – to influence voters' behavior in favor of a political party or candidate who pays for the campaign. From today's perspective, it is nothing new or surprising that political parties and candidates use advanced marketing techniques to carry out their campaigns, to deliver their messages to the right segments of the audience, and to win the hearts and minds of prospective voters.

However, during the whole 20th century, the approach of political parties to marketing politics changed quite dramatically. Together with the (technological) changes in the media sphere, campaigns became more and more sophisticated and financially demanding. These changes were perceived as evolutionary, at least in the West, where liberal democracies had a rather strong tradition. However, in Central and Eastern Europe, the political and societal development was different. The whole societies were suffocated by the authoritarian (sometimes even totalitarian) rule of the barbaric communist regimes. After their collapse, the respective states and societies had to adapt to the new situation – the newly acquired freedom brought up new challenges. To restore democratic institutions in the first place, of course, but also to teach political actors, media, and citizens how to enjoy and indulge in the new rights and responsibilities. A part of these revolutionary changes was learning and adopting marketing techniques in politics. Political parties were forced into learning by doing, often with the help of marketers and experts from abroad. Indeed, since the 1990s, professional election campaigns have been mainly carried out by American consultants due to the lack of a foundation in regions previously devastated by non-democratic regimes. This led to a boom in professional political marketing and local political consultants afterward.

In addition to the development of practice, (with a certain delay in time) political marketing has also become a popular subject of research and teaching at universities. Particularly in the late 20th and early 21st century, many universities began offering courses dedicated to political marketing, covering topics such as the personalization of politics and campaigns, advanced marketing techniques in politics, branding, effective persuasive communication, social media management for politics, and other tools deployed in political campaigns. Universities in Central and Eastern Europe were no exception. Two of the editors of this collection, Otto Eibl and Miloš Gregor, are perfect examples of such practice. They both teach at Masaryk University, a pioneer in the study of the political marketing discipline in the region. However, the teaching of political marketing at that time relied solely on texts by American (Pippa Norris and Bruce I. Newman among others), British (Jennifer Lees-Marshment, Heather Savigny, Robert Ormrod, Darren Lilleker, Nicholas O'Shaughnessy, Dominic Wring, and many others), and, to a lesser extent, German (Stephan Henneberg) or French (Philippe Maarek) authors. It is important to note that, similarly as political campaigns in the 1990s relied on foreign consultants because of the absence of domestic experts, even academia lacked scholars analyzing political campaigns and marketing. Studies of foreign authors typically focused on their countries of origin. There were only a few texts available on political marketing in Central and Eastern Europe. However, even that changed quickly. Scholars from Poland (especially Wojciech Cwalina, Andrzej Falkowski, and Robert Wiszniowski) were among the first who challenged this notion, and we were pleased to support their efforts later.

In 2012, one of the first Czech political marketing textbooks was published by teachers and students of Masaryk University. To celebrate the 30 years of the fall of the Iron Curtain, we decided to edit the book *Thirty Years of Political Campaigning in Central and Eastern Europe*, which was published in 2019. This comprehensive edited volume systematically maps and describes the development of political marketing in the region since 1989. It is the first and only publication of its kind – thanks to its scope, students and scholars of political marketing have a reliable source that reflects the history and development of political marketing and campaigns in the discussed regions. However, as the field of professionalizing election campaigns and political marketing is constantly evolving, we felt it necessary to include some of the latest trends that have emerged since 2019. To achieve this, we have enlisted the help of Bruce I. Newman, Editor-in-Chief of the *Journal of Political Marketing*, who has contributed to a special issue focused on the Central and Eastern European region in the journal. Bruce I. Newman has a strong connection to this region due to his long-term publishing collaboration, particularly with his Polish colleagues. We are pleased to introduce the special issue transmitted into this edited volume.

Recently, there have been several significant events that have had a profound impact on political events and election campaigns. It is important to maintain objectivity and avoid subjective evaluations in discussing these issues. Of course, the migration crisis, the coronavirus pandemic, the economic crisis, and especially the Russian aggression against Ukraine are frequently discussed in election campaigns. All of these topics can be strong emotional triggers and have the potential to divide and polarize entire societies, both in the East and the West. Political parties often try to gain an advantage by exploiting the misfortunes of others through fearmongering. These are challenges that Europe, the wider region, and the world must confront. And we have to carefully watch how political actors deal with these issues.

However, this book does not focus on these urgent issues especially for two reasons. Firstly, the call for abstracts on the special issue was published before the outbreak of the coronavirus pandemic in 2020. Secondly, apart from the pandemic that has significantly limited the contact form of election campaigns, these events affecting political development, the distribution of political forces, and the salience of topics in campaigns do not have a significant influence on the form of election campaigns and the use of political marketing tools. It is worth noting that propaganda and disinformation are more prevalent now than before (also because of the proliferation of modern digital communication means, especially the barely regulated environment of social networks). We can witness a larger part of campaigns moving online. However, these phenomena are not exclusively connected to the current crises but rather a longer-term development that we have been witnessing for more than the past ten years. The presented publication offers thought-provoking ideas and views on campaigns and political marketing in Central and Eastern Europe in the times before all the abovementioned crises struck. It consists of six case studies from six countries. These studies are presented in a framing chapter that outlines two seemingly contradictory lines of development in the region. However, as you read further, you will see that these phenomena often go hand in hand and their contradiction is only apparent.

We hope you find this publication both pleasant and inspiring.

Sincerely, Miloš Gregor, Otto Eibl,
and Bruce I. Newman.

Introduction: Professionalization and Democratic Backsliding? Political Campaigning in Central and Eastern Europe

Miloš Gregor and Otto Eibl

Over three decades have passed since the fall of the communist regimes in Central and Eastern Europe (CEE). Alongside these events, as part of a third wave of global democratization (Huntington 1993), free elections appeared after decades under non-democratic regimes wherein elections were just a façade and did not constitute the free choice of political representation. Free elections brought the need to attract voters through election campaigns. While these campaigns and political marketing already had a long tradition in Western democracies and were both a developed political discipline and a lucrative business, the emerging or renewed democracies were inexperienced in this field. Nevertheless, races involving political marketing began, and this gap was soon closed as electoral campaigns in CEE began to resemble those of Western democracies.

An eagerness for newly acquired freedom and a significant level of amateurism characterized the campaigns at the beginning of the 1990s. However, by the beginning of the twenty-first century, this was rather the opposite (Eibl and Gregor 2019). Most political parties operating in the region became quickly accustomed to the new approach to politics and a broad range of political marketing tools and techniques. Campaign materials are now predominantly professionally designed; parties organize media stunts to attract media attention; candidates are trained in rhetoric and, generally, on appearing in public; and campaign strategies have become less intuitive and more data-based. In other words, over the last 15–20 years, we have witnessed relatively rapid campaign management and communication professionalization.

However, that was not the only development observable in the region. Many scholars (Haerpfer 2003; Papaioannou and Siourounis 2008; Fagan and Kopecký 2020) have described and analyzed the democratization process in CEE, the evolution of new or renewed party systems, and the changing dynamics in relations among voters and political parties. In some of the region's countries, the democratization process was not completed; in others, it seemed finished at first sight, but upon closer examination, the stability, and quality of the democracy were somewhat fuzzier. The fragility of young and new democracies was exposed and constantly tested. Indeed, scholars (Bermeo 2016; Cianetti, Dawson, and Hanley 2018; Vachudova 2020) often noted democratic backsliding[1] in the discussed region.

Such a process can take the form of a revolution or even a violent coup, which, to be fair, is not common in the region. However, it can also occur through gradual changes applied by democratically elected representatives with autocratic tendencies who purposefully undermine the principles of liberal democracy. Based on several measurements, such as those from the Freedom House Economist Intelligence Unit, the Polity Project, and V-Dem, Haggard and Kaufman (2021, 13) identified 16 countries worldwide that had had a democratic backslide, six of which are from the CEE region: Hungary, Macedonia, Poland, Russia, Serbia, and Ukraine. The course, extent, and specific form of the backsliding vary from country to country, but what all of these cases have in common is their impact on elections, election campaigns, and political communication in general.

There are many ways in which an autocratic politician in charge may have an impact on competition within the electoral market, including restrictions on the number of parties, distortion of electoral rules and legislation in favor of the ruling party, misuse of the police and abuse of political opponents to control the media and its content, and the spread of a "right and only" interpretation of the world. In such an environment, it is particularly challenging for opposition formations that are allowed to exist and operate to be seen, heard, and perceived as a viable alternative to the actual government. In other words, when the government decides to cheat at the institutional level, it is hard to "really" challenge it, fight a biased media, and face all the technocratic obstacles. However, even in these states, political parties and candidates acquire and get used to the media logic of politics and use a broad range of advanced marketing and/or communication tools to approach and persuade their target groups. The fact that governing parties are taking clear advantage of their position does not imply that they do not understand the need and necessity for professional communication. Nevertheless, for political challengers—opposition candidates and parties—such conditions represent a severe and often unconquerable hurdle: How to approach election campaigns in an environment that is not equal, fair, or transparent? Even the best marketing strategy and well-chosen media mix will not necessarily guarantee satisfactory outcomes under such conditions.

In countries that are considered established and more or less stable democracies, the right strategy and attitude toward politics might play a significant role. Parties position themselves on the market and compete with others over competencies, attention, and, primarily, the votes of their target groups. Nevertheless, even these democratic countries show signs of slow and sneaky (but visible) democratic backsliding (Hungary and Poland being the most visible examples). The intensity of those unfavorable trends depends on the level of political culture in the given country and the party system's stability. As we can see, stability might be seen as an indicator of voter satisfaction with the performance of politicians, political parties, and the whole political system in general. If the level of trust in government or political parties drops, voters sooner or later desire new parties. In other words, the political market (semi-)opens, which creates windows of opportunity for new challenges to the "old" party (or even political) system. The semi-open character of political markets attracts numerous entrepreneurs and populists of all sorts who sense the opportunity to seize power.

Moreover, in the last couple of years, we have witnessed the emergence of numerous political parties whose selling point was rooted almost solely in their "newness" or in their effort to purify politics within the respective country (Sikk 2012, Hanley 2011, Bustikova and Guasti 2017, Havlík 2019, Kim 2021). Very little is needed to gain a substantial advantage over "old" or "traditional" parties. The "nonpolitical" character of these newcomers or their status as "politically intact" is something the old simply cannot offer. At the same time, at least some of these parties enjoy the "luxury" of not being based on any ideology. That provides them comfortable access to wider groups of voters and creates an unprecedented space for maneuvering across the left-right scale. Of course, the "nonideological" nature of their politics allows them to take positions on political issues based not on any set of solid values and beliefs but on popular demand. This is the moment when political marketing strategies, tactics, and techniques come into play; these newcomers recognize the need for and power of carefully crafted and meticulously disseminated messages.

Looking at the development of the party system in CEE countries (or of Europe in general) over the last 10–15 years, we see several examples of new parties that are very often labeled populist, entrepreneurial, or both (Hloušek, Kopeček, and Vodová 2020). Besides their ideological flexibility, such parties are also characterized by little or no internal democracy, an anti-elite rhetoric, and a high degree of personalization. Their top representatives are often persons with rich experience from various fields, such as business or even entertainment, trying to transfer their success from elsewhere to politics. They are goal and performance-oriented, and they manage parties in the same way as their firms—democratic values, deliberation, and inclusion are yielded to efficient governance. They have resigned any collective representation, and their political offer only meets the demands wrought by dissatisfied voters (Hloušek, Kopeček, and Vodová 2020). At the same time and in this context, they care about their image considerably, and they sometimes enjoy and support their status as celebrities. Furthermore, pollsters and marketers are becoming superior to partisans, and intra-party life is very limited. In extreme cases, partisans have only a limited opportunity to show signs of loyalty to the leaders during party conventions.

Although their leaders play a crucial role and present themselves as capable and competent problem-solvers or even visionaries, in reality, they are stuck in a state which could be described as "a follower mentality" (Ormrod and Henneberg 2010). Their strategic approach to marketing and communication can be described as "tactical populist" (Ormrod and Henneberg 2010), which means they have a short-term, goal-oriented approach to gaining and maintaining voter support, that is, to ensure that they closely and precisely track and trace their target groups' opinions and desires. When they know what the audience wants, they simply do their best (i.e., adjust their positions to the most salient issues at any given time) to satisfy their demands and deliver. We could (and should), of course, ask if such an approach to politics is sustainable over a longer period. Although there are partial results as to the effect on voter turnout in CEE (Leininger and Meijers 2021), we still do not have enough data and evidence to answer this question. However, the unfortunate events of the last couple of years have revealed that at least some of the "new political elites" are not able to handle a large-scale crisis. During the global COVID-19 pandemic, many politicians (not only but especially on the populist end of the political spectrum) did not perform well, regardless of their communication (Lilleker et al. 2021). Their poor performance was partly due to the nature of the crisis, which presented novel challenges. Additionally, they started losing the public's trust—they had to stop following the "will of the majority" and introduce restrictive measures that were not popular among voters. Moreover, politicians struggled to clearly explain what they were doing and why. The result was that populist leaders failed to deliver their promises of effective governance and quick solutions. Society could see that when facing similar challenges in most countries (if not all) around the world, the performance of populists was not better than that of "traditional politicians"—and in many cases, were worse. This damaged their image as popular leaders and forced their PR teams to work hard to restore it. The pandemic left populations more polarized than ever before, with anti-systematic and anti-democratic political forces rising in prominence.

Even after the pandemic, the general situation remains bleak. Russian aggression toward Ukraine, causing an energy crisis and inflation in many European countries, has created new divisions and cleavages, leaving people uncertain and threatened. Crises create significant pressure on many political actors, including populists. They are no longer solely competing amongst themselves but must also face new nonparliamentary, anti-systematic political forces and must combat disinformation and hybrid threats from abroad. The outcome of this struggle is uncertain, but it appears that some of the more established populists are changing their strategies, adopting the rhetoric and style of radical political forces, and becoming even more irresponsible in their competition for voters. The situation on the political market is becoming increasingly complex and challenging. Effective and efficient communication could be one of the keys (but not the only one) to resolving some of the current issues. Another crucial factor could be strong leadership and the courage of top representatives among relevant (democratic) parties. Here, we must ask again if populists are capable of offering and delivering such qualities. While we doubt this, we are also not witnessing their substantial decline. The truth is that whole societies remain divided and polarized, creating a very challenging environment. It seems that the (perceived) performance of the "new politicians" is better in "calm periods" but is insufficient in times of crisis. And this might be the long-awaited opportunity for "traditional parties" to restore their credit among voters (or open the political market to new political parties). However, populist appeals are not only fueled by the COVID-19 pandemic and Russian aggression against Ukraine. These two crises do not erase the problems that countries had to deal with before these turbulent years. Both unfortunate events prolong and deepen trends and issues present in societies and political environments years before. Where populists had a strong position, they were usually able to confirm and strengthen it further.

Besides (a lack of) values and the follower's logic, the populist style of politics brings a characteristic approach to the organizational aspect of politics and political communication. This new "style of politics" creates more and further opportunities for political consultants, and it forces political parties and candidates to professionalize their campaigns and communication (Strömbäck, Mitrook, and Kiousis 2010, Strömbäck and Kiousis 2014, Tenscher et al. 2016). To do so, business approaches are applied: centralization of communication, the absence of internal discussion accompanied by a top-down approach to decision-making, central control of the nomination process during intra-party primaries (if there are any), and direct influence of the party leader over the personnel policy of the party. Such processes are established with the intention being to control the party and its image. From this perspective, political parties are intended and perceived by their leaders as co-brands as opposed to viable independent entities. They serve their leaders, helping them initiate and maintain the relationship with voters. These politicians, thus, often gain the status of celebrities, who are then the centerpieces of political life (at least for the party and its voters). After all, celebritization (Street 2004, Lewis 2010, Wheeler 2013) is, together with personalization (Sara and Skogerbø 2013), another observable phenomenon (and not only) in the CEE region.

The lack of vision and focus on short-term goals are, of course, one of the many differences between them and old/traditional parties, which are often rooted in a set of values and beliefs stemming from more or less traditional political ideology. That makes them a little bit more "predictable." These "older" parties are limited in their actions by their ideological foundations and are closer to something we could describe as "convinced ideologists" (Ormrod and Henneberg 2010). However, we must bear in mind that Ormrod and Henneberg work with ideal types, and, in reality, we have to perceive their categories as defining a continuum. Thus, we are not saying that old parties must not use any marketing techniques or hire pollsters, political consultants, or strategists. The opposite is true: They must know what voters want to succeed in an extremely crowded political market. Nevertheless, their space for ideological maneuvering is very, very limited.

Of course, not every entrepreneurial or populist party is the same. Not every newcomer (i.e., wealthy and successful businessman) in politics wants to dismantle the whole political system and create something new. Through their actions, however, they transform the party/political arena into a market with voters understood as political consumers managed by slick political marketing. The personalization and mediatization of politics play into the hands of those able to deal with voters primarily as consumers of political products and related advertising activities. In some cases, blurring the behavioral differences between actors in the political system—the entrepreneurial or "nonpolitical" leader in their role as almighty savior—and a market economy threaten the tradition of liberal democracy as it was (re)built in the 1990s.

These are some of the issues we identify in today's CEE countries. Some are rather characteristic of the discussed region, and others are also visible across Western democracies. The saliency of the processes mentioned above as well as the issues correspond to the attention of political scientists and related scholars. Some issues are well described (i.e., mediatization, personalization, celebritization, populist communication), documented, and explained; others, however, lie on the fringes of research interest (campaign communication in semi-authoritarian states).

In this issue, we have collected a series of papers dealing with at least some of the aforementioned issues. In a sense, they represent a bridge between the known and the unknown and shed some light on current affairs in political marketing and campaign communication in CEE. We can divide this special issue of the *Journal of Political Marketing* into two parts: The first consists of case studies dealing with the professionalization of campaign communication, while the second bears witness to how difficult it is to succeed in a state that does not treat all parties equally.

Professionalization of political communication in CEE

In her paper, *Unikaitė-Jakuntavičienė* analyzes the development and professionalization of political marketing and the expenses of electoral campaigns in Lithuania from 1996 to 2020. The analysis is based on interviews with 46 political consultants and politicians and reviews of party spending in parliamentary campaigns. The author shows a trend valid for Lithuania and many countries in Central and Eastern Europe: campaigns have become an integral and essential part of elections and their professionalization over time while, at the same time, campaign spending has risen because of inflation, professionalization, and ad expenses.

Kolczyński and Mazur also deal with professionalization; however, they focus only on part of political campaigning—TV spots, and specifically, spots deployed in Polish parliamentary election campaigns from 2005 to 2019. The authors examine the speed of professionalization and analyze the personalization of political communication and the proportion of valence and position issue messages.

Grbeša's and Šalaj's paper aims to analyze the phenomenon of celebritization. The authors employ a modified concept of celebrity populism that combines the celebrity politician's communication style and the populist rhetoric of politicians. The paper's analysis consists of three case studies from Croatia and shows the way candidates take advantage of new opportunities that social media, especially Facebook, give them when communicating with supporters and voters. Celebrity politics is usually shown and analyzed as regards successful candidates; therefore, it may seem that this communication style determines electoral success. A similar pattern can be seen when focusing on populism. Grbeša and Šalaj show, however, that even deploying communication strategies with a combination of populism does not automatically bring these politicians the desired outcomes.

Party communication under semi-authoritarian rule

In their paper, *Ishiyama and Rybalko* elaborate on how (re)branding in regional election campaigns can be perceived as an opportunity for the opposition parties of authoritarian regimes, in this case, Russia's. The long-term suppression of political opposition at the national level and its ostracism from the center of political events mean that voters often cannot see an alternative to the ruling power. However, in regions further away from the center, opposition parties may grasp the opportunity to transform and rebrand themselves precisely as a voter-relevant alternative. The paper compares the rebranding of the Communist Party of the Russian Federation (CPRF) before the 2018 regional election campaigns in Russia to the National Action Party (PAN) in Mexico.

Bene, Petrekanics, and Bene focus on Hungary and second-order election campaigns in 2019. They aim to learn whether Facebook can serve as an effective political marketing tool in an illiberal context. The subject of their research is political advertising on Facebook, which is supposed to represent a channel through which opposition parties can communicate with their audiences in a country where mainstream communication channels are either formerly controlled or informally influenced by the governing party. The authors argue that social media raises their importance, especially in a country where information and the media environment are affected by the state or governing power's interventions. The paper also deals with the current topic of election expenses for online advertising and effective targeting.

Vučićević and Atlagić deal with the communication and campaigning of authoritarian presidents in a hybrid regime—the case in Serbia. The authors compare Milošević's and Vučić's styles of communication, perceived as a blurred area between political marketing and propaganda. Moreover, the paper describes how the COVID-19 pandemic is reflected in this campaign management style. While the example of Hungary shows how social media can be an opportunity for the opposition in a biased media environment, the Serbian example shows how government parties and candidates can control the media and media coverage with the help of, for example, online election meetings.

Of course, the list of these papers does not represent or cover all the processes observable in the region. Many countries with noteworthy and dynamic development in election campaigns and the use of political marketing are not included; moreover, the list of areas and spheres in which these changes occur are not exhaustive. However, we believe that the papers in this special issue represent a cross-section of broader phenomena that we can observe in Central and Eastern Europe, and they are not just isolated cases. The special issue does not provide answers to the further direction of development in the region. Rather, it is a somewhat open-ended question, providing insight into its current state. Nevertheless, we believe the issue can provide readers with exciting findings and provoke them into examining some of the processes further.

Note

1. In this context, backsliding can be perceived as an "erosion of democratic institutions, rules and norms that results from the actions of duly elected governments, typically driven by an autocratic leader" (Haggard and Kaufman 2021, 1).

ORCID

Miloš Gregor http://orcid.org/0000-0002-0796-7121
Otto Eibl http://orcid.org/0000-0002-4396-3136

References

Bermeo, N. 2016. "On Democracy Backsliding." *Journal of Democracy* 27 (1):5–19. https://doi.org/10.1353/jod.2016.0012
Bustikova, L., and P. Guasti. 2017. "The Illiberal Turn or Swerve in Central Europe?" *Politics and Governance* 5 (4):166–76. https://doi.org/10.17645/pag.v5i4.1156
Cianetti, L., J. Dawson, and S. Hanley. 2018. "Rethinking "Democratic Backsliding" in Central and Eastern Europe – Looking beyond Hungary and Poland." *East European Politics* 34 (3):243–56. https://doi.org/10.1080/21599165.2018.1491401
Eibl, O., and M. Gregor (Eds.) 2019. *Thirty Years of Political Campaigning in Central and Eastern Europe*. Cham: Palgrave Macmillan.
Fagan, A., and P. Kopecký. 2020. *The Routledge Handbook of East European Politics*. New York and London: Routledge.
Haerpfer, C. W. 2003. *Democracy and Enlargement in Post-Communist Europe*. New York and London: Routledge.
Haggard, S., and R. Kaufman. 2021. *Backsliding. Democratic Regress in the Contemporary World*. Cambridge: Cambridge University Press.
Hanley, S. 2011. "Dynamics of New Party Formation in the Czech Republic 1996-2010: Looking for the Origins of a Political Earthquake." *Czech Sociological Review* 47 (1):115–136.
Havlík, V. 2019. "Technocratic Populism and Political Illiberalism in Central Europe." *Problems of Post-Communism* 66 (6) :369–84. https://doi.org/10.1080/10758216.2019.1580590
Hloušek, V., L. Kopeček, and P. Vodová. 2020. *The Rise of Entrepreneurial Parties in European Politics*. Cham: Palgrave Macmillan.
Huntington, S. P. 1993. *The Third Wave: Democratization in the Late 20th Century*. Oklahoma: University of Oklahoma Press.
Kim, S. 2021. *Discourse, Hegemony, and Populism in the Visegrád Four*. New York and London: Routledge.
Leininger, A., and M. J. Meijers. 2021. "Do Populist Parties Increase Voter Turnout? Evidence from over 40 Years of Electoral History in 31 European Countries." *Political Studies* 69 (3) :665–85. https://doi.org/10.1177/0032321720923257
Lilleker, D., I. A. Coman, M. Gregor, and E. Novelli. 2021. "*Political Communication and COVID-19*." *Governance and Rhetoric in Times of Crisis*. New York and London: Routledge.

Ormrod, R. P., and S. C. M. Henneberg. 2010. "Strategic Political Postures and Political Market Orientation: Towards an Integrated Concept of Political Marketing Strategy." *Journal of Political Marketing* 9 (4) :294–313. https://doi.org/10.1080/15377857.2010.518106

Papaioannou, E., and G. Siourounis. 2008. "Democratization and Growth." *The Economical Journal* 118 (532):1520–51.

Sara, G., and E. Skogerbø. 2013. "Personalized Campaigns in Party-Centred Politics. Twitter and Facebook as Arenas for Political Communication." *Information, Communication & Society* 16 (5):757–74. https://doi.org/10.1080/1369118X.2013.782330

Sikk, A. 2012. "Newness as a winning formula for new political parties.." *Party Politics* 18 (4):465–486. https://doi.org/10.1177/1354068810389631

Street, J. 2004. "Celebrity Politicians: Popular Culture and Political Representation." *The British Journal of Politics and International Relations* 6 (4):435–52. https://doi.org/10.1111/j.1467-856X.2004.00149.x

Strömbäck, J., M. A. Mitrook, and S. Kiousis. 2010. "Bridging Two Schools of Thought: Application of Public Relation Theory to Political Marketing." *Journal of Political Marketing* 9 (1–2):73–92. https://doi.org/10.1080/15377850903472547

Strömbäck, J., and S. Kiousis. 2014. "Strategic Political Communication in Election Campaigns." In: Reinemann, C. (Ed.). *Political Communication*. Berlin and Boston: De Gruyter Mouton, 109–28.

Tenscher, J., K. Koc-Michalska, D. G. Lilleker, J. Mykkänen, A. S. Walter, A. Findor, C. Jalali, and J. Róka. 2016. "The Professionals Speak: Practitioners' Perspectives on Professional Election Campaigning." *European Journal of Communication* 31 (2):95–119. https://doi.org/10.1177/0267323115612212

Vachudova, M. A. 2020. "Ethnopopulism and Democratic Backsliding in Central Europe." *East European Politcs* 36 (3):318–40.

Wheeler, M. 2013. *Celebrity Politics*. Cambridge: Polity Press.

Political Campaign Professionalization in Lithuanian Elections

Ingrida Unikaitė-Jakuntavičienė

ABSTRACT
The article analyzes the extent to which the professionalization of Lithuanian political campaigns has changed over the last 30 years. To achieve this, the article employs two main methods. First, it reviews existing research on election campaign professionalization. Second, it presents the findings from a case study of Lithuanian political campaigns. The analysis draws on data from interviews with PR professionals and politicians conducted over the past two decades (46 interviews). The analysis also includes a data review of party spending in parliamentary campaigns. Through these methods, the analysis finds that both candidates and professional political consultants increasingly view political campaigns as important. Professional consultants play a significant role in campaign preparation and management in all parties, with major functions implemented by external campaign professionals being related to marketing strategies and communication management. Furthermore, contemporary Lithuanian political campaigns are often permanent and centralized, using a variety of marketing tools and instruments to research the electorate and prepare advertising campaigns and messages. The study concludes that Lithuanian election campaigns are gradually becoming more professionalized across all parties. However, the degree of professionalization varies depending on the financial and human resources available to specific party campaigns.

Introduction

In recent decades, electoral politics have experienced many changes: party identification, attachment, and membership have fallen; electoral volatility has increased; voters have appeared who are against political parties or are more critical of candidates and parties; political parties, instead of thinking about their ideologies, are more oriented toward product and sales (Mair, Müller, and Plasser 2004; Lees-Marshment 2001; Lees-Marshment 2009; Norris 1997; Wring 1996; Webb, Farrell, and Holliday 2002; Magin et al. 2017). Accordingly, we currently face the emergence of a new type of politics—*consumption politics*—and the growing importance of political marketing in election campaigns. This tendency is increasing (Lees-Marshment 2009a, b, 1), offering political parties and candidates a new way of campaigning.

As Lees-Marshment and Lilleker (2005, 7) define it, "Political marketing is about political organizations […] adapting techniques (such as market research and product design) and concepts (such as the desire to satisfy voter demands) originally used in the business world to help them achieve their goals." Political actors identify the needs of their potential supporters and attempt to meet those demands. Therefore, political actors need to be more responsive to their market and voters.

The use of political marketing is closely related with a process of campaign professionalization, which encompasses the growing importance of professional campaign management by including professional political consultants and PR experts (who do not belong to the party) more actively in election campaigns; increasing the required budgets for survey-based campaigns and the growing use of multiple communication channels (mass media, electronic media, and social media) in campaign communication (Plasser 2002, 244–248; Farell 2002); and the centralization of campaigns within political parties and permanent campaigning seeking to establish an interactive and individualized relationship between politicians and voters by using a marketing-oriented strategy (Lisi 2013). This global transformation in the nature and character of election campaigns has affected the rather new European democracies such as that of Lithuania.

The country's election campaign style has changed over the last three decades. The major factor influencing these changes has been a democratization process encouraging active competition between political parties and candidates and a modernization process offering a variety of new technologies and communication tools for campaigning. This study suggests that the changes are closely related to the increasing campaign professionalization as well. The first signs of professional campaigning were seen in Lithuania in the 1996 parliamentary elections, with larger political parties already having the possibility to involve professional political consultants in campaign management. Since then, the Lithuanian political campaign professionalization process has undergone several changes.

This article aims to present the major characteristics of contemporary election campaigns in Lithuania and to identify recent trends in political campaign professionalization by establishing how much the process of voter persuasion has changed over the last 30 years. The following questions will be addressed in the paper: How much has campaign management become professional and centralized? What roles do professional managers, PR consultants, and politicians perform during certain periods of campaigning? What political marketing techniques are increasing in use? How doesd communication change with voters during political campaigns? And how have the changes in political finance regulations affected campaigning?

Starting with a discussion of theoretical concepts such as political campaigns and communication professionalization, the article then provides contextual background information about Lithuanian elections followed by an explanation of the methods and sources of the study. A discussion of the research results is conducted in the fourth section reviewing the process of political campaign professionalization in Lithuania, as well as evaluating the campaigns according to contemporary election campaign characteristics. This section analyzes data from interviews with PR professionals and politicians made over the last two decades (45 interviews).

Professionalization of political campaign organization and communication

Since the collapse of the Soviet Union and the Socialist Bloc, Central and Eastern European countries have experienced fundamental changes in politics and political campaign communication. The changes followed the same pattern as in Western Democracies, but they started later and progressed faster. Processes like the "professionalization of politics and journalism, increasing market pressures, and technological developments such as the rise of television and the internet" (Vliegenthart 2012, 135–136) have led to a new style of political campaign organization and communication.

Political campaign and communication researchers usually conceive political campaign changes similarly but accentuate different campaign characteristics and aims. One way to classify and describe the major characteristics of various political campaigns is by using campaign evolution or phase models, dividing political campaign development into three phases: premodern, modern, and postmodern (Norris 2000; Plasser and Plasser 2002)—the "three ages of political communication" (Blumler and Kavanagh 1999). However, in the last decade, changes in political communication have already prompted reconsideration of this three-phase model of political campaigning, initiating research discussions of a fourth phase of political campaigning (Blumler 2016; Magin et al. 2017).

Premodern or first-age campaigns are characterized as decentralized campaigns relying on the work of volunteers. The party leader plays an important role in organizing the campaign with the party's professional assistants (Schmitt-Beck 2007, 744–745). Campaign communication in these campaigns primarily use personal contacts, door-to-door visits, public speeches in meetings, and partisan print media (Negrine and Papathanassoloulos 1996).

The critical period for the appearance of modern political campaigns, or the second age of campaigns, was the growing importance of television and public opinion polls in the 1960s–1990s period. Political campaigns gradually changed during this time from print media to television (Gianpietro 1987). Swanson and Mancini (1996) argue that campaigns became personalized—party leaders gradually began using personalized communication instead of problem-based communication. Modern electoral campaigns became centralized and thus organized from central party headquarters (Schmitt-Beck 2007, 746). Consequently, campaign centralization led to campaign professionalization when various professionals were invited to work on election campaigns and received more and different tasks than before. The beginning of campaign professionalization marks the growing involvement of pollsters, advertising and political marketing professionals in campaign organization, and the increased use of various tools and campaign practices in a more professional way. As Grusell and Nord (2020, 3) point out, "This trend toward *professionalization* of political campaigning is well documented in previous research and empirically supported by country studies and comparative studies (Gibson and Römmele 2009; Strömbäck 2009; Tenscher and Mykkänen 2013, Lilleker 2014)."

The third campaigning phase is called the postmodern campaign or third-age campaign. It has its beginnings in the last two decades of the twentieth century. Third-age campaigns is characterized by permanent campaigns using multiple channels of communication, narrowcast messages, targeted advertisements, marketing logic, more specialized political consultants, and so on (Strömbäck 2007, 52).

A few years ago, researchers initiated discussions about the beginning of a fourth age of political communication and fourth phase of political campaigns (Blumler 2016; Magin et al. 2017; Lilleker, Tenscher, and Štětka 2015) related to the emergence of Web 2.0 and its offer of new communication channels and microtargeting. Researchers mention 2008 as the starting point of this fourth age and stress the success of Barack Obama's 2008 presidential campaign, considered the first campaign to exploit all of the potential of online communication and social media utilization (Magin et al. 2017; Lilleker, Tenscher, and Štětka 2015). This fourth age campaign is also called an individual-centered campaign, as it is based on personalized data, microtargeting, message distribution within social networks, and direct party and candidate communication with voters (Magin et al. 2017, 1701).

Contemporary election campaigning suggests some trends, which Strömbäck and Kiousis (2014) summarize: Campaign communication remains concentrated on television as the most important source of information; campaigning is focused on individual candidates and leaders instead of the parties; the internet and various communication platforms are growing in importance; microtargeting and narrowcasting become more popular campaign strategies; increasing media choices make it more difficult to reach new and inattentive voters; and political parties become increasingly marketing and sales oriented. Because of these trends, the need for professional campaigning and communication has increased. Thus, we may notice a process of increasing professionalization, "defined by continuous efforts at improving the use of different campaign strategies and tactics as well as by increasing use either of internal campaign staff or outside consultants" (Strömbäck and Kiousis 2014, 123). All these characteristics of contemporary campaigns makes them more expensive and financially demanding.

As professionalization is regarded as one of the main characteristics of a contemporary campaign, it is important to discuss the concept of professionalization in detail. Political campaign and communication professionalization is a process with many aspects and conceptualizations;

the characterization of campaigns as professionalized varies depending on the conceptualization of the concept. However, some basic conceptualizations can be identified.

On a general level, campaign professionalization is described as a "process by which the political actors adapt their strategies to changes in society and in the political systems as well as to the changes in the media system" (Holtz-Bacha 2002, 23). This conception lists several attributes describing this adaptation process: social and political changes related to modernization, media system changes, de-ideologization of political parties versus personalization and privatization of politics relying on image strategies, and experts taking on tasks once held by party members.

A review of the literature indicates that campaign professionalization might be described as a process toward the greater involvement of campaign professionals—experts in different aspects of campaign management, communication, and strategy (Plasser and Plasser 2002; Negrine 2008; Holtz-Bacha 2002; Strömbäck and Kiousis 2014). Internal professionalization is related to the growth of staff working within the parties who have greater knowledge and expertise in election campaigning. External professionalization is related to a process wherein political parties hire more professionals, experts, and consultants from outside the party for special tasks (Gibson and Römmele, 2009).

The third campaign professionalization concept is related to a process wherein campaign professionals become more specialized at certain tasks related to campaigning and communication (Strömbäck and Kiousis 2014). Usually, campaign experts offer different, specialized services for campaigns—preparation of advertising materials, analysis of opinion polls, media analysis and advertising in media, social media communication strategies, and others.

On the other hand, campaign professionalization may be conceptualized as a process of growing the use of strategies and tools aimed at maximizing the number of electorates. Campaign strategy is associated with tools used to analyze the polls and other research data, to manage various channels of media, and to develop targeted communication and advertising plans for segmented electorates (Tenscher, Mykkänen, and Moring 2012). The struggle for power encourages political parties to place less emphasis on various extreme ideological principles and thus increase the numbers of potential voters. The desire to expand the electorate is manifested in the growing use of political marketing tools, characterized by the transition from pre-prepared party or candidate image-"selling" to listening to the changing needs of voters and constantly adjusting political campaigns (Schmitt-Beck 2007). The dominant campaign paradigm is marketing logic using narrowcast targeted messages. A marketing-oriented campaign "should concentrate on giving the targeted consumers in the selected markets what they want or need" (Strömbäck 2007, 56).

Another characteristic of a professionalized campaign is increasing the centralization of political campaigns, concentrating decision-making power in the party's central headquarters (Scammell, 1998; Lisi 2013).

The professionalization of campaigning may be based on party or candidate campaign processes related to structures and strategies (Grusell and Nord 2020). On the one hand, campaigns become more professional the more financial and personal resources there are available. The campaign budget usually dictates the number of professionals hired for campaign management, public relations, polling, advertising, and other expert areas (Norris 2000). Thus, campaign spending is closely related to campaign professionalization.

This paper relies on the campaign professionalization definition provided by Strömbäck (2007, 54) summarizing all the previously mentioned conceptions of professionalization and focusing on the core characteristics of professionalized campaigns: "Professionalized political campaigning is characterized by being permanent, although with varying intensity; by the central campaign headquarters being able to coordinate the messages and the management of the campaign; and by using expertise in analyzing and reaching out to members, target groups and stakeholders, in analyzing its own and the competitors' weaknesses and strengths and making use of that knowledge, and in news management."

Real campaigns may vary from country to country and do not necessarily have all the features of a professionalized campaign, but the tendencies may indicate the direction and degree of the process under analysis.

The characteristics of contemporary professionalized political campaigns will now be discussed in the article sections that follow, attempting to assess trends of campaign professionalization in the case of Lithuania. Campaign spending will be addressed first. The campaigning period in the country is longer and is gradually becoming permanent. This has led to a growth in campaign budgets. Second, the thoughts of experts and politicians concerning the de-ideologization and personalization aspects of campaigning, closely related to strategies used in professionalized campaigns, are reported. Psychological factors here become more important, leading to political tension, presenting campaigns as political shows, and distorting political reality. The personalization of politics forces the election campaign to focus on image strategies and the presentation of candidates in their private environment rather than in their political role and environment. The involvement of professionals in campaigning will be discussed third. The campaign professionalization process encourages the control of actions, professionalized campaign management, and the involvement of various professional political consultants in campaign organization. Fourth, professionalization is associated with the use of opinion polling in campaigning and various market-oriented strategies. Thus, the growing importance and intensity of using marketing techniques will be discussed. Fifth, social media—the major characteristic of the fourth age of professionalized campaigns—will be addressed. A noticeable trend is the growing use of social media channels for campaign communication, thus allowing more personalized communication for politicians with the public. From this, the question is posed as to whether these new communication channels are replacing traditional media or complementing campaign communication.

Lithuanian parliamentary elections

Lithuania, being a democratic parliamentary republic with elements of a semi-presidential republic, holds two important national elections: direct presidential elections and parliamentary elections, with turnouts ranging from 50% to 78%. The Seimas is a unicameral parliament with 141 members who are elected in direct and secret elections for a four-year term (The Constitution of the Republic of Lithuania 1992). Parliament members are elected using a mixed electoral system: 70 seats are elected *via* proportional representation (PR; in one multi-member district) and the remaining 71 are elected in separate constituencies (single-member districts; SMDs). To win PR seats, party lists and coalitions must surpass thresholds of 5% and 7%, respectively. In the SMDs, if no candidate wins more than 50% of the first-round votes, a second round takes place. This type of electoral system determines the electoral campaign format in both districts. "Parties are the central players in electoral campaigns, but individual candidates are equally important, especially when competing in the SMDs. Lithuanians are more likely to trust leaders and personalities instead of parties. This tendency is noticeable from the results of public opinion polls and SMD election results" (Unikaite 2008, 33; Unikaite-Jakuntavičienė 2019, 66). How Lithuanian political parties and candidates adapt to this situation and what political campaign tools they use in campaigning will be discussed in the analysis of Lithuanian campaign development and professionalization.

The 1990 founding parliamentary election in Lithuania was based on the inherited Soviet majority system of representation. A new electoral system was introduced in the 1992 parliamentary election. Since these elections, through to 2021, eight parliamentary elections have taken place in Lithuania. On October 11, 2020, the last ordinary parliamentary elections took place. Over the past decades, on average, six to eight parties have been represented in the parliament. Governments are composed of multiple parties—usually of three or more.

Lithuanians are not inclined to trust political parties. Public opinion polls indicate that only 5–6% have trust in political parties as institutions, whereas more than 60% distrust them (15min.lt, February 2, 2020). Political campaigns prior to elections are therefore concentrated on intensive communication, advertising, and voter persuasion and are of great importance for political parties seeking better voting results. Political campaign events and content may be decisive for certain political parties seeking to pass the election threshold. This motivates parties and politicians to make a tremendous effort in preparation for election campaigns.

The first signs of campaign professionalization in Lithuania were already visible in the 1996 elections when major political parties, having bigger budgets, hired advertising professionals in the campaign (Unikaite-Jakuntavičienė 2019, 69–70). To what extent the election campaigns have become professionalized will be discussed in the analysis of interviews with representatives of Lithuanian political parties and professional political consultants.

Methodology

This political campaign professionalization development study uses a qualitative case study approach and is based on personal interviews with campaign managers and party politicians actively participating in national election campaigns as well as professional campaign consultants. The interviews were conducted as elite, semi-structured interviews from 2004 to 2018. As Armannsdottir, Carnell, and Pich (2020, 83) write, "Elite interviews can be characterized as comprehensive discussions with a small number of experts or participants with specialist knowledge designed to capture insightful perceptions." A portion of the interviews were conducted face-to-face during the campaign period before the 2004, 2012, and 2016 elections; others were conducted between elections. The interviews lasted from 40 to 90 min. The interview-guiding questionnaires—one for politicians and another for PR consultants—were prepared by the author of this study after a literature review on campaign communication and professionalization. The questionnaires served as a guide, with the possibility to change the questions and adapt them to the conversation and person being interviewed. The guiding questions were related to the following thematic blocks: election campaign characteristics and strategies, campaign management, political marketing, campaign finance, and the role of PR consultants in campaigning. The interviews with politicians were aimed at identifying the basic characteristics of contemporary political campaigns related to communication, organization and marketing, and the degree of campaign professionalization as well as assessing how important campaigns are for politicians. The PR consultants were asked about their work with political parties, how many functions they perform in political campaigning, and how they evaluate Lithuanian political campaigns in terms of professionalization.

The informants/politicians were selected for the interviews using a purposive sample, aiming to represent major political parties of a certain period. The specific personalities were selected according to one important criterion: Politicians had to be working in the central election campaign headquarters of the party or were themselves running their election campaigns in a single mandate district. The PR consultant informants were selected according to their involvement with the election campaigns of different political parties. In total, 35 interviews with politicians and 10 interviews with political consultants and political commentators/journalists were conducted. All interviews were conducted in Lithuanian and recorded and transcribed in extenso. The citations from the interviews were translated into English by the researcher.

In addition to the elite interviews, reports of political parties on campaign finances and spending for certain activities were reviewed and analyzed. This spending information helped to identify some changes in campaigning practices.

Election campaign professionalization development in Lithuania

In the following section, the Lithuanian election campaigns will be analyzed regarding the general degree of campaign professionalization development in terms of the basic characteristics, organization, campaign strategies, and communication of contemporary campaigns.

First, the informants view toward campaigns will be assessed, suggesting that greater emphasis on campaign significance may be a sign of campaign professionalization. Second, campaign organization matters will be discussed, analyzing the duration of campaigning, campaign centralization, the use of political marketing techniques, the involvement of PR consultants in the preparation of campaigns by identifying the roles of PR consultants in political campaigns, and the politician's views toward PR consultancy work. Third, campaign communication changes will be analyzed. Finally, changes in campaign financing will be reviewed, and the campaign professionalization process in Lithuania will be evaluated.

Importance of election campaigns for voting results

Prior to 1996, parliamentary political parties organized their campaigns by relying more on the party membership, trying to use the different expertise of politicians. Political parties combined a few methods of communicating their ideas with voters: direct meetings with voters and political advertising on television and radio as well as in print media. Professionals were hired just for campaign material preparation. It was a popular view among politicians that campaigns are necessary but do not play a decisive role. Thus, we may classify these campaigns as having the characteristics of modern campaigns. The importance of campaigning started to grow in Lithuania during the 1996 parliamentary elections when the first professional campaigns were run and election campaign spending increased (Unikaitė-Jakuntavičienė 2019, 68; Unikaitė 2007, 76). When asked to evaluate how important campaigns are to today's elections, there was little doubt among. The parties emphasized a few reasons why election campaigns are of great importance and why they should be well prepared: (1) Lithuania is among the countries where political parties have a volatile electorate. Therefore, election campaigns may influence the voting decisions of undecided voters, sometimes even causing changes in previous voting decisions (Adomėnas 2014; Vyšniauskas 2015; Auštrevičius 2012, etc.). (2) In Lithuania, according to survey data and the experience of political parties, approximately 25–40% of voters make their final voting decisions during the campaign period or at the end of the campaign (Vyšniauskas 2015; Labanauskas 2004; Valinskas 2012; Auštrevičius 2012). (3) Election campaigns introduce the candidates and manifestos of political parties and serve as a time for "selling the product":

> This is a period before elections when people are likely to be more interested in political candidates. Accordingly, candidates have the possibility to tell the voters more information about themselves, their ideas. We may compare politicians with products. Products have their marketing plans if we wish them to be well-known and people have a wish to buy them. Politicians must be recognizable, and their ideas must be well-known to the voters if they wish "to be bought" by the voters' votes (Palionis 2015).

(4) Campaigns generate voting results—"There are no results without campaigns" (Požėla 2014). (5) "The best indicator of campaign importance is the success of new parties in elections" (Pagojus 2014). Since the 2000 parliamentary elections, every election cycle has seen new parties elected to the Seimas. They usually organize an intensive campaign and, in a short period of time, collect large numbers of votes (as was the case for New Union, the Labor Party, Order and Justice, the National Resurrection Party, and the Way of Courage).

In summary, politicians do not try to deny the significance of campaigns nor do they seek arguments as to why campaigning should not be taken seriously. On the contrary, a number of politicians directly acknowledge they use political marketing and try to organize sales-oriented and marketing-oriented campaigns. The next section will discuss the specifics of campaign organization in Lithuania.

Campaign organization in Lithuania: Centralization, duration, and the involvement of professionals

The campaign organization process is a long process involving active members of political parties and professional consultants. As analysis of the interviews indicates, there have been changes in political campaign organization when compared with the first professional campaigns in Lithuania.

The first change is related to the centralization of campaign organization, a feature of a professionalized campaign. The first interviews with leaders of the Social Democratic Party in 2004 indicated that this party tried to decentralize campaigning, especially in single mandate districts (SMD), allowing regional branches of political parties and candidates in SMDs more freedom and possibility to concentrate campaigning on regional issues. The party prepared basic advertising materials with the party symbols and campaign ideas (Kirkilas 2004). Candidates received leaflets from the central election headquarters but had the possibility of planning SMD events themselves (Vėsaitė 2004). The most recent interviews, however, show that the Social Democratic Party has been trying to centralize campaigns and control the entire advertising and communication process. Individual SMD candidates can still provide some specific ideas or use different means of communication related to the specifics of any given region (Požėla 2014; Pagojus 2014).

Homeland Union—Lithuanian Christian Democrats (a conservative party) always tries to differentiate two types of campaigns: (1) an election campaign organized by the central election headquarters, responsible for the national campaign strategy and budget (national communication channels, events organized by the party, advertising materials, election manifesto preparation), and (2) campaigns organized by individual candidates themselves with the help and consultation of central headquarters (Kubilius 2004). Due to the specifics of SMDs, freedom in organization of regional campaigns was allowed (Jukneviciene 2004). All SMD candidates have their own election headquarters and decide on how to campaign and how to obtain finances (Kupčinskas 2004). The same tendency has remained in recent campaigns. Major organization work is centralized, but candidates have their own supplementary campaigning as well (Adomėnas 2014; Mikulėniene 2014). The 2020 elections show that this party still follows the same model. One change however is that the party partially finances the candidate campaigns in SMDs. As the leader of the central elections' headquarters mentioned, "Every candidate in an SMD received a €5,000 donation in the first round of the elections and €2,000 in the second round" (Homeland Union 2020). Single candidates follow the recommendations of the central party headquarters regarding the election program and use prepared templates for visual advertising materials, slogans, and information in advertisements.

Other parties try to combine centralized national campaigns with decentralized campaigns in SMDs as well (Vėgėlė 2004; Valiukevičiūtė 2004; Rimšelis 2004; Šilgalis 2004). However, priority is given to the higher centralization of campaign management even in SMDs. Thus, a clear trend of national campaign centralization is noticeable among all the parties, with some small exceptions due to the mixed election system demanding that candidates prepare more targeted messages in the SMDs.

Election campaign duration varies among political parties and among the different elections. The first interviews in 2004 revealed a tendency toward a rather short campaign preparation and campaigning period—usually six months to a year. Recent interviews with political party representatives indicate that major parties with a long tradition of election campaigning are more likely to start their preliminary preparations for the next election two or even three years before the official campaign. A representative of Homeland Union (2020) argues, "We started analysis of the electorate at the beginning of 2017. In 2018, the election headquarters were established, but real, concrete preparation for the 2020 elections started just one year before." The informant confirmed the statement that campaigning has become permanent because, between the national parliamentary elections, the other elections serve as a test of various strategies. When it comes to the smaller or newer parties lacking financial and human resources, most of them usually start their campaigning around three to five months and up to a year before the elections. Overall, we notice the signs of permanent campaigning among the bigger parties in Lithuania, but this tendency is not common and depends on the financial resources and leadership of the political parties.

When looking at the involvement of campaign professionals in the preparation and organization of election campaigns, from outside as well as inside the party, we can note some changes.

As the results of the interview data analysis indicate, the first Lithuanian political campaigns were organized by party leaders and active members, avoiding experts from outside. The first professionals from outside were invited when organizing the second, 1996 parliamentary elections in Lithuania. These professionals were asked to implement technical work regarding advertising materials and strategy. Gradually, various professionals from outside delivered more and different work.

The interviews with PR consultants explained what the roles these consultants had within the political parties' campaign headquarters. First, all informants agreed that political consultants do specific tasks and do not work with the political agenda of the parties: "Decisions are always made by the clients. Consultants prepare arguments, positions, and possible methods. If we choose this way, we implement that strategy, with these pluses and minuses" (Gudelis 2014); "Political consultants must help to achieve results, but ideas and aims are to be formulated by the politicians" (Kontrimas 2014). All the interviewed politicians further confirmed these statements, arguing that politicians should be active campaign participants and should listen to various advice from experts, but it is they who must decide what direction to take on their own. However, some differences in the roles of professionals are apparent when it comes to the campaigns of new and smaller political parties. As M. Lapinskas argues:

> The roles depend on the parties. The parties with a long tradition, such as Homeland Union, the Social Democrats, Liberal Movement, make the final decisions themselves. The Labour Party, which do very good campaigns, may have a different model. It seems that decisions are made by professionals in their party. (Lapinskas 2014)

Evaluating the tasks of professionals in Lithuanian political campaigns, we notice that professional consultants are an important part of campaign organization, but solely for technical or specialized work. This suggests that political parties either do not trust political consultants or lack the finances to hire PR companies.

Furthermore, all informants were asked whether politicians are likely to use the advice offered by political consultants. Various informants had different opinions. Politicians mentioned that they listen to the advice, but a "politician is independent and may make the final decision" (Adomėnas 2014; Pagojus 2014): "Politicians are more likely to trust and give the right to make a decision to the consultants in technical matters, for instance, where to place a poster" (Pagojus 2014). Some politicians value the advice of PR consultants and say that sometimes they are useful (Auštrevičius 2014). Many informants mentioned that "Lithuania is a small state," arguing that "this leads to a deficit in agencies specializing in political campaigning." The answers reveal that Lithuanian politicians have no wish to lose leadership in campaigning and are still unlikely to rely on political consultants and agencies, especially when Lithuanian companies are not specialized only in political PR.

Examining the share of work during campaigns, there a tendency for members of the political party's central election headquarters to perform a majority of the work—prepare an election manifesto, generate basic campaign ideas, form the political part of a campaign, and decide which PR consultants will be invited to work together. Politicians, however, are likely to minimize the importance PR consultancy work. As V. Gapšys argues, the "work of consultants comprises only about 5% of campaign work" (Gapšys 2014). Many politicians acknowledge that political parties have many experts inside, and a lot of work is implemented by people from within the parties. A representative of Homeland Union (2020) stated that "some political party members may have more expertise and experience in political campaigning than experts from outside." Accordingly, the major political parties—Homeland Union, Order and Justice, and the Social Democrats—think about professional political consultants as they do about technical specialists and use their services selectively for certain tasks.

In contrast to Lithuanian politicians, interviewed professional PR consultants have a slightly different view regarding the share of work on a campaign. Many consultants argue that work share depends on the maturity of the political party (Kontrimas 2014; Gudelis 2014; Jurgelionytė

2014). Parties with long political histories are more likely to implement several tasks themselves. Parties lacking leadership, without an analytic center, and with a smaller membership will employ political consultants for a broader spectrum of tasks, such as manifesto writing, situational analysis, political event organization, and so forth (Kontrimas 2014). Additionally, consultants noticed a recent tendency among parties to place more trust in professionals and to ask consultants not only for political marketing work but also for strategic campaign communication consultation (Gudelis 2014). This type of work indicates changes in campaign organization and more trust in PR consultants. In brief, political parties usually listen to the advice of consultants, but they do not always evaluate them positively. This stems from a belief that political leaders and party campaign headquarters know how to communicate with voters better and are cautious in regard to the work of PR consultants.

What is more, the interviews indicate that political consultants usually implement functions related to campaign communication (PR, marketing, information analysis). As the political party representatives mentioned, professional consultants are involved in work with television, internet, and printed advertising material preparation (Adomėnas 2014; Pagojus 2014; Morkūnaitė-Mikulėnienė 2014). Meetings with voters are coordinated by the politicians themselves. As the interviewed consultants explained, many communication services are offered to politicians in Lithuania, including "election strategy, preparation of campaign manifestos, public communication consultations, preparation of agitation materials, media planning, etc." (Kontrimas, Lapinskas, and Jurgelionytė 2014). However, politicians decide themselves which services they need. Small and new political parties, as already mentioned, are more likely to order a broader spectrum of services.

It is usual for political parties to buy certain services from professional consultants but not employ them (Vyšniauskas 2015; Homeland Union 2020; Gustainis 2015; Gapšys 2014). Political parties also have different traditions of hiring one or several PR companies; the Liberal Movement or Order and Justice, for instance, usually work with just one company (Auštrevičius 2014). Homeland Union and the Social Democratic Party are more likely to work with more than one company, and the recent elections indicated that many parties are more likely than not to buy services from individual freelancers than buy services from actual PR companies (Homeland Union 2020). In this way, they save money, attract more qualified experts, and receive service that is adjusted to the needs of the party.

A few PR consultants think their work is more visible during the campaign but are more active before the campaign starts (Gudelis 2014; Lapinskas 2014). Others think that professionals work equally before and during the campaigns (Jurgelionytė 2014; Kontrimas 2014). Lithuanian political campaign organizations are dominated by political party leadership and by members of central election headquarters, modeling the political part of the campaign: creating election manifestos, generating election messages and slogans, composing the electoral lists, and so on. A significant activity among party members is in campaign logistics and technical work: political agitation, leaflet distribution, and door-to-door activities (Mikulėnienė 2014; Gapšys 2014; Požėla 2014; Šivickas 2012; Baškienė 2012).

The informants were asked to evaluate the quality of Lithuanian professional political consultancy work. Different politicians presented various opinions. However, two basic tendencies were expressed: (a) Politicians think that professionals have rather high costs, and (b) there is a shortage of good political consultants in Lithuania. As V. Mazuronis points out, "The bad point is that professionals are very expensive, and there are not enough—lots of parties but just a few companies working with politicians, expensive and not always sincere and wanting to know what a client really needs". P. Auštrevičius argues, "Consultants work for a short period and do not always understand the real situation. They are expensive, but the party is without guarantees with regard to results. Parties accept the risk" (Auštrevičius 2014). A. Pagojus stresses, "The costs are high, but it is good that work is implemented by professionals who know their jobs" (Pagojus 2014). J. Požėla mentions the shortage of political consultants and provides example that the same consultant works with several parties. He thinks it is a matter of discretion and confidentiality (Požėla 2014).

Political consultants were asked how they work with parties that have different ideological positions from themselves. All of the informants argue that political consultants are unbiased specialists, able to evaluate the chances of winning elections from outside and, thus, may provide the best proposals during election campaigns (Kontrimas 2014; Gudelis 2014). However, one consultant said congruence of ideological values between client and consultant makes the work easier (Jurgelionytė 2014).

Overall, the country's political parties are satisfied with the work of political consultants but would like to have the possibility of more choice among professional political consultants—many PR companies decide to work only with businesses and refuse to provide political consultation—and receive less expensive services. This issue is partially overcome by buying services from individual freelancers offering marketing and communication services.

When looking at the evaluations of Lithuanian election campaign professionalism, political consultants were likely to confirm that they are rather professional. D. Gudelis argues, "Campaigns are professional because they have all the necessary elements for communication: strategic planning, public opinion polls, permanent PR communication, events organization, professional advertising, messages, slogans, etc." (Gudelis 2014). Another consultant thinks that "campaigns have characteristics of professionalism but will become really professional when the services of political consultants are needed by professional politicians, not by amateurs" (Kontrimas 2014). Many consultants argue that election campaigns are not attractive and rather boring due to the passivity of voters and the lack of desire to participate in campaigning (Kontrimas 2014; Jurgelionytė 2014). Some consultants are more likely to evaluate every campaign separately because their professionalism depends on the circumstances, participants, and organizers (Žakas 2015). Lapinskas agrees and says that "not every party uses all the elements of election campaigns" (Lapinskas 2014). To summarize then, there is no agreement about the professionalism of campaigns among political consultants. The possibility for professional contemporary campaign preparation exists, but everything depends on the financial resources, contextual factors, and the understanding of political party leaders as to the importance of professionalized contemporary campaigns.

In conclusion, as we notice from all the interviews, campaign organization professionalization is visible in Lithuania: Campaigns are becoming longer, centralized, and controlled by party leadership, and they involve external political consultants in campaign organization more extensively.

Marketing orientation of contemporary election campaigns

Another indicator of campaign professionalization is the use of different campaign marketing strategies and tactics to research and segment the electorate, of different advertising materials, and of different communication strategies. Changes in the sphere of political advertising and communication are visible in the campaigns of Lithuanian political parties. First, before the 2004 and 2012 elections, all the informants argued that the most important media channel of communication with voters was television. This channel could spread information to large groups of voters (Vėsaitė 2004; Kirkilas 2004; Muntianas 2004). A few politicians were critical of campaigning on television, mentioning that TV channels are influential but much of the information provided is artificial, made by imagemakers and PR specialists, and thus creates a mistaken public opinion (Muntianas 2004). More than half of the informants stressed the important role of discussions and debates on TV but were skeptical about advertising through the medium (Valinskas 2012; Kupčinskas 2004; Starkevičius 2004; Velička 2004; Kubilius 2004). This negativity about ads on TV might be a consequence of changes in campaign advertising regulations—television advertisements were previously forbidden for a certain period, seeking to cut down on campaign expenditures, but a few years ago, these ads were again allowed.

Before the 2016 elections, social media and news media portals became one of the fastest growing channels of communication with voters during election campaigns. Earlier, the internet has been used by the parties to intensely focus communication on the young electorate, attracting this targeted group of younger voters; however, more recent campaigns indicate, and politicians confirm, that internet channels and social media have gradually become an effective channel for attracting other target groups (except the elderly). The growing use of social media platforms, such as Facebook or Instagram, for campaign communication is related to the possibility of microtargeting and narrowcasting. I. Paludnevičiūtė, head of the Freedom Party's 2020 parliamentary election campaign headquarters, explained the party's decision to rely on social media communication:

> We did some research, evaluated our voter characteristics, and simply assessed where we can best reach more voters and target our constituents most rationally, rather than just wasting money on advertising that is less effective and less relevant to us. We assumed that our voter is more accessible in the electronic space, and advertising there is still a bit cheaper than in other channels. (Naprys 2020)

The other political parties (among them Homeland Union) endeavored to choose different communication channels for different target groups and tried not to rely on any one channel. As chief of Homeland Union's 2020 parliamentary election campaign headquarters, A. Vyšniauskas, argues, "Such a healthy mix of different channels, and a correspondingly even distribution of funds between the national campaign, the single members, and all the instruments and channels, is justified" (Naprys 2020). Accordingly, three central motives may be listed for using social media in recent election campaigning: (1) marketing, "meaning that the political parties used it to increase the visibility of their candidates in the public sphere" (Unikaitė-Jakuntavičienė 2019, 74) and to reach young voters who are not users of traditional media channels; (2) mobilization of voters to come to elections or to meetings with politicians and increase interest in various party campaign activities during the campaign; and (3) direct communication engagement with voters who are not participating in personal meetings (Jurgelionytė 2012).

A further argument for using social media in campaign communication is the personalization of communication. Political parties are more likely to present leaders and personalities in campaigns instead of extensively discussing ideological issues; personalities usually help a party get elected rather than the popularity of a party's ideas. Moreover, Lithuanian voters are more likely to trust individual candidates than political parties. Accordingly, individual candidates in SMDs and political party leaders relying on the analysis of the electorate are trying to be more actively involved on social media platforms and perform personalized communication.

If we examine the popularity of advertising on other channels based on the interviews and campaign spending reports, one can remark that overall other communication channels and advertising instruments are still popular as well. All of the informants, whether describing the first campaigns in Lithuania or those most recent, unanimously argue that the best way to communicate with and persuade voters is personal contact—meeting voters personally *via* door-to-door activities, visiting them in various regions, and meeting with them in small groups. Therefore, political parties try to start campaigning as early as possible and visit as many voters as possible within their living environments. This personal communication, that is, visits by party leaders and candidates to all the Lithuanian regions, started to be used more widely in the 2000 elections and has continued growing in popularity to the present.

Many politicians argue that this type of communication is not easy or cheap. Furthermore, it is time-consuming. But it is effective. As one politician mentioned, "The more handshakes you make, the more votes you get" (Valinskas 2012). Personal communication is effective for a few reasons: (a) Voters do not waste time going to meetings but are happy to meet politicians who come to their homes. One politician, for instance, mentioned the words of a voter he visited to explain why it was important: "It's rare that politicians come to us to ask us how we live" (Kupčinskas 2004). Thus, one of the most important arguments for using direct communication with voters is showing that politicians are in close contact with ordinary people.

(b) Personal visits help to better understand the electorate and speak the same language, to show interest in the voters' opinion instead of only presenting your own ideas (Velička 2004; Jurgelionytė 2012; Valiukevičiūtė 2004; Muntianas 2004; Labanauskas 2004; Valinskas 2012; Kubilius 2004). Door-to-door visits are now inevitable characteristics of every election campaign, implemented by bigger political parties with significant human resources, as well as by the candidates organizing their campaigns in SMDs. Homeland Union started the 2020 campaign by investing resources on personal meetings with voters in both large and small cities and using advertising campaigns as a way of polling the electorate, asking them what issues the new government should concentrate on and then providing leaflets with advertising for the party and candidates (Homeland Union 2020; Naprys 2020).

As Lithuanian political parties and candidates have a need to make campaigns more responsive to the voters and offer proposals for *all* the targeted groups, a growing importance and intensity concerning public opinion polls during the campaign preparation and implementation process is noticeable. During the 2004 informant interviews, only the major parties stated that they used public opinion polls in preparation for an election campaign so that they could get to know their possible electorate better and then adjust the campaign ideas according to those demands (Homeland Union—Lithuanian Christian Democrats; Social Democratic Party; Labor Party; Order and Justice; Liberal and Center Union). As representatives of the parties mentioned, the main target audiences of these parties are loyal electorates and swing/undecided voters. Other political parties explained that they use public opinion polls if they have money (Lithuanian Christian Democrats, Lithuanian Peasants Party). The most recent interviews indicated that all parties with the finances to support it use public opinion polls during all stages of campaign preparation and organization (Auštrevičius 2012; Jurgelionytė 2012; Špakauskas 2012; Pagojus 2014; Žemaitaitis 2012; Baltraitienė 2012; Dalinkevičius 2012, Lapinskas 2012; Homeland Union 2020). Public opinion polls are used by the parties not only for measuring party preferences but also to understand the interests of the electorate, to facilitate the campaign's strategic planning, and to prepare the political messaging. Meetings and visits with small groups of voters before the preparation of a campaign, as well as special public opinion polls, help the parties create a product and find the best ways to sell it.

According to the interview data, Lithuanian campaign organizers use multiple methods of increasing their knowledge about potential voters and their political preferences in order to create targeted communication, implement a number of political marketing strategies, and use the newest advertising instruments. This is a characteristic of campaign professionalization.

Election campaign budgets and spending on political advertising

The discussion of Lithuanian party orientation toward the active use of various political marketing techniques, together with polling, is closely related to changes in political finance regulation in Lithuania. When state subsidies were introduced for political parties in 2000, political parties which had amassed 3% or more of the votes in parliamentary and municipal elections were eligible for a state subsidy (Unikaitė 2008, 34–37). Big and popular political parties had no need to ask for money from legal persons and were able to maintain stable finances. This allowed political parties to hire more professionals for campaign organization and introduce more marketing strategies in campaigning. Accordingly, campaign expenses started growing rapidly (see Table 1).

However, political parties expressed an opinion that despite state subsidies allowing more transparency in party and campaign finances, the need for larger amounts of money did not disappear. Every election, professional campaign services became more expensive and budgets increased, especially for those wishing to prepare a professional campaign (Muntianas 2004; Gapšys 2014; Gustainis 2014).

The growth of spending is related to the following processes: electorate passivity and disinterest in politics; the involvement of external professionals in campaigning; growth of

Table 1. Party spending for Lithuanian Parliamentary Campaigns (1996–2020).

Year	Party spending (EUR)	Inflation rate (%)
1996	654,018	13.1
2000	1,584,343	0.98
2004	3,265,837	1.16
2008	5,525,895	10.93 (global financial crisis)
2012	7,490,651	3.09
2016	7,061,338	0.91
2020	7,747,000	1.3

Source: Prepared by the author using data from the Central Electoral Commission of the Republic of Lithuania (www.vrk.lt), data from the PhD dissertation of the author (Unikaite 2007, 76, 94, 112), data from macrotrends.net (2021), and the Bank of Lithuania yearly report (1996).

various media channels for advertising; and rising rates of services due to inflation rate changes.

During the first two parliamentary election campaigns, voters were more interested in politics and more actively participated in campaign events than in the second decade of Lithuanian independence. Therefore, campaigns relied on the active participation of party members in campaign information distribution rather than media advertising. By the 2000 election campaign, new political parties had entered the political arena and state subsidies were available. Party spending began increasing election after election before stabilizing in the 2012 campaigns after spending limits were introduced. The budgets of the last three parliamentary election campaigns varied from €7 to 8 million.

Looking at the parties' expenditure for advertising in parliamentary elections over the 1996–2020 period, it is worth emphasizing two tendencies. First, the proportion of spending for advertising materials and services comprises the largest segment of the expenses. It seems that political parties have employed their financial resources mainly toward preparing different kinds of campaign materials and distributing them through different communication channels. Second, spending on advertising increased from 40% of the campaign budget to between 85–90% in the last four elections (see Figure 1).

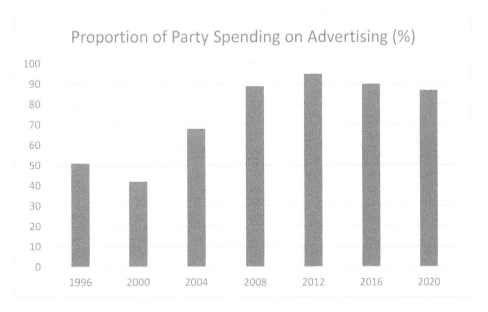

Figure 1. Proportion of Party Spending on Advertising in Lithuanian Parliamentary Campaigns (1996–2020).
Source: Prepared by author using data from the Central Electoral Commission of the Republic of Lithuania (www.vrk.lt) and data from the author's PhD dissertation (Unikaite 2007, 76, 94, 112)

Analysis of the available data regarding party spending for different types of advertising during the 2020 elections shows that the political parties decided to spend their money accordingly: €1.6 million on external advertising (leaflets, posters, etc.), €1.1 million on advertising in print media, and €2 million on other means of advertising (special leaflets sent by post to voters, advertising *via* online media and television).

Despite the overall picture, there are important differences between parties. Homeland Union decided to use various types of advertising and disbursed the largest funding (approx. 50%) on other advertising (direct communication, polling, leaflets); external advertising as well as advertisements in print media, the internet and television were used (Naprys 2020). The former governing party, the Lithuanian Peasants and Greens Union, used practically no television advertising, with the majority of their finances going to external and other types of advertising (newspapers, leaflets etc.). Only the newest political party, the Freedom Party, having no state subsidies, invested most of its finances into internet advertising due to its orientation toward the youngest voters. These tendencies in the distribution of advertising spending reflect the aim of the political parties to use scarce financial resources purposively after careful analysis of the electorate and marketing strategies.

To conclude, the overall spending of party campaigns and distribution of advertising spending confirm a growing professionalization of contemporary campaigns in Lithuania. Every election campaign becomes more expensive, and the share of spending for campaign advertising is high.

Do Lithuanian election campaigns have the characteristics of fourth-age professionalized campaigns?

Analysis of the data collected in interviews and in the campaign spending reports allow one to summarize the results and assess whether Lithuanian political campaigns can be classified as professionalized in the fourth age of election campaigns. The guiding interview questions were linked to the ten characteristics of contemporary professionalized campaigns. Each characteristic was evaluated as to whether or not it was a typical campaign attribute. The results are provided in Table 2.

The table indicates that only four characteristics were evaluated at the highest level. All of the informants confirmed the importance of campaigning for the results, the growth of campaign budgets, and the use of external professionals for various services as well as the growing importance of marketing strategies in campaigning. In the evaluation, only two points were given for the length of campaign, taking into consideration smaller parties which began their campaigns just before the official campaign and without long preparation. Other characteristics to which two points were given were due to the fact that the representatives of both bigger and smaller parties had a differing of opinions about certain campaign characteristics. For instance, television

Table 2. Evaluation of Lithuanian Political Campaigns according to contemporary professionalized campaign characteristics.

Contemporary professionalized campaign characteristics	Characteristic presence intensity[a]
Election campaign importance for election results evaluation	3
Growth of election campaign budgets and spending for advertising	3
Longer campaigns/permanent campaigns	2
Professional political consultants and experts hired for election campaigns	3
Involvement of experts in the broad spectrum of campaign work/specialization of consultants	2
De-ideologization and personalization of campaigns	2
Growing use of marketing techniques (polls, targeting, narrowcasting, etc.)	3
Television as a main communication channel with voters	2
Growing importance of communication with voters by using internet channels	2
Growing use of social media in election campaigning	2
Total:	**24/30**

[a] A 3-point scale was used for evaluation, with 0 signifying the absence of a characteristic, 1—used sometimes, 2—characteristic is present in campaigns rather often, 3—the characteristic is typical and visible during campaigns.

was given only two points because, while politicians stressed the influence of TV, they also said that they may not always use television advertising due to a lack of financial resources. Online communication is growing but is also getting more expensive as well and not every political party uses it. Parties relying on elderly voters still show a preference for print advertising and direct meetings instead of active communication on social media platforms.

Overall, 24 points were scored on the table. This expresses a gradual development of Lithuanian political campaigns and a gradual growth of campaign professionalization. As Lithuanian professional consultants have no possibility to make strategic decisions, are not responsible for the political part of campaigning, and have limited functions and influence within central campaign headquarters, we may argue that Lithuanian election campaigns have more characteristics associated with third-age election campaigns than fourth-age. However, we cannot deny the changes and potential to have more professionalized contemporary campaigns in the future.

Conclusion

This study has examined the development and basic characteristics of contemporary Lithuanian political campaigns regarding the professionalization process. The first group of questions in this analysis inquired as to the organizational aspects of campaigns, concentrating on the duration of campaigning and the involvement of professional political consultants within the election campaign organization. The results indicate that professionals play an important role in campaign preparation and management in all the parties. Though all the politicians stressed the technical functions of political consultants, it seems that the major functions implemented by the outside professionals are related to marketing strategies and communication management. Lithuanian political parties hire professionals not only during the campaign preparation and implementation periods but in between elections as well. Political leaders tend to trust political consultants and listen to the proposed advice but are more likely to make final strategic decisions themselves. However, the role of professional consultants may differ among parties. As all the PR experts agreed, the larger parties demand fewer functions or tasks of them, whereas smaller or new parties usually buy all the necessary services for campaign organization.

The second group of questions in this study were related to the basic characteristics of Lithuanian political campaign communication and political marketing strategies. The results indicate that contemporary Lithuanian political campaigns use a variety of tools and instruments—meetings and discussions with voters between elections, public opinion polls, focus groups—to research the electorate and specific interests of targeted voter groups. Therefore, they may prepare campaign advertising and messages according to the voting predispositions and communication preferences of the voters. The parties are likely to use the same logic as in business marketing: "to know the characteristics of consumers and prepare the product for selling." Among the communication channels, the most extensively used is personal communication: door-to door visits and meetings with small groups of voters. Television remains the major media channel, together with the growing popularity and use of social media, especially during the last two parliamentary elections. Print media is used in campaigns for communication with elderly voters and voters living on the periphery, where regional media is popular. Other advertising instruments like leaflets, posters, and billboards are still popular and treated as effective instruments for making candidates and parties recognizable and known.

The changes to political finance regulations introducing state subsidies for the parties and a ban on corporate donations in Lithuania affected campaigning in the following way: It initiated spending growth among parties on campaigning, increasing the possibilities for organizing more professionalized campaigns. An analysis of campaign spending shows that in the last three elections, overall spending on campaigning stabilized and varies from €7 to 8 million. Spending on advertising reached 80–90% of all expenditures. This indicates growing use of professionalized campaign instruments among the parties.

In closing, the results of the study show that Lithuanian election campaigns are developing gradually and are generally becoming more professionalized across all parties. Lithuanian campaigns have all the conditions to be professionalized. However, the professionalization process may differ from party to party. Major political parties, being more mature and having more financial and human resources, more political experience, and more professionals inside the party, are organizing more professionalized campaigns than smaller and newer parties without political experience. Structural and financial party conditions seem to matter for the level of campaign professionalization, as does the professional leadership of the party since this is where strategic decisions are made. If party leadership is professional, leaders may make the right choices regarding the advice of political consultants.

In addition, this study evaluated Lithuanian campaigns according to the characteristics of contemporary professionalized campaigns. As the analysis indicates, political campaigns do not develop progressively among all political parties. Some party campaigns might be considered third-age political campaigns, and some already have almost all the characteristics of fourth-age professionalized campaigns. Thus, generally, we conclude that Lithuanian campaigns have many features of professionalized campaigns and the potential to become contemporary professionalized campaigns in the near future.

Studies in election campaign professionalization development trends need to be conducted in various contexts, allowing for the possibility for comparison. Future studies of Lithuanian campaign professionalization should continue with interviews before each new election and extend the research, including additional methods of data gathering. Interviews with politicians and campaign consultants should be combined with a survey of party members and detailed campaign spending analyses. Additionally, an analysis of party campaign communication and campaign materials should be made.

ORCID

Ingrida Unikaitė-Jakuntavičienė http://orcid.org/0000-0001-8756-7306

References

Armannsdottir, Guja, Stuart Carnell, and Christopher Pich. 2020. "Exploring Personal Political Brands of Iceland's Parliamentarians." *Journal of Political Marketing* 19 (1–2):74–106. doi: 10.1080/15377857.2019.1680931.
Blumler, Jay G. 2016. "The Fourth Age of Political Communication." *Politiques de Communication* 6 (1):19–30. doi: 10.3917/pdc.006.0019.
Blumler, Jay G., and Dennis Kavanagh. 1999. "The Third Age of Political Communication: Influences and Features." *Political Communication* 16 (3):209–30. doi: 10.1080/105846099198596.
Farell, David M. 2002. "Campaign Modernization and the West European Party." In *Political Parties in the New Europe*, edited by Luther Kurt R. and F. Müller-Rommel, 63–83. Oxford: Oxford University Press.
Gianpietro, Mazzoleni. 1987. "Media Logic and Party Logic in Campaign Coverage: The Italian General Election of 1983." *European Journal of Communication* 2 (1):81–103. doi: 10.1177/0267323187002001005.
Gibson, Rachel K., and Andrea Römmele. 2009. "Measuring the Professionalization of Political Campaigning." *Party Politics* 15 (3):265–93. doi: https://doi.org/10.1177/1354068809102245.
Grusell, Marie, and Lars Nord. 2020. "Setting the Trend or Changing the Game? Professionalization and Digitalization of Election Campaigns in Sweden." *Journal of Political Marketing* 19 (3):258–78. doi: 10.1080/15377857.2016.1228555.
Gyventojų Pasitikėjimas Partijomis Išlieka Itin Žemas//Citizen Trust in Political Parties Remains Very Low. 2020, 15min.lt, Accessed May 23. https://www.15min.lt/naujiena/aktualu/lietuva/gyventoju-pasitikejimas-partijomis-islieka-itin-zemas-56-1107114.

Holtz-Bacha, Christina. 2002. "Professionalization of Political Communication." *Journal of Political Marketing* 1 (4):23–37. doi: 10.1300/J199v01n04_02.

Lees-Marshment, Jennifer. 2001. *Political Marketing and British Political Parties*. Manchester: Manchester University Press.

Lees-Marshment, Jennifer. 2009a. "Marketing after the Election: The Potential and Limitations of Maintaining a Market Orientation in Government." *Canadian Journal of Communication* 34 (2):205–27. doi: 10.22230/cjc.2009v34n2a2031.

Lees-Marshment, Jennifer. 2009b. *Political Marketing: Principles and Applications*. London: Routledge.

Lees-Marshment, Jennifer, and Darren G. Lilleker. 2005. *Political Marketing: A Comparative Perspective*. Manchester: Manchester Press.

Lilleker, Darren G. 2014. *Political Communication and Cognition*. Basingstoke: Palgrave.

Lilleker, Darren G., Jens Tenscher, and Václav Štětka. 2015. "Towards Hypermedia Campaigning? Perceptions of New Media's Importance for Campaigning by Party Strategists in Comparative Perspective." *Information, Communication & Society* 18 (7):747–65. doi: 10.1080/1369118X.2014.993679.

Lithuanian Bank Yearly Report. 1996. (Lietuvos banko ataskaita (1996)). Accessed March 09, 2021. https://www.lb.lt/lt/leidiniai/metu-ataskaita-1996-m.

Mcrotrends.net. 2021. Accessed March 09, 2021. https://www.macrotrends.net/countries/LTU/lithuania/inflation-rate-cpi.

Magin, Melanie, Nicole Podschuweit, Jörg Haßler, and Uta Russmann. 2017. "Campaigning in the Fourth Age of Political Communication: A Multi-Method Study on the Use of Facebook by German and Austrian Parties in the 2013 National Election Campaigns." *Information, Communication & Society* 20 (11):1698–719. doi: 10.1080/1369118X.2016.1254269.

Mair, Peter, Wolfgang C. Müller, and Fritz Plasser. 2004. *Political Parties and Electoral Change: party Responses to Electoral Markets*. London: Sage Publications Ltd.

Naprys, Ernestat. 2020. "Kam per Seimo rinkimus išleisti 8 mln. eurų: išlaidžiausios partijos ir kandidatai" ("Where 8 mln euros have been spent during the Seimas elections: the most expensive parties and candidates"), delfi.lt. Accessed February 10, 2021. https://www.delfi.lt/verslas/verslas/kam-per-seimo-rinkimus-isleisti-8-mln-euru-islaidziausios-partijos-ir-kandidatai.d?id=85934873

Negrine, Ralph. 2008. "The Transformation of Political Communication. Continuities and Changes in media and politics." Houndsmills and New York: Palgrave MacMillan. doi: 10.1177/1081180X96001002005.

Negrine, Ralph, and Stylianos Papathanassopoulos. 1996. "The Americanization of Political Communication: A Critique." *The Harvard International Journal of Press/Politics* 1 (2):45–62. doi: 10.1177/1081180X96001002005.

Norris, Pippa. 1997. *Electoral Change since 1945*. Oxford: Basil Blackwell.

Norris, Pippa. 2000. *A Virtuous Circle: Political Communications in Postindustrial Societies*. Cambridge: Cambridge University Press.

Plasser, Fritz, and Gunda Plasser. 2002. *Global Political Campaigning: A Worldwide Analysis of Campaign Professionals and Their Practices*. Westwood: Praeger Publishers.

Scammell, Margaret. 1998. "The wisdom of the war room: US campaigning and Americanization." *Culture & Society* 20 (2):251–275. doi: 10.1177/016344398020002006.

Schmitt-Beck, Rüdiger. 2007. "New Modes of Campaigning." In *The Oxford Handbook of Political Behavior*, edited by R. J. Dalton and H. Klingemann, 774–64. Oxford: Oxford University Press.

Strömbäck, Jesper. 2007. "Political Marketing and Professionalized Campaigning." *Journal of Political Marketing* 6 (2–3):49–67. doi: 10.1300/J199v06n02_04.

Strömbäck, Jesper. 2009. "Selective Professionalization of Political Campaigning: A Test of the Party-Centred Theory of Professionalized Campaigning in the Context of the 2006 Swedish Election." *Political Studies* 57 (1):95–116. doi: 10.1111/j.1467-9248.2008.00727.x.

Strömbäck, Jesper, and Spiro Kiousis. 2014. "Strategic Political Communication in Election Campaigns." In *Political Communication*, edited by I. C. Reinemann, 109–28. Berlin: Walter de Gruyter.

Swanson, David L., and Paolo Mancini. 1996. *Politics, Media, and Modern Democracy: An International Study of Innovations in Electoral Campaigning and Their Consequences*. Westport, Conn: Praeger.

Tenscher, Jens, and Juri Mykkänen. 2013. "Transformations in Second-Order Campaigning: A German-French Comparison of Campaign Professionalism in the 2009 European Parliamentary Elections." *Central European Journal of Communication* 6 (2):171–87.

Tenscher, Jens, Juri Mykkänen, and Tom Moring. 2012. "Modes of Professional Campaigning: A Four-Country Comparison in the European Parliamentary Elections 2009." *The International Journal of Press/Politics* 17 (2):145–68. doi: 10.1177/1940161211433839.

Unikaite-Jakuntavičienė, Ingrida. 2019. *Lithuania". in Thirty Years of Political Campaigning in Central and Eastern Europe*, edited by O. Eibl, and M. Gregor, 65–82. London: Palgrave Macmillan.

Unikaite, Ingrida. 2007. "Rinkimų Kampanijos Sąsajos su Rinkimų Rezultatais: LR Seimo Rinkimų (1996-2004) Atvejis//Election Campaign's Links with Electin Results: LR. Seimas Elections Cases (1996–2004)." PhD. diss., Vytautas Magnus University.

Unikaite, Ingrida. 2008. "Lithuania: Political Finance Regulation as a Tool of Political Manipulation." In *Public Finance and Post-Communist Party Development*, edited by J. Ikstens and S. Roper, Aldershot: Ashgate.

Vliegenthart, Rens. 2012. "Professionalization of Political Communication? A Longitudinal Analysis of Dutch Election Campaign Posters." *American Behavioral Scientist* 56 (2):135-50. doi: 10.1177/0002764211419488.
Webb, Paul D., David M. Farrell, and Ian Holliday. 2002. *Political Parties in Advanced Industrial Democracies*. Oxford: Oxford University Press.
Wring, Dominic. 1996. "Political Marketing and Party Development in Britain: A 'Secret' History." *European Journal of Marketing* 30 (10/11):92-103. doi: 10.1108/03090569610149818.

Interviews

(1) Interview with PR expert Jurgelionytė, Aušrinė. May 8, 2012. Vilnius.
(2) Interview with PR expert Špakauskas, Jaunius. May 7, 2012. Kaunas. Prepared by J. Nosovas and V. Sviderskis.
(3) Interview with journalist Slauskis, Žilvinas. May 4, 2012. Kaunas. Prepared by L. Migonis and A. Butkutė.
(4) Interview with journalist/political analyst Bačiulis, Audrius. May 8, 2012. Vilnius. Prepared by G. Jazdauskas.
(5) Interview with Velička, Dominykas (member of Seimas 2000–2004, member of Liberal Union of Lithuania). May 10, 2004. Vilnius. Prepared by I. Butėnaitė.
(6) Interview with Kubilius, Andrius (member of Seimas 1990–2019, member of Homeland Union—Lithuanian Christian Democrats). June 3 2004. Kaunas. Prepared by J. Alauskaitė.
(7) Interview with Starkevičius, Kazimieras (member of Seimas 2004–2020, member of Homeland Union—Lithuanian Christian Democrats). June 2, 2004. Kaunas. Prepared by S. Arminaitė.
(8) Interview with Kupčinskas, Andrius (member of Seimas 2018–2020, member of Kaunas city council 2000-2018, member of Homeland Union—Lithuanian Christian Democrats). September 5, 2004. Prepared by M. Barauskas.
(9) Interview with Juknevičienė, Rasa (member of Seimas 1990–2019, member of Homeland Union—Lithuanian Christian Democrats). May 10, 2004. Prepared by I. Filipova.
(10) Interview with Vėgėlė, Ignas (head of election committee of Lithuanian Christian Democratic Party). October 14, 2004. Vilnius. Prepared by J. Tylaitė.
(11) Interview with Valiukevičiūtė, Ona (member of Seimas 2004–2016, 2018–2020, member of Order and Justice). October 6, 2004. Šakiai. Prepared by G. Čiečkius.
(12) Interview with Kirkilas, Gediminas (member of Seimas 1992–2020, member of Lithuanian Social Democratic Party). September 20, 2004. Vilnius. Prepared by M. Juška.
(13) Interview with Labanauskas, Gintautas (member of Lithuanian Social Democratic Party). October 6 2004. Kaunas. Prepared by Eglė Urbonaitė.
(14) Interview with Vėsaite, Birutė (member of Seimas 2000–2016, member of Lithuanian Social Democratic Party). October 4, 2004. Kaunas. Prepared by L. Tamulynas.
(15) Interview with Martinkaitienė, Vilma (member of Seimas 2004–2008, member of Labour Party). September 22, 2004. Kaunas. Prepared by E. Sagatauskaitė.
(16) Interview with Muntianas, Viktoras (member of Seimas 2004–2008, member of Labour Party). September 24, 2004. Kaunas. Prepared by E. Alijevaitė.
(17) Interview with Padaiga, Žilvinas (member of Seimas 2004–2008, member of Labour Party). October 20, 2004. Kaunas. Prepared by A. Tamulevičiūtė.
(18) Interview with Rimšelis, Klemensas (member of Liberal and Centre Union). October 6, 2004. Kaunas. Prepared by A. Pikšrytė.
(19) Interview with Šilgalis, Žilvinas (member of Liberal and Centre Union, head of election committee). October 5 2004. Vilnius. Prepared by J. Brazauskaitė.
(20) Interview with Tamašauskas, Erikas (member of Liberals and Centre Union). September 30, 2004. Kaunas. Prepared by D. Plėvytė.
(21) Interview with Baltraitienė, Virginija (member of Seimas 2005–2016, member of Labour Party). April 30, 2012. Kėdainiai. Prepared by A. Garbaliauskaitė and V. Pugalskytė.
(22) Interview with Valinskas, Arūnas (member of Seimas 2008–2012, Speaker of the Seimas, leader of National Resurrection Party). April 24, 2012. Vilnius. Prepared by A. Sankauskas and R. Žvirblys.
(23) Interview with Šivickas, Mindaugas (member of Liberal and Centre Union). May 2, 2012. Kaunas. Prepared by L. Mukaitė.
(24) Interview with Mikaitis, Rimantas (member of Liberal Movement). April 24, 2012. Kaunas. Prepared by R. Baranauskas and K. Dackevičius.
(25) Interview with Teišerskytė, Dalia (member of Seimas 2004–2016, Liberal Movement). May 2, 2012. Kaunas. Prepared by D. Sližytė and L. Lapatinskaitė.
(26) Interview with Baškienė, Rima (member of Seimas 2004–2020, member of Lithuanian Peasants and Greens Union). April 30, 2012. Kuršėnai. Prepared by M. Matukaitytė.
(27) Interview with representative of Liberal Movement, PR expert. April 27, 2012. Vilnius. Prepared by G. Vasilaiuskaitė and A. Stankutė.

(28) Interview with Dalinkevičius, Gediminas (member of Labour Party, member of Seimas 2000–2004). April 20, 2012. Vilnius. Prepared by I. Žukauskaitė and L. Paukštytė.
(29) Interview with Auštrevičius, Petras (member of Seimas 2004–2014, member of EP 2014–2020, member of Liberal Movement). April 23, 2012. Vilnius. Prepared by O. Movsesjan.
(30) Interview with Žemaitaitis, Remigijus (member of Seimas 2009–2020, member of Order and Justice). May 14, 2012. Kaunas. Prepared by K. Tamašauskas and A. Martinkėnaitė.
(31) Interview with Jankauskas, Donatas (member of Seimas 2004–2016, member of Homeland Union—Lithuanian Christian Democrats). May 17, 2012. Kaunas. Prepared by J. Butkus and P. Murinas.
(32) Interview with Ulevičius, Liutauras, independent PR consultant, November 2015. Interview made by e-mail. Prepared by E. Petručionis.
(33) Interview with Jurgelionytė, Aušrinė, project manager at PR company Socialiniai partneriai. April 2014. Interview prepared by I. Unikaitė- Jakuntavičienė
(34) Interview with Lapinskas, Mindaugas (head of PR company Brandscape). March 19, 2014. Vilnius. Prepared by E. Petručionis.
(35) Interview with Kontrimas, Linas (head of PR company PR Service). March 2014. Prepared by E. Petručionis. Prepared by E. Petručionis.
(36) Interview with Gudelis, Darius (head of VIP Communications). March 19, 2014. Vilnius. Prepared by E. Petručionis.
(37) Interview with Žakas, Arijus (head of Socialus marketingas advertising agency). November 18, 2015. Vilnius. Prepared by E. Petručionis.
(38) Interview with Palionis, Andrius (vice-mayor of Kaunas, member of Vieningas Kaunas, head of election committee). November 4, 2015. Kaunas.
(39) Interview with Gapšys, Vytautas (head of election committee of Labour Party, member of Seimas). February 26, 2014. Vilnius.
(40) Interview with Pagojus, Julius (head of election committee of Lithuanian Social Democratic Party). February 26, 2014. Vilnius.
(41) Interview with Požėla, Juras (member of election committee of Lithuanian Social Democratic Party). March 19, 2014. Vilnius.
(42) Interview with Gustainis, Šarūnas (member of Liberal Movement, member of Seimas). November 17, 2015. Vilnius.
(43) Interview with Adomėnas, Petras (member of election committee of Homeland Union—Lithuanian Christian Democrats). February 28, 2014. Vilnius.
(44) Interview with Morkūnaite-Mikulėniene, Radvilė (vice-chair of Homeland Union—Lithuanian Christian Democrats). February 11, 2014.
(45) Interview with Vyšniauskas, Andrius (member of Homeland Union—Lithuanian Christian Democrats). November 10, 2015. Prepared by E. Petručionis.
(46) Interview with member of Homeland Union—Lithuanian Christian Democrats. October 27, 2020.

Professionalization of Campaign Communication beyond Communication Forms. An Analysis of Poland's Political Spots

Mariusz Kolczyński ⓘ and Marek Mazur ⓘ

ABSTRACT
Previous studies on the professionalization of campaign communication concentrated on forms of communication, ignoring the important question of how election campaigns vary in terms of the content of their election messages. The article intends to partially fill this breach by dealing with the case of Poland's parliamentary election campaigns in the years 2005–2019. Therefore, it not only describes the main groups of determinants (systemic, competitive, technological, and social) influencing the speed and direction of the process of professionalization in Poland but also attempts to verify the extent to which a party's electoral messages include certain content that can be treated as manifestations and effects of professionalization. Based on an analysis of audiovisual political advertising during five parliamentary campaigns, the study shows the dominance of valence issues (comparing them to position issues) in spots and the presence of centralized personalization (but not beyond simple party labeling). No linear increase or decrease of trend intensity has been observed regarding the above issues during the five elections. While the overall occurrence of these phenomena remains stable in the campaigns under study (meaning a significant, usually predominant share of party spots in a given year), their intensity varies.

Introduction

The process of change in the form and concept of election campaign management has drawn the attention of political communication researchers for several decades. They have described and explained these changes in categories of modernization (Swanson and Mancini 1996; Farell 2002), Americanization (Blumler and Gurevitch 2005; Bowler and Farell 1992; Xifra 2011) and professionalization (Negrine et al. 2007). The last of these conceptualizations, which relates to Weber's category of purposive rationality of organization (Weber 2002), seems to be the most analytically useful approach to the observation of global trends, and most thoroughly describes what is common and specific in the evolution of campaign communication among contemporary parties (Holtz-Bacha 2007, 63). This perspective locates campaign transformation within the framework of a process that can be described as "a process of change, in the field of politics and communication as elsewhere, that, either explicitly or implicitly, brings about a better and more efficient—and more studied—organization of resources and skills in order to achieve desired objectives, whatever they might be" (Papathanassopoulos et al. 2007, 10).

Among the important conditions necessary for the gradual and unidirectional process of political communication professionalization, one has to mention social and structural modernization (Swanson and Mancini 1996), mediatization of politics (Blumler and Kavanagh 1999; Strömbäck 2008; Strömbäck and Esser 2014; Esser 2019), marketization of politics (Newman 1994; Lilleker and Lees-Marshment 2005; Wring 2009) involving the participation of campaign experts in politics (Plasser and Plasser 2002) as well as institutional and legal determinants of greater competitiveness in the political market.

Professionalization expresses the adaptation of political parties to the above-mentioned changes in the campaign environment, which is part of a process involving the structural-functional transformation of political parties (Farell 2006). At the same time, it is the result and cause of an evolving process, which is reflected, in particular, in the organizational norms and values of electoral parties, encompassing catch-all parties (Kirchheimer 1966), professional-election parties (Panbianco 1988), cartel parties (Katz and Mair 1995), and the most advanced model in this respect: the business-firm party model (Krouwel 2006; Sobolewska-Myślik and Kosowska-Gąstoł 2017).

Embarking on a path toward professionalization of campaign communication is a consequence of parties' decreasing ability to ensure a loyal electoral base sufficiently enough to achieve their electoral goals (Mair et al. 2004). The effects of the dealignment process (Dalton et al. 2000) are illustrated by lower indicators of party membership, party identification (Berglund et al. 2005), and increased electoral volatility, as well as an increase in the number of late voters (McAllister 2002) and undecided voters.

It should be emphasized that campaign professionalization cannot be interpreted simply in terms of a party's reaction to socio-political changes. What also matters in this context is the behavior of individual parties in party systems, their characteristics, and the current context of their strategic decisions (Gibson and Römmele 2001).

Campaign transformation studies usually refer to the three-phase evolution model (Norris 2000; Farell and Webb 2000; Negrine 2008), which is based on the assumption of a political party's growing strategic sophistication of campaign communication at its planning level (i.e., its use of the latest research techniques), concept development and its implementation, reflecting the desire to reach the target groups of the campaign in the most precise and effective way. The overriding goal of growing campaign specialization is to maximize electoral support.

In the search for what is common in these models, regardless of their different labels, we shall refer to the paradigm of professionalization, which at the highest level of the campaign means: "the intensive use of multiple instruments of communication (including new ICTs), a marketing-oriented strategy of campaigns through continuous activities, a centralization of power within parties and, finally, an interactive and individualized relationship between candidates and voters" (Lisi 2013, 260).

Studies of professionalization prove its universal nature which is dependent on specific, systemic conditions (Negrine et al. 2007), which are particularly important in the emerging democracies in Central and Eastern Europe (Eibl and Gregor 2019). The focus of researchers is often on the degree of campaign professionalization defined mainly in terms of parties' use of selected campaign management techniques. Several studies on the party-centered theory of professionalized campaigning have confirmed the differences between parties in this respect (Strömbäck 2009; Gibson and Römmele 2009; Lisi 2013), as well as between types of campaigns (Tenscher and Mykkänen 2014).

These empirical analyses provide excellent information about the process of professionalization, showing its determinants and different stages of advancement. However, by focusing on campaign forms, they ignore the important question of how election campaigns vary in terms of the content of election messages, which is important for understanding the systemic consequences of professionalization.

In our article, we will attempt to partly fill this gap by dealing with the case of Polish parliamentary election campaigns in the years 2005–2019. Scientists studying campaign professionalization in Poland since 2005 agree that this process has significantly intensified (Cwalina and Drzewiecka 2019; Brodzińska-Mirowska 2013; Jacuński 2016). In reference to Strombach's conceptualization (2010, 56), there has been an increase in the use of marketing techniques and campaign experts, a prolongation of the campaign, and a concentration of power in the central campaign headquarters. Our first objective is to identify the key systemic conditions of this process and its specificity with regard to party expenditure on campaigns.

Second, in order to better understand the characteristics of campaign transformation, a study of the audiovisual political advertising content of the 2005–2019 parliamentary campaigns will be conducted. Referring to the concepts of political advertising prevailing in literature (Katz and Mair 1995; Kaid 2004; Trent and Friedenberg 2000), we want to verify the extent to which a party's electoral messages include content that can be treated as manifestations and effects of professionalization. We attempt to perform this type of analysis while being aware of the difficulties it entails, i.e., taking into consideration the contextual and unique character of each campaign. In order to achieve the best election result, professionalizing parties communicate different electoral offers, and their content results from their positioning and targeting strategies, which are shaped by an analysis of their current position and resources, as well as by numerous elements in various proximity to the campaign.

Nevertheless, we assume that some implications of the marketing concept of a campaign can be identified, which are manifested in the electoral messages of professionally advanced parties. Since the marketing approach is a party's response to the progressive destructuring of the voter market and results in the blurring of axiological and platform-specific differences between parties, it can be assumed that with the increase in the degree of professionalization, a party's sensitivity to demands coming from interest groups and voters who do not yet relate to the party increases. In the new conditions, parties more often than previously seek ways to mobilize voters who identify with the party to attract volatile voters and undecided voters. The classic dilemma inherent in political marketing (Ormrod and Henneberg 2006; Strömbäck 2007), which consists of the need to ensure an optimal combination in electoral offers of what is important for party identity according to the results of opinion polls, with due consideration of the needs and attitudes of voters from the target groups, is of particular importance in this context.

For the above reasons, rival groups who communicate through the mass media and the Internet with a broad socio-political spectrum of voters, especially groups competing for election victory, are more likely to resort to issues that are important, popular and that can bring together diverse voter target groups. This selective approach in defining campaign issues specific to party competition can be interpreted in terms of the salience theory (Budge and Farlie 1983), according to which parties focus on such general problems which put the parties in a privileged competitive position. Farell et al. (1998) link such a strategic party approach directly to the influence of political consultants.

Due to the fact that campaign professionalization in Poland during the analyzed period is happening under conditions of a more unpredictable electoral market than in Western European democracies and in constantly evolving and rather flexible identities of political groups operating in the catch-all formula, their communicated electoral messages should be characterized by a special focus on valence issues at the expense of position issues (Green 2007), which derive from Downs' tradition of defining party competition in the categories of spatial theory (1957). The latter mainly serves to mobilize voters with strong party identification by confronting other parties in axiological and problematic disputes. Valence issues, on the other hand, do not divide socially, making it easier to gain the support of a wide range of voters (Smith 2006). Additionally, they can better serve to implement the concept of political branding, which emphasizes the symbolic dimension of political brands (Scammell 2007, 2015) and is oriented toward building an emotional relationship between the party and voters who are less interested in politics and less politically conscious. This type of strategy may be particularly useful in democracies such as Poland, where the percentage of voters who do not identify with parties is higher (at about 50% of voters in Poland since 1990—CBOS 2019a) than in political systems with a longer history, a tradition of mass parties and a party system founded on clear socio-political divisions affecting the political preferences of voters. We have therefore formulated a hypothesis that states that in most advertising spots of the parties competing in the parliamentary elections under analysis, the emphasis is on valence issues at the expense of position issues.

The development of the branding concept in politics can also be identified as one of the basic reasons for the popularization of strategic personalization, which we consider in our study to be the second feature of electoral message content in professionalized campaigns. According to this context, in campaign communication, individuals gain importance at the expense of parties, collective identities, and political issues (Karvonen 2010; Rahat and Sheafer 2007). Strategic personalization may also mean an increase in the role of attributes of a politician at the expense of attributes related to a politician's work (Adam and Maier 2010; Aelst et al. 2012). As part of the study of this phenomenon, party campaigns usually emphasize centralized personalization (Balmas et al. 2014), according to which in the concept of creating a party's brand, its leader plays a particularly important role. This typical marketing approach results from a party's adaptation to the market logic of the media and the assumption that the leaders are particularly effective in attracting media attention and the attention of the general public (Stromback 2008; Plasser and Lengauer 2009). Media logic is conducive to personalization due to the growing commercialization of the media, increasing journalistic deprofessionalization resulting in the less substantive reporting of politics, and the development of media technology (Strömbäck and Esser 2014). There is no doubt about the impact of television on personalization. In addition, the logic of network media (Klinger and Svensson 2015; Adamik-Szysiak 2018), by promoting messages that are appealing to and chosen by the general public, as well as distributed without the intermediation of professional gatekeepers, creates particularly favorable conditions for increasing the informative value of simple and emotionally engaging political content featuring prominent politicians and enhancing image self-creation (Manning et al. 2017; Serazio 2017). Hence, our second hypothesis in the spot content study is that, in most spots, the leader is featured as the speaker and an important subject of the spot.

In light of the progression of professionalization, we assume that the occurrence of the types of problems raised and those concerning strategic centralized personalization will increase in subsequent campaigns.

Determinants of parliamentary election campaign professionalization in Poland

The evolutionary process of changes in the preparation and organization of election campaigns (marketization and mediatization of elections) taking place in Poland since 1989 is developing in a way peculiar to the Polish socio-political context, hence the subsequent stages of the process should not be considered solely from the perspective of global modernization processes (Holtz-Bacha 2002, 28–29). Therefore, the contextual determinants of the observed changes include all the factors related to the process, namely: the functioning of the political system, the development of the party system (presented in two dimensions: organization and competition) and its stability, structure, and competitiveness of the political market, legal regulations concerning the operation of political entities—including electoral regulations, the schedule of national elections and the general attitude of citizens to the world of politics—measured, among other things, by the degree of approval for the groups in power and an assessment of the political class' style of action. The degree of approval was reflected in the successive phases of Poland's systemic transformation in changes occurring among the electorate (level of structuring, party loyalty, support flow tendencies).

The transformations taking place within the media system are also significant, most importantly the pace of its development and shaping rules according to which political entities have access to particular media communication channels. All of the abovementioned characteristics point to the specificity of campaign professionalization in Poland being more akin to the transformations observed in recent democracies (Lisi 2013) than to those described in Anglo-American literature (Stromback 2009, 96). The main differences stem from the fact that, in recent democracies, the influence exerted by external determinants (systemic environment) is incomparably greater than in established democracies. Systemic determinants had a decisive influence on the shape of the Polish political market and the development opportunities of political parties particularly in the initial period of democratic transformation.

The intensity and speed of implementing new methods of running election campaigns (in the strategic and executive dimensions) can be correlated with subsequent stages of party system development. It should be assumed that the shape of Poland's party system after 1989 is a result of adopting a number of fundamental systemic solutions, most importantly the principle of political pluralism (1989), the proportional electoral system (1991, 1993—introducing a 5% electoral threshold for political parties or election committees, with an 8% electoral threshold for coalition entities) and a system of financing political parties from state budget subsidies (1997). In this context, three phases of party system development can be identified: (1) initial organization (1990-1993), (2) early stabilization (1994-2000), and (3) stabilization (since 2001). In the first two phases, the key role in the professional transformation of political parties was played by exogenous factors, while endogenous factors prevailed in the third phase (intra-party).

In the short history of Polish transformation, many organizational ideas can be observed; however, a significant part of newly formed political groups faced fundamental issues in determining their market identity. In the axiological dimension, the orientation around two groups of values prevailed: values associated with the past (in the case of most right-wing parties) or instrumental values considered to be an essential basis for current political activities. On the other hand, due to the existence of a "post-socialist axiological gap" and the socially perceptible consequences of economic transformation (in particular mass unemployment), the few groups that referred to liberal capitalist values were completely disregarded by most segments of the electorate. Thus, in the first and second phases of the development of the party system, despite the high dynamics of the system transformation process (and sometimes even the turbulent nature of the transformation), the process was random and in isolation from social reality. As a consequence, it did not lead to any permanent diversification and structuring of the political market.

The year 1997 constituted a clear turning point in the development of the party system, marked on the one hand by the adoption of a new Constitution and a new law on political parties, and the pre-election consolidation of right-wing groups on the other. These changes built the foundations for further systemic transformation. The parliamentary elections in 1997, featuring a highly effective maneuver to concentrate the fragmented forces of the right side of the political scene into one group (Solidarity Electoral Action [Akcja Wyborcza Solidarność, abbr. AWS]), led to the creation of a clear structure of the political market, enabling voters to choose from among three clearly defined (at least for Polish conditions) political offers: left, center and right—opening the way for the stabilization of the political scene. Symbolically, the parliamentary elections in 2001 closed the period of the initial adaptation of political parties to the rules of the functioning of a democratic state, at the same time opening a phase of gradual organizational consolidation and professionalization of projects carried out within the framework of political competition (especially by the newly created political entities: the Civic Platform [Platforma Obywatelska, abbr. PO] and the Law and Justice [Prawo I Sprawiedliwość, abbr. PiS] parties).

The market stabilization and consolidation of party organizations were largely due to the adopted solutions concerning the financing of political and electoral parties. Since the parliamentary elections, there has been a trend toward an increase in campaign spending among parties competing for victory. In the 2010s, the financial gap between the leading and remaining parties became particularly visible (see Table 1).

The 2005 parliamentary elections, which took place in the specific context of an unprecedented combination of presidential and parliamentary elections (with a strongly personalized electoral message) and a de facto decomposition of the dominant political group of the post-communist left—the Democratic Left Alliance [Sojusz Lewicy Demokratycznej, abbr. SLD]—is considered

Table 1. Spending of the top three parties/electoral committees on parliamentary campaigns (in PLN)*.

Election date	Election result		
	1st place in the elections	2nd place in the elections	3rd place in the elections
2001	26 995 002	15 319 017	1 861 247
2005	29 908 733	27 180 444	25 733 930
2007	29 424 920	28 285 522	26 114 878
2011	29 274 776	30 119 644	1 748 565
2015	29 656 020	29 415 998	2 877 178
2019	30 220 938	30 029 089	9 641 495

*own work based on State Election Commission data, www.pkw.gov.pl.

to be a breakthrough in the process of professionalization. New solutions were introduced by right-wing parties fighting to consolidate their market position (Law and Justice and Civic Platform), presenting modern strategic solutions (especially in the field of electoral communication) prepared by external political service providers on the basis of the results of large-scale political market research (polls, focus groups). Taking into account the temporal dimension, the 2005 campaign can be considered the first to meet the basic criteria for a permanent campaign. Thus, three key (and interdependent) areas of activity in political campaigns have been significantly modified: (1) the field of campaign planning and preparation (gradual extension of campaign duration, progressive professionalization of campaign preparation), (2) the field of campaign management (strengthening the decision-making position of party leaders and increasing the importance of the role of the professional bureaucratic system, as well as using external/professional staff and advisory departments to take on successive decision-making powers) and (3) the field of communication (Farrell and Webb 2000).

Changes in the way of communicating with potential voters have been of particular importance for professionalization. On the one hand, there was a radical increase in the use of mass communication, while on the other hand, a far-reaching change occurred in the way the electoral message was formatted: from narrowly addressed (targeted) messages referring to fundamental party values to messages instrumentally using universal values to achieve the maximum possible reception range (marking the beginning of the evolutionary disideologization of the electoral offer). In other words, by taking advantage of the weakening market position of left-wing parties, the dominant right-wing parties managed to seamlessly adopt strategies typical of Western European catch-all parties.

Generally speaking, the new solutions applied during the 2005 parliamentary campaign (proven in practice in the campaign preceding the early parliamentary elections in 2007) have shaped a specific market model in the Polish context, whose main determinants are: the popularization of strategic marketing orientation, the formation of teams of election campaign specialists within the party, an increase in the importance of political market research, the generality and broad social range of political offers and an increase in the costs of election campaigns (Kolczyński and Mazur 2007, 2009).

Expenditure on paid projects implemented through means of mass communication constitutes a major part of the rising costs of campaigns. An analysis of the spending structure in this area makes it possible to determine the nature and reorientation of election campaign mediatization in Poland. It also allows for a reflection on the specificities of utilizing media channels by entities competing in the election process. The key factor (apart from technological development) determining which communication channels are chosen is the funding an entity has at its disposal (a dependence well visible in the case of groups with low financial resources, limiting their possibilities of multichannel media impact).

Table 2 shows how the allocation of financial resources has changed for tasks carried out through the mass media by two political parties dominating the Polish market in the parliamentary campaigns conducted between 2005 and 2019.

In the case of the Civic Platform, what draws attention is the stabilization (at a relatively high level: 53%–55% of the campaign budget) of expenditure on campaign projects carried out

Table 2. Media expenditure in the election campaign of the Civic Platform and the Law and Justice party (share in %)*.

Election date	Party	Campaign expenditure (in PLN)	Expenditure on mass media (share in %)	TV expenditure (share in mass media expenditure in %)	Press expenditure (share in mass media expenditure in %)	Radio expenditure (share in mass media expenditure in %)	Internet expenditure (share in mass media expenditure in %)
2005	PiS	29 908 755	55	65	5	8	x*
	PO	27 180 444	48	63	23	8	x*
2007	PO	29 424 920	37	70	20	5	x*
	PiS	28 285 522	68	49	8	2	x*
2011	PiS	30 119 644	53	23	18	8	7
	PO	29 274 776	54	51	8	1	13
2015	PiS	29 656 020	46	53	11	4	9
	PO	29 415 998	53	49	6	1	16
2019	KO (PO, N, I.Pl, Greens)	30 220 938	55	14	4	1	34
	PiS	30 029 089	41	16	8	9	22

*Source: own work based on State Election Commission data, www.pkw.gov.pl.

by means of mass communication. There is also a clear trend in how the strategic position of individual media has changed: a significant decrease in the role played by television (max. 70% of spending on media in 2007—min. 14% in 2019) and a significant increase in spending on Internet projects (from 14% in the 2011 campaign to 34% in the 2019 elections). Expenditure on Internet campaigns in 2019 perfectly indicates a further increase in the role of external, professional, and highly specialized political service providers and a high degree of concentration of decision-making powers (Internet campaigns were both conceptually and executively dominated by two large providers whose services consumed 74.5% of the funds allocated for Internet campaigns). The qualitative change in the approach to communication during the campaign is also evidenced by the fact that the costs of broadcasting spot ads on television constituted only 42% of the costs of promoting electoral committees on the Internet.

The Law and Justice party's media strategy was shaped in a slightly different way; since the elections in 2005, we can observe a gradual decrease in funding for the campaign conducted in the mass media. The visible lack of regularity in the way individual media channels are used is not incidental. Law and Justice communication strategies have a multi-faceted character: they are based on seeking a balance between activity in the conventional media, high exposure by means of outdoor advertising, and direct communication (as much as 15.8% of expenditure in 2019 went on organizing election conventions and meetings with voters). The exception is the Internet since its use generated higher costs in subsequent campaigns (up from a 7% share in spending on mass communication in 2011 to 22% in 2019).

Analyzing media spending by parties holding a secondary position on the political market is difficult as we are dealing with two different types of organizations: those with a relatively stable market position (Democratic Left Alliance, Polish People's Party [Polskie Stronnictwo Ludowe, abbr. PSL]) and newly formed groups whose life cycle on the market includes at most two or three consecutive parliamentary elections. It should also be remembered that their financial resources allocated to election campaigns are significantly lower than those of the large dominant parties (in 2015: PSL party –44.2%, Modern party [Nowoczesna] – 38.9%, SLD party –27%, Kukiz'15 party –9.7%, KORWIN party –5.5%, Together party [Razem] – 1.2% of the winning Law and Justice party's budget; in 2019: SLD –32.1%, PSL –28.2%, Confederation [Konfederacja] – 5.8% of the winning Law and Justice party's budget). Despite these differences, in 2015, a similar share of media spending in the campaign budget can be observed (from 33% to 45%). On the other hand, the limited budget of the campaign clearly affects the choice of main media channels, with a visible limitation of the role of television and increased Internet exposure among parties with the lowest financial resources (31% of the media budget—Together party, 26%—Kukiz'15).

In the 2019 elections, the shift in campaign communication toward the Internet is more visible and clearly indicates a strategic reorientation of communication activities, since the share of funds allocated for online promotion in media spending is very high; in the extreme case of the right-wing Confederation party, it exceeds 57% (see Table 3).

Valence issues and strategic centralized personalization in audiovisual political advertising

In order to verify our hypotheses about Polish parties' greater emphasis in mass media on valence issues at the expense of position issues, the high degree of strategic centralized personalization, and an increase in the intensity of these features in subsequent campaigns, we conducted a content analysis of political spots that were broadcasted during the parliamentary election campaigns of 2005–2019. According to declarations made by Poles, spot ads are one of the most popular sources of information about committees and candidates running in the elections (since 2011 they have only fallen slightly short of TV news and current affairs programs—CBOS 2019b). Therefore, it should not come as a surprise that the campaign strategies of Poland's main parties, it represents the main form of communication, ensuring control over the message and the effectiveness of influencing voters, as evidenced by the course of the parliamentary election campaigns of 2005–2007, which constituted a marketing breakthrough. In both elections, the final success was largely determined by audiovisual advertisements with a properly formatted message, professionally selected form, placed in a carefully prepared manner in the schedule of strategic activities, and broadcasted with high frequency in carefully selected time and television brackets. The potential of audiovisual advertising was significantly increased thanks to the possibilities of broadcasting ads on the Internet, as in the first period mainly on the parties' websites (2011). In subsequent campaigns, it was disseminated on a commercial basis in various communication channels on the Internet offering access to the target political audience.

For the purpose of this study, 94 audiovisual ads of the parties that received at least 5% support from all the voters were analyzed. Two main criteria were adopted for the selection of the sample: the frequency of broadcasting and the number of broadcasts on Internet channels. This allowed for the selection of spots of key strategic importance for a given political party or election committee and those that resonated best among potential voters. The number of ads

Table 3. Media expenditure in the election budget of small parties in the 2015 and 2019 parliamentary elections (% share)*.

Election date	Party	Campaign expenditure (in PLN)	Expenditure on mass media (share in %)	TV expenditure (share in mass media expenditure, in %)	Press expenditure (share in mass media expenditure, in %)	Radio expenditure (share in mass media expenditure, in %)	Internet expenditure (share in mass media expenditure, in %)
2015	PiS	29 656 020	46	53	11	4	9
	PO	29 415 998	53	49	6	1	16
	PSL	13 122 215	42	22	36	6	7
	Modern	11 551 946	45	11	9	6	17
	SLD (as United Left Coalition)	8 027 474	44	6	18	4	7
	Kukiz'15	2 887 178	33	11	30	8	7
	KORWIN	1 644 243	45	34	12	1	31
	Together	353 526	6	0	55	4	26
2019	KO (PO, N, IPl, Greens)	30 220 938	55	14	4	1	34
	PiS	30 029 089	41	16	8	9	22
	SLD	9 641 495	49	4	12	4	23
	PSL	8 468 107	40	4	31	4	19
	Confederation	1 729 900	32	1	14	1	57

*Source: own work based on State Election Commission data, www.pkw.gov.pl.

of a single party analyzed in one election ranged from two to five; 45% of all the ads lasted a maximum of 30 s, 31% of them lasted between 31 and 60 s, and 24% lasted over 60 s. The study was conducted based on a categorization key prepared by the authors (see Appendix 1).

In light of our studies, we can conclude that the main topic of the majority of the ads, which are crucial for a given election campaign, deal with contextually selected socio-political issues, enabling reference to values fundamental for a political broadcaster (54% of the ads examined). Thus, the axiological plane can be considered the main area of electoral competition; in other words, a certain set of values constitutes the core of the political offer, complemented by the organizational and personal dimensions of the offer (see Figure 1). However, it should be stressed that political values in ads tend to define the identity of a party in general terms that elude a party's (model) ideological profile. They can therefore be regarded as typical for catch-all parties.

The results of our study have confirmed the first hypothesis, which claims that there is more emphasis in ads on valence issues (issues seen uniformly as bad or good by voters) than on position issues (issues relating to disputes between parties and divergent political attitudes among voters, see Table 4). Namely, parties tended to focus voter attention on such general positions and values that are widely accepted and which, due to their importance and the party's image to date, may help them compete in the elections. The most popular problems cited in the spots included the fiscal policy (lowering of various tax burdens, i.e., in the 2005 and 2019 campaigns), the fight against corruption (in the 2007 campaign), social support programs for various social groups (families, pensioners) and environmental protection (in the 2019 campaign). Emphasis on position issues dominated 19% of the spots, which resulted from two goals set by the parties: image confrontation concerning current issues viewed differently by the public, and, less frequently, axiologically determining one's position on the left-right continuum. In 10% of the spots, the parties emphasized both types of issues to a similar degree, while in 15% of the ads, there was no emphasis on any of the described types.

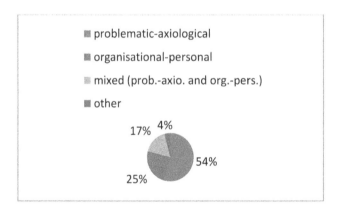

Figure 1. The main topics of audiovisual advertising spots in the parliamentary campaigns of 2005–2019 (n = 94)*.
*Source: based on own research

Table 4. Emphasis on issues in audiovisual spots*.

Types of issues	Parliamentary campaign/year					
	2005 (n = 17)	2007 (n = 15)	2011 (n = 17)	2015 (n = 24)	2019 (n = 21)	Sum (n = 94)
Position	1	7	5	3	2	18 (19%)
Valence	11	7	9	14	12	53 (56%)
Mixed (position and valence)	1	1	3	4	0	9 (10%)
None	4	0	0	3	7	14 (15%)

*Source: based on own research.

Analysis of ad content in subsequent election campaigns points to a relatively constant pattern of message formatting. In more than half of the ads in a given year, valence issues turned out to be more significant than position issues. The content of the ads deviates significantly from this pattern only in 2007, which can be explained in particular by the confrontational style of competition in the only early elections in this group. This was associated with an attempt by the opposition parties to discredit the ruling party (PiS) and to emphasize the differences between these parties in the problematic and axiological dimensions.

As a result of the study, we are also able to confirm the hypothesis concerning the occurrence of centralized personalization in ads, although only in part. For this study, we have distinguished two dimensions of strategic personalization: the formal-symbolic, and the substantive dimensions. The former reflects the leader's exposure in the visual layer (the leader dominates this layer or it is shown in the ad) and his/her role as an important conveyor of verbal content in the ad (she/he is the main speaker and/or addresses the camera directly). The second refers to a situation where the characteristics of the leader are an important or dominant subject of the ad.

The combined results show that the focus on the leader in most ads is limited to the symbolic-formal dimension (See Table 5). This evaluation of our results corresponds to the conclusions of long-term studies of political advertising in other countries (Holtz-Bacha 2004; Scammell and Langer 2006; Langer 2011), which prove that leaders primarily play the role of the "face of a campaign." The leaders serve the purpose of visual identification, effectively concretizing and emotionally saturating the party image. After becoming the key spokesman for a party, they reinforce the coherence and clarity of their message. Rarely does this message apply to the leaders themselves, meaning their qualities as politicians and individuals (the leader appeared as an important subject in no more than 12% of the ads).

The model of strategic personalization in ads is not common, since a significant percentage of ads have not shown any of its manifestations.

In subsequent campaigns, the degree of strategic personalization in ads varied. In 2005, it was relatively high, while in the years 2007 and 2019, it was the lowest. It appears evident that a leader's exposure depends on the context of elections determined by the political strength of individual leaders and the system of competition inherent in the social and political situation. The involvement of leaders in the ads of the first elections studied may result from the fact that they directly preceded presidential elections, in which some of the leaders also participated. In the 2011 and 2015 elections, the reasons for the high degree of personalization should be sought in the strategic approach of new parties entering the political market, which resorted to the credibility of their leaders—the party founders—in the creation of their political brand. The messages communicated by these parties, including their names, were to trigger strong, emotional, and positive associations among voters: in 2011—with the political history of the scandalous media politician Janusz Palikot (Palikot Movement), in 2015—with the courage and intransigence of the celebrity politician, popular singer Paweł Kukiz, who won 20% of the vote in the recent presidential elections (Kukiz '15), and in the same year—with the economic education and professionalism of Ryszard Petru (Modern Party of Ryszard Petru).

Table 5. Exposure of a leader in spots*.

Types of exposure of a leader	2005 ($n=17$)	2007 ($n=15$)	2011 ($n=17$)	2015 ($n=24$)	2019 ($n=21$)	Sum ($n=94$)
Formal-symbolic	11	7	4	13	7	43 (46%)
Substantive	2	0	1	1	0	5 (5%)
Formal-symbolic and substantive	1	0	5	0	1	6 (6%)
None	72 3	43 8	59 7	58 10	38 13	41 (44%)

*Source: based on own research.

In presenting the results of our analysis, it is worth emphasizing in this context the fact that in 2007 and 2019, no new group entered parliament except for one, which, acting in a confederacy formula, avoided promoting a single political leader (the Freedom and Independence Confederation in 2019). The degree of the leader's exposure in 2011 was most likely also determined by the strategy assumed by the Civic Platform which won the elections. The strategy was built around the positive opinion of the majority of the public regarding the competences and personal qualities of the popular Prime Minister Donald Tusk (CBOS (Centrum Badania Opinii Społecznej) 2011a), who clearly enjoyed more positive support than the leader of the largest opposition party (CBOS (Centrum Badania Opinii Społecznej) 2011b).

Summarizing our analysis of election communication in the years 2005–2019, we can venture to conclude that it was dominated by problem positioning with a clear predominance of valence issues over position issues, and by the leader constituting an essential part of a party's brand image. No linear increase or decrease of trend intensity has been observed concerning the above issues throughout the five elections. While the overall occurrence of these phenomena remained stable in the campaigns under study (a significant, usually predominant share of party spots in a given year), their intensity varied.

Conclusion

The analysis of election campaign professionalization in Poland allows us to identify four main groups of factors influencing the speed and direction of the observed changes: (1) systemic determinants—in the first period of democratic transformation (1989–2001), (2) competitive determinants—the market duopoly of the dominant parties (since 2005) favoring adopting the "follow" strategy (i.e., replicating market solutions of the market-leading competitor in a given period in order to neutralize its competitive advantage), (3) technological determinants—the Internet guarantees strategic advantages which can be described as "technological effectiveness," i.e., with comparable inputs, it offers more campaign intensity than traditional media (ultimately, multi-channel communication strategies on the Internet offer a greater range of impact than television), (4) social determinants—the growing number of voters with unstable party preferences necessitates the use of sophisticated methods of impact, appropriate to the current campaign context, and of nonparty motives for potential electoral engagement (Cwalina and Drzewiecka 2019, 139–140).

The causes of valence issues and strategic centralized personalization appearing in key strategic messages should be attributed to the last of the above groups of factors. From a party's marketing perspective, an electoral message's form seems to be most effective in the context of winning the votes of voter groups with diverse political preferences and of various social profiles, and in the mobilization and persuasion of undecided, centered voters, with political attitudes that are not yet fully defined.

Based on the assumption that the Polish political parties that received more than 5% support represent a high level of professionalization of election campaigns, our analysis confirms that campaign transformation in Poland expresses above all the ability of the parties to adapt their electoral communication to the current socio-political context and entails flexible, contextual positioning of the electoral offer with reference to instrumental values. This conclusion applies to all parties, and the way election spots are constructed remains independent of the size of the party and its age. The marketing differentiation of offers with a predominance of valence issues, at least at the electoral communication level in the last weeks of the campaign, is most often achieved through references to the party image, communication style, and simple personal party labeling.

In such circumstances, the dilemma described by researchers of professionalization is of particular significance in the context of Poland's political system (Papathanassopoulos et al. 2007, 19). According to it, party decision-makers are confronted with having to choose between achieving greater electoral efficiency through professionalization by implementing short-term catch-all communication strategies, or ensuring the greater integrity of their party by applying long-term strategies for building their political identity (which is better served by position issues).

The choice of the first of these paths by recent democracies, as illustrated by our research on Poland, may have significant systemic consequences, such as an increase in the level of instability and unpredictability in the context of interparty competition, and, above all, in its structural dimension. Undoubtedly, the largest parties are in a more privileged position thanks to their financial advantage and other resources at their disposal allowing them to exercise power over other parties (Gibson and Römmele 2001, 2009). However, without a strong electoral base, they too are confronted with the risk of losing a great deal of support in the face of the dynamic changes taking place in the system of political competition.

ORCID

Mariusz Kolczyński http://orcid.org/0000-0002-0355-4004
Marek Mazur http://orcid.org/0000-0002-6684-9790

References

Adam, Silke, and Michael Maier. 2010. "Personalization of Politics. A Critical Review and Agenda for Research." *Annals of the International Communication Association* 34 (1):213–57. https://doi.org/10.1080/23808985.2010.11679101

Adamik-Szysiak, Małgorzata. 2018. *Strategie Komunikowania Podmiotów Politycznych w Polsce w Mediach Społecznościowych*. Lublin: Wydawnictwo Uniwersytetu Marii Curie-Skłodowskiej.

Aelst, Peter Van., Tamir Sheafer, and James Stanyer. 2012. "The Personalization of Mediated Political Communication. A Review of Concepts, Operationalizations and Key Findings." *Journalism* 13 (2):203–20. https://doi.org/10.1177/1464884911427802

Balmas, Meital, Gideon Rahat, Tamir Sheafer, and Shaul R. Shenhav. 2014. "Two Routes to Personalized Politics: Centralized and Decentralized Personalization." *Party Politics* 20 (1):37–51. https://doi.org/10.1177/1354068811436037

Berglund, Frode, Sören Holmberg, Hermann Schmitt, and Jacques Thomassen. 2005. "Party Identification and Party Choice." In *The European Voter*, edited by J. Thomassen, 106–24. Oxford: Oxford University Press.

Blumler, J. G., and D. Kavanagh. 1999. "The Third Age of Political Communication: Influences and Features." *Political Communication* 16 (3):209–30. https://doi.org/10.1080/105846099198596

Blumler, Jay G., and Michael Gurevitch. 2005. "'Americanization' Reconsidered: U.K.—U.S. Campaign Communication Comparisions Cross Time." In *Mediated Politics: Communication in the Future of Democracy*, edited by L. Benett and R. N. Entman, 380–405. Cambridge: Cambridge University Press.

Bowler, Shaun and David M. Farell, Eds. 1992. *Electoral Strategies and Political Marketing*. London: Macmillian Press Ltd.

Brodzińska-Mirowska, Barbara. 2013. *Marketing Międzywyborczy w Teorii i Praktyce*. Przypadek Platformy Obywatelskiej. Toruń: Wydawnictwo UMK.

Budge, Ian, and Dennis Farlie. 1983. "Party Competition – Selective Emphasis or Direct Confrontation? An Alternative View with Data." In *Western European Party Systems: Continuity and Change*, edited by H. Daalder and P. Mair, 267–306. London: Sage.

CBOS (Centrum Badania Opinii Społecznej). 2019a. *Struktura sceny politycznej: partie bliższe i dalsze* Komunikat z badań no 37/2019.

CBOS (Centrum Badania Opinii Społecznej) . 2019b. *Odbiór kampanii wyborczej i aktywność polityczna w internecie przed wyborami parlamentarnymi* Komunikat z badań no 152/2019.

CBOS (Centrum Badania Opinii Społecznej). 2011a. *Portret Donalda Tuska po ponad trzech latach sprawowania urzędu premiera*. Komunikat z badań no 83/2011.

CBOS (Centrum Badania Opinii Społecznej). 2011b. Wizerunki liderów partyjnych. Komunikat z badań no 114/2011.
Cwalina, Wojciech, and Milena Drzewiecka. 2019. "Poland." In *Thirty Years of Political Campaigning in Central and Eastern Europe*, edited by O. Eibl and M. Gregor, 131–40. Palgrave Macmillan, Cham, Palgrave Mcmillan. https://doi.org/10.1007/978-3-030-27693-5_10
Dalton, Russell J., Ian McAllister, and Martin P. Wattenberg. 2000. "The Consequences of Partisan Dealignment." In *Parties without Partisans: Political Change in Advanced Industrial Democracies*, edited by R. Dalton and M. P. Wattenberg, 37–63. Oxford: Oxford University Press.
Eibl, Otto and Miloš Gregor, Eds. 2019. *Thirty Years of Political Campaigning in Central and Eastern Europe.* Palgrave Macmillan, Cham, Palgrave Mcmillan. https://doi.org/10.1007/978-3-030-27693-5_10
Esser, Frank. 2019. "Comparative International Studies of Election Campaign Communication: What Should Happen Next?" *Journalism* 20 (8):1124–38. https://doi.org/10.1177/1464884919845450
Farell, David M. 2002. "Campaign Modernization and the West European Party." In *Political Parties in the New Europe. Political and Analytical Challenges*, edited by K. R. Luther, F. Müller-Rommel, 63–83. Oxford: Oxford University Press.
Farell, David M. 2006. "Political Parties in Changing Campaign Environment." In *Handbook of Party Politics*, edited by Katz R. and W. Crotty, 122–33. Los Angeles: Sage.
Farell, David M., and Paul Webb. 2000. "Political Parties as Campaign Organizations." In *Parties without Partisans: Political Change in Advanced Industrial Democracies*, edited by R. Dalton and M. P. Wattenberg, 102–28. Oxford, Oxford University Press.
Farell, David M., R. Kolodny, and S. Medvic. 1998. "The Political Consultant/Political Party Relationship: A Health Warning for Representative Democracy or a Welcome Advance?." Paper Presented at the Annual Meeting of the American Political Science Association, Boston, September 3–6.
Gibson, Rachel, and Andrea Römmele. 2001. "Changing Campaign Communications: A Party-Centered Theory of Professionalized Campaigning." *Harvard International Journal of Press/Politics* 6 (4):31–43. https://doi.org/10.1177/108118001129172323
Gibson, Rachel, and Andrea Römmele. 2009. "Measuring the Professionalization of Political Campaigning." *Party Politics* 15 (3):265–93. https://doi.org/10.1177/1354068809102245
Green, Jane. 2007. "When Voters and Parties Agree: Valence Issues and Party Competition." *Political Studies* 55 (3):629–55. https://doi.org/10.1111/j.1467-9248.2007.00671.x
Holtz-Bacha, Ch. 2002. "Professionalization of Political Communication." *Journal of Political Marketing* 4:23–37.
Holtz-Bacha, Christina. 2004. "Germany: From Modern to Postmodern Campaign." In *The Politics of Representation*, edited by J. Roper, Ch. Holtz-Bacha, and G. Mazzoleni, 77–97. New York: Peter Lang.
Holtz-Bacha, Christina. 2007. "Professionalization of Politics in Germany." In *The Professionalization of Political Communication*, edited by R. Negrine, P. Mancini, Ch. Holtz-Bacha, and S. Papathanassopoulos, 63–79. Bristol: Intellect.
Jacuński, Michał. 2016. *Sieciowe Komunikowanie Polityczne w Polsce: perspektywa Aktorów Politycznych*. Wrocław: Wydawnictwo Uniwersytetu Wrocławskiego.
Kaid, Lynda Lee. 2004. "Political Advertising." In *Political Communication Research*, edited by L.L. Kaid. Mahwah, 155–202. New Jersey-London: Lawrence Erlbaum Associates, Publishers.
Karvonen, Lauri. 2010. *The Personalization of Politics: A Study of Parliamentary Democracies*. Colchester: ECPR Press.
Katz, Richard S., and Peter Mair. 1995. "Changing Models of Party Organizations and Party Democracy. The Emergence of the Cartel Party." *Party Politics* 1 (1):5–28. https://doi.org/10.1177/1354068895001001001
Kirchheimer, Otto. 1966. "The Transformation of the Western European Party Systems." In *Political Parties and Political Development*, edited by J. LaPalombara and M. Weiner, 177–200. Princeton: Princeton University Press.
Klinger, Ulrike, and Jakob Svensson. 2015. "The Emergence of Network Media Logic in Political Communication: A Theoretical Approach." *New Media & Society* 17 (8):1241–57. https://doi.org/10.1177/1461444814522952
Kolczyński, Mariusz, and Marek Mazur. 2007. *Wojna na Wrażenia. Strategie Polityczne i Telewizja w Kampaniach Wyborczych w 2005 Roku*. Warszawa: Wydawnictwo Sejmowe.
Kolczyński, Mariusz, and Marek Mazur. 2009. *Broń Masowego Wrażenia*. Warszawa: Wydawnictwo Sejmowe.
Krouwel, André. 2006. "Party Models." In *Handbook of Party Politics*, edited by Katz R. and W. Crotty, 249–69. Los Angeles: Sage.
Langer, Ana Ines. 2011. *The Personalization of Politics in the UK. Mediated Leadership from Atlee to Cameron*. Manchester: Manchester University Press.
Lilleker, Darren G. and Jennifer Lees-Marshment, eds. 2005. *Political Marketing. A Comparative Perspective*. Manchester: Manchester University Press.
Lisi, Marco. 2013. "The Professionalization of Campaigns in Recent Democracies: The Portuguese Case." *European Journal of Communication* 28 (3):259–76. https://doi.org/10.1177/0267323113475463
Mair, Peter, Wolfgang C. Müller, and Fritz Plasser. 2004. "Conclusion: Political Parties in Changing Electoral Markets." In *Political Parties and Electoral Change. Party Responses to Electoral Markets*, edited by Mair P., W. C. Muller, and F. Plasser, 264–74. London: Sage.

Manning, Nathan, Ruth Penfold-Mounce, Brian D. Loader, Ariadne Vromen, and Michael Xenos. 2017. "Politicians, Celebrities and Social Media: A Case of Informalisation?" *Journal of Youth Studies* 20 (2):127–44. https://doi.org/10.1080/13676261.2016.1206867

McAllister, Ian. 2002. "Calculating or Capricious? The New Politics of Late Deciding Voters." In *Do Political Campaigns Matter? Campaign Effects in Elections and Referendums*, edited by D. M. Farell and R. Schmitt-Beck, 22–40. London: Routledge.

Negrine, Ralph. 2008. *The Transformation of Political Communication. Continuities and Changes in Media and Politics*. Basingstoke: Palgrave Macmillan.

Negrine, Ralph, Paolo Mancini, Christine Holtz-Bacha, and Stylianos Papathanassopoulos, Eds. 2007. *The Professionalization of Political Communication*. Bristol: Intellect.

Newman, Bruce I. 1994. *The Marketing of the President. Political Marketing as Campaign Strategy*. California: Sage.

Norris, Pippa. 2000. *A Virtuous Circle. Political Communications in Postindustrial Societies*. Cambridge: Cambridge University Press.

Ormrod, Robert, and Stephan C. Henneberg. 2006. "'Are You Thinking What We're Thinking' or 'Are we Thinking What You're Thinking?' an Exploratory Analysis of the Market Orientation of the UK Parties." In *The Marketing of Political Parties. Political Marketing at the 2005 British General Election*, edited by D. G. Lilleker, N. A. Jackson, and R. Scullion, 31–58. Manchester: Manchester University Press.

Panbianco, Angelo. 1988. *Political Parties: Organization and Power*. London: Cambridge University Press.

Papathanassopoulos, Stylianos, Ralph Negrine, Paolo Mancini, and Christina Holtz-Bacha. 2007. "Political Communication in the Era of Professionalisation." In *The Professionalization of Political Communication*, edited by R. Negrine, P. Mancini, Ch. Holtz-Bacha, and S. Papathanassopoulos, 9–25. Bristol: Intellect.

Plasser, Fritz, and Günther Lengauer. 2009. "Television Campaigning Worldwide." In *Routledge Handbook of Political Management*, edited by D.W. Johnson, 253–71. New York: Routledge.

Plasser, Fritz, and Gunda Plasser. 2002. *Global Political Campaigning. A Worldwide Analysis of Campaign Professionals and Their Practises*. Westport: Preager.

Rahat, Gideon, and Tamir Sheafer. 2007. "The Personalization(s) of Politics: Israel, 1949–2003." *Political Communication* 24 (1):65–80. https://doi.org/10.1080/10584600601128739

Scammell, Margaret. 2015. "Politics and Image: The Conceptual Value of Branding." *Journal of Political Marketing* 14 (1–2):7–18. https://doi.org/10.1080/15377857.2014.990829

Scammell, Margaret, and Ana Inés Langer. 2006. "Political Advertising in the United Kingdom." In *The Sage Handbook of Political Advertising*, edited by L. L. Kaid and Ch. Holtz-Bacha, 65–82. Thousand Oaks: Sage.

Scammell, Margaret. 2007. "Political Brands and Consumer Citizens: The Rebranding of Tony Blair." *The ANNALS of the American Academy of Political and Social Science* 611 (1):176–92. https://doi.org/10.1177/0002716206299149

Serazio, Michael. 2017. "Branding Politics: Emotion, Authenticity, and the Marketing Culture of American Political Communication." *Journal of Consumer Culture* 17 (2):225–41. https://doi.org/10.1177/1469540515586868

Smith, Gareth. 2006. "Competetive Analysis, Structure and Strategy in Politics: A Critical Approach." *Journal of Public Affairs* 6 (1):4–14. https://doi.org/10.1002/pa.40

Sobolewska-Myślik, Karatzyna, and Beata Kosowska-Gąstoł. 2017. "„Partie Politycznych Przedsiębiorców" – Nowy Model Partii?" *Athenaeum Polskie Studia Politologiczne* 55 (3):108–29. https://doi.org/10.15804/athena.2017.55.06

Strömbäck, Jesper. 2010. "Political Market-Orientation in a Multi-Party System: The Swedish Case." In *Global Political Marketing*, edited by J. Lees-Marshment, J. Strömbäck, and C. Rudd, 16–33. London: Routledge.

Strömbäck, Jesper. 2007. "Political Marketing and Professionalized Campaigning." *Journal of Political Marketing* 6 (2–3):49–67. https://doi.org/10.1300/J199v06n02_04

Strömbäck, Jesper. 2008. "Four Phases of Mediatization: An Analysis of the Mediatization of Politics." *The International Journal of Press/Politics* 13 (3):228–46. https://doi.org/10.1177/1940161208319097

Strömbäck, Jesper, and Frank Esser. 2014. "Introduction." *Journalism Studies* 15 (3):243–55. https://doi.org/10.1080/1461670X.2014.897412

Strömbäck, Jesper. 2009. "Selective Professionalization of Political Campaigning: A Test of the Party-Centred Theory of Professionalised Campaigning in the Context of the 2006 Swedish Election." *Political Studies* 57 (1):95–116. https://doi.org/10.1111/j.1467-9248.2008.00727.x

Swanson, David L. and Paolo Mancini, ed. 1996. *Politics, Media and Modern Democracy: An International Study of Innovations in Electoral Campaigning and Their Consequences*. Westport: Praeger.

Tenscher, Jens, and Juri Mykkänen. 2014. "Two Levels of Campaigning: An Empirical Test of the Party-Centred Theory of Professionalisation." *Political Studies* 62 (1_suppl):20–41. https://doi.org/10.1111/1467-9248.12104

Trent, Judith S., and Robert V. Friedenberg. 2000. *Political Campaign Communication*, 319–49. Westport-London: Praeger.

Wring, Dominic. 2009. "The Modern British Campaign." In *Routledge Handbook of Political Management*, edited by D. W. Johnson, 283–94. New York: Routledge.

Xifra, Jordi. 2011. "Americanization, Globalization, or Modernization of Electoral Campaigns? Testing the Situation in Spain." *American Behavioral Scientist* 55 (6):667–82. https://doi.org/10.1177/0002764211398086

Appendix 1

Categorization key in spot content analysis

1. Name of the committee
2. Name of the spot
3. Duration of the spot
    3.1 up to 30 s;
    3.2 31-60 sec;
    3.3 over 60 sec.
4. A catalogue of issues appearing in the verbal layer of the spot
    4.1 state foreign policy
    4.2 fiscal policy
    4.3 social policy
    4.4 employment and unemployment
    4.5 agriculture
    4.6 investment in infrastructure
    4.7 education and the educational system
    4.8 healthcare
    4.9 crime and protecting citizens
    4.10 law and justice
    4.11 culture
    4.12 environmental protection and ecology
    4.13 external security and defence
    4.14 State—Church relations
    4.15 corruption
    4.16 immigration policy
    4.17 others (which?) _____
5. The main topic of the spot (regardless of the spot's function: self-presentation or attack on a political opponent) in the verbal layer
    5.1 problematic and axiological issues
    5.2 organizational-personal issues (description of the party, mainly in terms of the people who make it up) mixed—problematic/axiological and personnel/organizational issues to the extent that they have been addressed
    5.3 others: _____
6. Problematic and axiological emphasis in the verbal layer of the spot is placed on:
    6.1 position issues
    6.2 valence issues
    6.3 position and universal issues to a similar extent
    6.4 problematic and axiological matters do not appear in the spot or do so only marginally
7. Appearance of the leader in the spot of the party (broadcasting the spot) in the visual layer:
    7.1 dominates the spot
    7.2 is shown
    7.3 does not appear
8. The leader of the party is present in the verbal layer
    8.1 is the main speaker
    8.2 is the speaker
    8.3 does not appear
9. The leader speaks to the camera (0/1)
10. The leader in the verbal layer:
    10.1 is not the subject of the spot
    10.2 is a subject only marginally (i.e., only one leader feature mentioned)
    10.3 is quite an important topic (among other things)
    10.4 dominates the spot.

"Send in the Clowns": The Rise of Celebrity Populism in Croatia and Its Implications for Political Marketing

Marijana Grbeša and Berto Šalaj

ABSTRACT
In recent years, celebrity populism has become increasingly prevalent in politics worldwide. However, the relationship between populism and celebrity politics is not straightforward, and more research is needed to understand how these two concepts intersect. The authors of this paper argue that a more nuanced understanding of celebrity populism is necessary to identify and analyze its various forms. By analyzing the communication strategies of the three populist candidates in the 2019–2020 Croatian presidential election, this paper empirically investigates how celebrity populism manifests in practice. The authors use their proposed conceptualization to classify the candidates based on their use of populist and celebrity strategies. This allows for a more granular understanding of the different ways in which celebrity and populism can be combined in politics. The findings suggest that celebrity populism can take on different forms depending on the specific context and characteristics of the candidates. Moreover, the authors argue that celebrity populism is a strategy that can be effective in gaining popularity and mobilizing voters, particularly in countries where trust in political institutions is low.

Introduction

In May 2019, the front page of the Croatian daily *Jutarnji list* featured a photo of Miroslav Škoro, one of the most famous Croatian singers and entertainers, with the headline: "Presidential candidate? If that is what my people want". A few weeks later, Škoro officially announced his presidential candidacy for the 2019–2020 election. At about the same time, a major political focus was on the victory of the famous comedian Volodymyr Zelensky in the Ukrainian presidential election. Zelensky ran with his party "Servant of the People", named after the homonymous Netflix series in which Zelensky plays an kindhearted teacher who runs for president. Zelensky won the presidency with 73% of the votes. Škoro received 24.45% of the votes and came in third.

Despite numerous contextual differences, Škoro and Zelensky shared more than one similarity: they were both political outsiders who relied on their fame as show business stars to run for political office, and they both campaigned by communicating strong populist messages. In this paper, we argue that these similarities are the features of *celebrity populism*, a phenomenon that has been gaining strength across the world but still lacks solid conceptual underpinning. The goal of this paper is to discuss the idea of *celebrity populism* and to examine if and how it was present in the 2019–2020 Croatian presidential election.

In the theoretical section, we first define the concepts of populism and celebrity politics and discuss their relationship. We consider populism to be a thin-centered ideology that is built on the idea that society is divided into two homogenous and mutually-conflicted groups: honest people and corrupt elites (Freeden 1996; Mudde 2004). This conflict between the honest people and the elites permeates populists' highly personalized, media-oriented and vastly affective communication. We then examine the arguments about "celebritization" of politics and provide an overview of different types of celebrity politicians (West and Orman 2003; Street 2004; Marsh, 't Hart, and Tindall 2010). We draw on David Marsh, Paul 't Hart and Karen Tindall's (2010) typology of celebrity politicians to ground our conceptualization of *celebrity populism* and its two main types – *celebrity populists* and *populist celebrities*. A *celebrity populist* is a celebrity who acquires populist discourse to run in an election. A *populist celebrity* is a populist politician who adopts celebrity strategies to attract public attention and sway voters.

The theoretical segment is followed by an overview of the Croatian context to situate the argument. The overview focuses on the emergence of populism and the specifics of populist campaigning in Croatia. In the empirical part, we analyze the Facebook communication of the three populist candidates in the 2019–2020 presidential election, Mislav Kolakušić, Ivan Pernar and Miroslav Škoro. We aim to establish if and how their populist narratives merged with celebrity cues into different types of *celebrity populism*. Finally, we indicate implications of populist campaigning and celebrity populism for Croatian political marketing.

Populism and populist communication

Contemporary accounts usually conceptualize populism as a "thin-centered" political ideology (c.f. Mudde 2004; Kaltwasser 2014). This understanding builds on Mudde's seminal definition of populism as "an ideology that considers society to be ultimately separated into two homogeneous and antagonistic groups, 'the pure people' versus the 'corrupt elite', and which argues that politics should be an expression of the *volonté générale* (general will) of the people" (2004, 543). Although people-centeredness and the antagonistic relationship toward elites represent the central core of populism, it needs additional values to make sense of the political world in which it acts, which is why populism is commonly considered a "thin-centered ideology" (Freeden 1996, 2003).

Populists have influenced many of the established practices of contemporary election campaigns, most notably in terms of narratives, communication styles and campaign strategies. The populists' narrative is built around dramatic antagonism between "corrupt elites" and "honest people", whom they claim to represent. This construction of systemic conflict between the people and elites is coupled with the "crisis talk" described by Homolar and Scholz (2019) and, in some cases, with the rage against the "dangerous others" who are, along with elites, responsible for "the crises" (i.e., migrants, minorities, financial institutions, the European Union and others, depending on the ideological leaning of the populists in question). Populists know how to utilize a mediatized political environment to their own advantage (Aalberg et al. 2017; Mazzoleni and Bracciale 2018) and cleverly combine lavish performances with controversial language to attract news media that crave scandals, sensation and spectacle. In Mazzoleni's (2008, 53) view, populists are "strong personalities that perfectly fit the news media's demand for the spectacular and emotional treatment of social reality, including political life".

Apart from being media savvy, one of the central features of populist communication is the efficient and creative use of digital technology, which has been commonly regarded as one of the culprits responsible for the rise of contemporary populism (Groshek and Koc-Michalska 2017; Schroeder 2018). The commonly addressed features and functions of digital technology that allegedly facilitate the rise of populist options are: (1) the unmediated nature of social media that allows populists to communicate directly with their supporters while bypassing the filter of the mainstream media (Manucci 2017); (2) the agenda-setting effect(s) of social media

(Mazzoleni 2016); (3) the organizational potential of the internet that enables political newcomers to build their party structures, implement decision-making procedures and mobilize supporters (Miconi 2015; Borge Bravo and Santamarina Sáez 2016); and finally, (4) microtargeting (Bodo, Helberger, and de Vreese 2017).

Celebrity politics

Celebrity politics is a phenomenon that is closely linked to processes of mediatization (Esser and Stromback 2014), personalization (Langer 2012) and re-styling of politics (Corner and Pels 2003). Corner and Pels (2003, 2) argue that "[t]he mass visibility that is afforded by modern mediated politics has foregrounded issues of 'style, appearance, and personality', breaking down some of the fences that separate politics from entertainment and political leadership from media celebrity". They maintain that "celebrity power is progressively being translated from the popular entertainment industries toward more 'serious' fields such as business, politics, art and science" and that "the only future for political personality is that of celebrity" (Corner and Pels 2003, 8). Similarly, Driessens (2013, 641) argues that "[c]elebrity has become a defining feature of our mediatized societies". He suggests that we have been witnessing "diversification of celebrity", which means that celebrities are no longer confined to the world of entertainment or sports, but that other social fields, including politics, may also produce celebrities (Driessens 2013, 644). Driessens contends that "celebritization" of society is driven by the processes of "mediatization, personalization and commodification" (2013, 649).

In his seminal work on the power of celebrities, David Marshall (1997, ix) defines celebrities as those people who "enjoy a greater presence and wider scope of activity and agency than those who make up the rest of the population. They are allowed to move on the public stage while the rest of us watch". Building on Marshall's (1997) understanding of celebrity, scholars have been trying to describe the different types of relationships between political and celebrity spheres and to categorize celebrity politicians accordingly. The pioneering conceptualizations developed by West and Orman (2003), Street (2004) and the later works of 't Hart and Tindall (2009) and Marsh, 't Hart and Tindall (2010) have influenced numerous scholarly attempts to describe and categorize the roles(s) of celebrity politicians. West and Orman (2003, 2–4) base their classification on the source of fame. Thus, West and Orman (2003, 2–4) differentiate among the following categories: "political newsworthies", who rely on their performance to engage with the public; "legacies", who were born into a well-known family; "famed nonpoliticos (elected officials)", who were well-known before being elected; "famed nonpoliticos (lobbyists and spokespersons)", who are, basically, celebrities who endorse or advocate certain causes; and finally, "event celebrities", who become famous because of an event (a scandal, tragedy or similar).

Street's (2004) relatively simple, yet influential, classification is based on the relationship between politics and popular culture. He argues that the convergence between politics and popular culture translates into two types of celebrity politicians. The first type, CP1, is a celebrity originating from the world of show business or sports who becomes an elected politician, such as Arnold Schwarzenegger. The second variant of CP1 is a traditional, elected politician who engages with celebrity techniques that typically belong to the world of pop culture in order to gain sympathies and attract voters. The second type, CP2, includes celebrities who engage for a common cause and use their celebrity power to influence political decisions, such as Bono Vox, Angelina Jolie etc. CP2s also go by the name "celebrity diplomats" or "celebrity activists "(Cooper 2008; Tsaliki, Frangonikolopoulos, and Huliaras 2011).

Based on 't Hart and Tindall's (2009) original conceptualization, Marsh, 't Hart and Tindall (2010, 327) further distinguish among five categories of celebrity politicians: celebrity advocate, celebrity endorser, celebrity politician, politician-turned-celebrity (politician celebrity), and politician who uses someone else's celebrity. Their typology is based on two criteria: the sphere of origin and the nature of the relationship with the other sphere (2010, 327). The celebrity advocate is a nonpolitical actor who wishes to influence the public agenda or advocate for a certain policy; the celebrity endorser is a nonpolitical celebrity who endorses a candidate or a party, while the politician who uses others' celebrity is an elected politician who relies on someone else's celebrity or fame. In our paper, we rely on the remaining two categories, *celebrity politicians* and *politician celebrities*, who are contained in other conceptualizations. *Celebrity politicians* are celebrities from nonpolitical spheres who become elected politicians (Street's CP1, subtype 1). Driessens (2013, 644) identifies this process as a celebrity "migration." *Politician celebrities* are those actors whose sphere of origin is politics; however, their public behavior, personal life or connections to celebrities change their public appeal to the extent that they no longer exclusively belong to the political sphere but also to the celebrity sphere (Street's CP1, subtype 2). This is what Driessens (2013, 644) recognizes as a "diversification of celebrity". Politician celebrities are constantly adapting their political communication strategies to an increasingly mediatized and personalized political environment (Marsh, 't Hart, and Tindall, 2010, 325). The implementation of highly personalized media-centered communication that celebritizes politicians' image is typical of, albeit not limited to, populist politicians.

Celebrity populism

The connection between celebrity politics and populism has often been regarded as inherent or intuitive, since performance and style are central to both (i.e., Moffitt 2016; Pels 2003; Street 2004, 2019). Street (2019, 2) even claims that celebrity politics is a feature of the rise of populist politics. However, studies that explicitly address the relationship between these two phenomena and analyze how populists or populist-like politicians construct their celebrityhood, are still rather modest (for exceptions see Alomes and Mascitelli 2021; Bartoszewicz 2019; Enli 2017; Giglioli and Baldini 2019; Schneiker 2019; Street 2019; Wood Corbett and Flinders 2016).

Enli (2017) and Schneiker (2019) use the case of former United States President Donald Trump to demonstrate how political discourse may be celebritized by strategically promoting a de-professionalized, authentic and amateurish style of communication. Schneiker (2019) binds populism and celebrity politics into the concept of a "superhero anti-politician celebrity". Wood, Corbett and Flinders (2016) also build on the idea of authenticity, ordinariness and humanization in political communication to develop a concept of an "everyday celebrity politician", as opposed to a distant "superstar celebrity politician". They argue that in the age of anti-politics, appearing "normal", "ordinary", "human" and in touch with the people may be crucial for achieving celebrity fame. This assumption is closely linked to the idea that the power of celebrities stems from the impression that they are both "ordinary and extraordinary" (Driessens 2013, 643), "one of us" and "very special at the same time" (van Zoonen 2005, 82). In Enli's (2017), Schneiker's (2019) and Wood, Corbett and Flinders' (2016) accounts, social media is central to the promotion of the discourse of authenticity and ordinariness.

Giglioli and Baldini (2019) cite Waisboard (2018) to argue that there is a certain "elective affinity" between populism and celebritized politics. Populists, like celebrity politicians, have the power to energize and mobilize otherwise apathetic publics (Marsh, 't Hart, and Tindall 2010). Furthermore, emotional appeal is central to both celebrities and populists. Marshall (1997) argues that celebrities originating from the entertainment industry rely on affection, emotions and irrationality to build relations with their audiences, which is exactly the kind of bond that politicians seek to establish with the people. Wirz (2018, 1131) shows that "populist communication is inherently more emotion-eliciting than nonpopulist communication and therefore especially persuasive". Street (2019, 9) similarly points out that populists tend to elicit adoration that resembles behavior of fans but also warns that fans may lack critical thinking. Thus, the central concern for scholars is to understand "how the passions of citizen-fans are elicited and orchestrated" (Street 2019, 10).

Another straightforward parallel between celebrity politics and populism is the issue of distrust in political elites. Wheeler (2013) and Cooper (2008) argue that involvement of celebrities in politics has been inspired by a distrust in the political elites in the first place. Celebrity politicians, like populists, often play the card of "political outsiders" who are not part of the resented establishment: "they are new, they are exciting, they are unpredictable" (Marsh, 't Hart and Tindall 2010, 324). t'Hart and Tindall (2009) indicate that the more dissatisfied the publics are with traditional politics, the greater the opportunities for celebrities to successfully run for office. The same idea holds true for populists (Grbeša and Šalaj 2018a).

Although the connection between celebrity politics and populism may seem apparent, a demanding mission to combine them into a solid concept that would identify specific features of the celebrity-populist blend, as opposed to celebrityhood of traditional non-populist politicians, is still far from accomplished. Building on Marsh, 't Hart and Tindall's (2010) distinction between celebrity politicians and politician celebrities, we propose a definition of *celebrity populists* vs. *populist celebrities*.

The *celebrity populist* is a celebrity who acquires populist rhetoric to run for elected office and in some cases, maintains this rhetoric while holding elected office. The *populist celebrity* is a populist politician who engages with different celebrity techniques to mobilize supporters and celebritize his/her image. Both types of celebrity populism merge populism and celebrityhood into a powerful communication mix that combines attractiveness of populist messages with the awe of celebrity culture. This proposition upgrades Marsh, 't Hart and Tindall's (2010) typology by setting populism against mainstream politics. In addition to the celebrity sphere, we introduce two political spheres of origin: mainstream politics and populist politics. Figure 1 demonstrates how these different spheres (the sphere of mainstream politics, populist politics and the celebrity sphere) merge into different types of celebrity politics (celebrity politics and celebrity populism) and generate four different types of celebrity politicians.

Such conceptualization enables us to distinguish between: (1) political celebrities, mainstream politicians who resort to celebrity discourse to construct their celebrity persona; (2) celebrity politicians, celebrities who come from the celebrity sphere (usually entertainment or sports) and run for elected office using mainstream, non-populist discourse; (3) populist celebrities, populist politicians who adopt elements of celebrity discourse to acquire and/or retain public support; and (4) celebrity populists, celebrities who come from the celebrity sphere and rely on populist discourse (rhetoric of anti-elitism and people-centeredness) to win an election and/or maintain public support.

We see this typology as an incentive to develop an elaborate conceptual framework of celebrity populism that is still largely missing from scholarly work on celebrity politics.

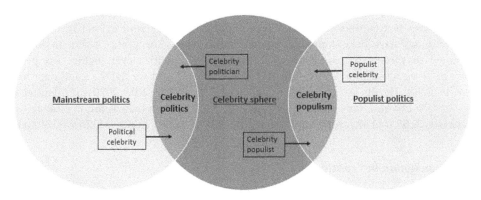

Figure 1. Spheres of origin and types of celebrity politicians.

The context: Populism and populist campaigning in Croatia

Ever since achieving independence, Croatia has been interchangeably governed by two major parties – the Croatian Democratic Union (*Hrvatska demokratska zajednica*, HDZ) and the Social Democratic Party (*Socijaldemokratska partija*, SDP). However, in the last couple of years supremacy of the HDZ and the SDP has been challenged by a number of populist options. The advent of populism in Croatia has been inspired by resentment toward the established political elites (Grbeša and Šalaj 2018a) and one of the lowest levels of trust in institutions within the EU (Eurobarometer 2019; Henjak 2017).

Although populist ideas have been present in Croatian politics since the 2000s (Grbeša and Šalaj 2018a), the real advent of populism began in 2015 with the rise of the Bridge (*Most*) and Human Shield (*Živi zid*), two populist parties that challenged the duopoly of the HDZ and the SDP. *Most* won nineteen seats in the 2015 parliamentary election and thirteen in the 2016 snap election. *Živi zid* won one seat in the 2015 and eight seats in the 2016 parliamentary election. *Živi zid* won one seat in the 2019 European election, while *Most* did not make it to the European Parliament.

Most and *Živi zid* avoided the dominant left-right divide issues in Croatian politics by criticizing all mainstream parties and condemning the bipolar nature of the Croatian party system. While *Most* is best described as a borderline case between centrist populism and an anti-establishment party (Grbeša and Šalaj 2018b), *Živi zid* is a blend of social populism, soft-Euroscepticism and right-wing anti-immigrant messages.

Most first started as a national network of local independent politicians. After their unexpected success in 2015, *Most* became minor partner in two HDZ governments (2015–2017). However, their conflict with the HDZ's Prime Minister Andrej Plenković in 2017 pushed them to the opposition. *Živi zid* is Croatia's most rigid populist party, with a range of radical solutions to social and political problems. Unlike *Most*, they have refused to partner with any of the mainstream parties. The party emerged out of a civic organization *Živi zid's* political rise began when one of the party's leaders, Ivan Vilibor Sinčić, a young engineering student at the time, stood in the 2014 presidential election. He won 16.4% of the votes, which was a respectable score given that he was completely unknown. Ivan Vilibor Sinčić used his newly acquired visibility to lead *Živi zid* to the Parliament in 2015 and 2016. Apart from Sinčić, the most prominent party figure was Ivan Pernar, an eccentric architect of *Živi zid*, a Member of the Parliament (from 2016 to 2020) and a controversial antivaxxer.

The rise of *Most* and *Živi zid* paved the way for the emergence of other populist options and candidates, with Mislav Kolakušić and Miroslav Škoro being the most successful. Mislav Kolakušić was a judge of the Commercial Court of Zagreb who resigned in order to be eligible to stand as a candidate in the 2019 election for the European Parliament with his independent list. Kolakušić campaigned by conveying strong populist messages targeting national political elites and addressing corruption. His campaign was almost exclusively focused on digital media. He won the mandate with 7.89% of the vote, despite his low visibility in the mainstream media and discouraging support in the polls of only 2.8% just one month before election day (Index 2019).

Miroslav Škoro is a famous Croatian singer and entrepreneur with a PhD in Economics. His hit patriotic songs have been topping Croatian radio charts for years. Although his career is mostly linked to show business, Škoro was flirting with politics even before his presidential candidacy in 2019; he was an MP on the HDZ's list in 2007 and the HDZ's candidate for Mayor of Osijek in 2008. He ran as an independent candidate in the 2019/2020 presidential election and won 24.45% of votes, only slightly less than the HDZ's incumbent Kolinda Grabar Kitarović, who garnered 26.65% of the votes and eventually lost to SDP's Zoran Milanović in the runoff.

Populist campaigning in Croatia

Personalization is one of the main features of political campaign communication in Croatia (Grbeša 2009; Kunac, Lalić, and Andrijević 2013) and, like many other post-socialist countries (see Petrovova and Eibl 2019; Bartoszewicz 2019; Hašić 2020), Croatia has embraced celebrity politics. It has been exercised mainly through humanization, popularization and celebrity endorsement (Grbeša and Šalaj 2019).

Until recently, Croatian politicians predominantly relied on traditional forms of advertising, such as billboards, posters, newspaper ads, and television and radio commercials. However, in recent years, mainstream parties and candidates have recognized the importance of digital campaigning that, at first, was most enthusiastically embraced by populist parties and candidates (Grbeša and Šalaj 2019).

In order to provide an overview of the populist campaigning that set the stage for the 2019–2020 presidential election, we focus on the populist narrative, attention-grabbing communication and the use of digital media by *Živi zid* and Mislav Kolakušić in the 2015 and 2016 parliamentary elections and the 2019 European election.

Živi zid and its two leading figures, Ivan Vilibor Sinčić and Ivan Pernar, have been using strong populist rhetoric ever since they first appeared on the political stage in 2014 (Grbeša and Šalaj 2016; Mustapić and Hristić 2016; Čular and Grbeša 2020). Albertini and Vozab (2017, 15) argue that most of the party's activities - protests, social media campaigning, attacks on media or other politicians - were primarily aimed at attracting media attention and increasing public visibility. The most successful politician in this respect has been Ivan Pernar, who strategically branded himself as a showman and *enfant terrible* of Croatian politics. Pernar has been tactically using mischievous stunts to attract the media and enchant his supporters: he was dragged from the Parliament for interrupting the proceedings on several occasions and each of these incidents was streamed live on Facebook, and he once ate pizza during a parliamentary sitting. He has been aggressively using social media, especially Facebook, to mobilize and energize his supporters. Barišić (2020, 305) observes that Pernar's entire Facebook communication strategy has been strongly anti-elitist, while on "the people" side, he adopted strategy of posing as "the people's" ombudsman or the "voice of the deprived". Barišić (2020, 304–307) notes that Pernar often uses formats not typical of Croatian mainstream politicians, such as selfies, and that he willingly adopts the language of the "younger generation." Vuković (2019) likewise suggests that Pernar usually posts about "everyday things" several times a day, which is typical of social media influencers, rather than politicians. Vuković (2019, 15), therefore, argues that Pernar is a "reality-style" celebrity politician, while Klauški (2016) refers to him as a "good television" and brands him a "Jerry Springer of Croatian politics". Even *The New York Times* identified Pernar as a "Trump-like figure" because he is, like Trump, "a political outsider who uses social media and attention-grabbing attacks on opponents" (Lyman 2017). When asked in a talk show if he is a comedian or a serious politician, Pernar replied: "If the media are ready to make a circus and show, I am ready to be a clown and have fun with them" (N1, 24sata.hr. 2016).[1] In one of his Facebook posts (22 February 2017), Pernar wrote: "If I wanted to be 'serious' like other politicians, I could be, but that wouldn't be me and you wouldn't be interested in what I am saying because I would be boring, like everybody else".

Similarly, *Živi zid* demonstrated an impressive use of digital media in the 2015 and 2016 parliamentary elections. In the 2015 election campaign, *Živi zid* generated more content on Facebook than any other party. They published twenty posts a day on average, and also had the most fans and most interactions with their fans (Biberović 2015). In the 2016 snap election, *Živi zid* replicated their digital strategy, which presumably paid off since they won eight seats in the Parliament. They published an average of ten posts a day on Facebook, had the most shares and twice as many as the second-best rated party (SDP) and enjoyed the most interactions (Glavinić 2016). In the 2019 election for the European Parliament, most parties focused the majority of their resources on digital campaigning, including mainstream parties (EEMC Report 2019). *Živi zid* campaigned almost entirely online, but its online presence was not superior to other main parties anymore. It was preceded by the HDZ, the SDP and *Most* (EEMC Report 2019).

Digital media also played a crucial role in the rise of Mislav Kolakušić, a political outsider who unexpectedly won a seat in the European Parliament in the 2019 European election.

Kolakušić campaigned by conveying strong populist messages targeting national political elites and addressing corruption with the slogan, "Every mafia meets its end!" He announced that the European election was just a first step toward him becoming president and then eventually Prime Minister and Minister of Justice and Internal Affairs (Romić 2019). This became his campaign mantra. Kolakušić's success was phenomenal, given his exceptionally low presence in the mainstream media and overall absence of conventional campaigning. Interestingly, unlike *Živi zid,* whose campaign strategy had always been to attract the mainstream media's attention, Kolakušić kept refusing to talk to journalists, but at the same time, he complained about his low media visibility (Romić 2019). The central focus of his campaign was the Facebook page "Citizens for Mislav Kolakušić" that had supposedly been created by "citizens" who supported Kolakušić. However, communication on the page clearly suggests that it has been professionally managed by Kolakušić's campaign team. In a talk show interview preceding the European election, Kolakušić explained that he was using Facebook to target disenchanted voters of other parties and turn them into his supporters (Biberović 2019a). Digital media expert Petar Tanta (Biberović 2019a) outlined that Kolakušić wisely combined three communication channels: Facebook communication, a web page allegedly dedicated to fight against corruption (antikorupcija.com) and Google Display Network. Tanta also noted that every one of Kolakušić's Facebook posts starts with a disclaimer "Share!" that contributed to the broad organic reach of his messages.

In 2015, 2016 and 2019, *Živi zid* and Mislav Kolakušić strongly relied on three campaign strategies. First, they campaigned by communicating strong populist messages, which tend to contribute to the popularity of politicians who use them (Wirz 2018; Blassnig et al. 2019). Second, they all adopted distinct variants of performative communication. Finally, they used digital media in an innovative and clever way to mobilize supporters and target voters.

Methodology and research design

In the analytical section of the paper, we combine quantitative and qualitative content analysis to examine the Facebook campaign communication from the three populist candidates who ran in the 2019-2020 presidential election – Mislav Kolakušić, Ivan Pernar and Miroslav Škoro – and to establish if and how their populist narratives merged with celebrity cues into different types of *celebrity populism*.

The first round of the election was held on 22 December 2019 and the second round on 5 January 2020. Ivan Pernar won 2.31% of votes, Mislav Kolakušić 5.87% and Miroslav Škoro 24.45%. None of them advanced to the second round. The content analysis is focused on their respective Facebook pages because digital media is confirmed to be well-suited for the promotion of both populist and celebrity discourse (i.e., Manning et al. 2017; Enli 2017). In addition, evidence from previous elections shows that Facebook was central to both Živi zid's and Mislav Kolakušić's campaigns. Finally, according to The Reuters Institute Digital News Report (2020), social media is the main source of news for 55% of citizens in Croatia, with Facebook being convincingly the most popular social media platform (for 74% of citizens).

The content analysis included all posts published on Kolakušić's, Pernar's and Škoro's Facebook fan pages in the period of the official election campaign, from 9 to 22 December 2019. We first examined the presence and valence of populist cues, including: (1) presence and valence of references to the people; (2) presence and valence of references to elites; (3) presence of attacks on individual politicians, given that they are often used as a proxy for "political establishment," and (4) presence of references to "dangerous others" other than political elites. We used binary codes, "yes" or "no," to detect presence and "positive," "negative" or "neutral" codes to establish valence. We then coded posts for the presence of various elements of celebrity politics: (1) references to the candidate's personal life, including elements of humanization and (2) references to popular culture or show business. In defining indicators of celebrity politics, we relied on van Zoonen's (2006) conceptualization of celebrity politics as a phenomenon constituted by both popularization and personalization. Both celebrity categories were coded with binary codes, "yes" or "no."

Finally, we coded the Facebook posts for the presence of visual elements (videos, photos and graphics) and links, with binary codes, "yes" or "no." Since many videos were more than twenty minutes long, we decided to code only textual parts of the posts and to use additional content to qualitatively substantiate the findings.

The analysis included Pernar's and Škoro's Facebook fan pages and Kolakušić's page "Citizens for Mislav Kolakušić", which remained his primary communication hotspot even after the European election[2]. The agreement between coders was strong across all categories. It ranged from Cohen's kappa = 0.82 to 1.00.

Findings

Mislav Kolakušić: a populist messiah

Mislav Kolakušić campaigned with the slogan "For Mislav. It's either Mislav, or it's the same". He published 31 posts during the analyzed period. A curiosity about this page is that all of the posts have been written in third person, quoting or praising Kolakušić. Tanta (Biberović 2019b) notes that, unlike in the European election when Kolakušić relied on paid content, in this election he relied only on the organic reach of his Facebook messages. Like in the European election, his every post had a disclaimer "Share!".

The people are mentioned in seventeen posts, mostly neutrally (fifteen posts), while one post contains positive mention of *the people* and one is very harsh toward *the people*: "This election is the test of intelligence of Croatian citizens, Croatian people. (…) This time you have to vote, otherwise you will be responsible for everything that will happen" (Facebook 18 December 2019). *The people* are labeled as "citizens" or "Croatian citizens" in the majority of posts and only in one post as "the people". Almost half of the posts (fourteen) demonstrate strong resentment toward political elites, mainly toward the "HDZSDP" (the blended acronym of HDZ and SDP used to refer sardonically to their presumed duopoly) and "state corruption": "Every normal, responsible person who is not part of the HDZSDP's network is aware of the devastating effect of the HDZSDP's candidates in this and every other election. It is up to citizens to demonstrate if they want changes or a continuation of the HDZSDP's destruction of Croatia" (Facebook 11 December 2019). Five posts contain attacks on other candidates (Milanović, Grabar Kitarović and/or Škoro). In two posts, Kolakušić identifies media companies and public relations industry as the dangerous others who "deceive and violently create public opinion" (Facebook 20 December 2019). The analyzed posts do not contain references to Kolakušić's private life, pop culture or show business. Another distinctive feature of Kolakušić's Facebook communication is the use of two established propaganda techniques, unwarranted extrapolations (voting for the HDZ, the SDP or any other option other than Kolakušić leads to a downfall of Croatia) and generalizations: "Mislav Kolakušić's views are the views of most of us, citizens. It's time to confirm that on election day" (Facebook 15 December 2019). Pundits assessed Kolakušić's rhetoric as "authoritarian". Political analyst Žarko Puhovski (Danas 2019) called him "Hitler from our neighborhood," and argued that those who criticize Kolakušić will be considered "either traitors or idiots". In the analyzed period, twelve photos were published, and the only person featured in them was Kolakušić. All but one photo was staged, and the rest were professionally captured studio portraits. Five videos were posted and all were clips from television shows featuring Kolakušić. "Ordinary people" or supporters did not appear in any photo or video. Links were present in four posts and textual graphics in ten posts.

Kolakušić's populism was mostly expressed though his vociferous resentment toward corrupt elites but significantly less so in terms of identification with the people. He mentioned citizens in more than half of his posts. Nevertheless, Kolakušić's communication toward the people was detached, moralizing and even intimidating. A complete absence of a "one of us" moment was further reinforced by the absence of "ordinary people", or any other people whatsoever, other than Kolakušić in the visual materials. The content of the Facebbok page was generally aggressive and dramatic, both in language and style. The use of the third person format is unusual and undermines the authenticity of "socially mediated populism" (Mazzoleni and Bracciale 2018). However, the stunning success of Mislav Kolakušić in the European election suggests that this format, if managed and marketed properly, has significant campaign potential. The perceived goal of the Facebbok page in both elections was to build a personality cult of Mislav Kolakušić, and to promote his messianic mission of saving Croatia. Curiously, this goal may represent a connection to celebrity politics: the Facebook page that served as Kolakušić's main campaign outlet was designed and managed as a page created by fans who gather to worship their idol. According to Tsaliki, Frangonikolopoulos and Huliaris (2011, 9), the "unconditional admiration" that celebrities enjoy stems from their charisma and an impression that they have "capacities that are superior to other people". It seems "unconditional admiration" is exactly the kind of celebrity aura that Kolakušić's campaign advisers were trying to achieve, albeit with far less success than in the 2019 European election.

Ivan Pernar: a reality TV populist

Ivan Pernar competed in the 2019–2020 election as a candidate of Ivan Pernar's Party since he fell out with *Živi zid* after the European election and established his own party. Pernar posted 69 posts in the analyzed period. He made five references to the people, positive or neutral, and he referred to them mostly as "the people". He made three negative comments about political elites in general and attacked other presidential candidates in six posts (Milanović, Grabar Kitarović, Kolakušić and/or Škoro). Pernar mentioned "dangerous others" in eight posts (media and the EU in three, migrants in one and the USA in one), often in relation to different conspiracy theories. Every post contained a video (58), a photo (7) or a link (4). Most videos were filmed by Pernar himself (52), while six were clips from television shows that hosted Pernar. His photos and videos commonly featured him in the company of "ordinary people", where he acquired different roles: a celebrity surrounded by fans, a candidate who is "one of us", a reality star who stalks pedestrians or a documentarist who is filming troubled people and acting as their ombudsmen. Pernar made one reference to his personal life on election day when he posted a video of himself and "the First Lady" driving to the polling station. He made no references to pop culture or show business.

Pernar's Facebook communication mostly relied on videos, while many of the posts did not contain any text at all. This is why the frequency of populist indicators was sporadic, although a populist narrative permeates the majority of his videos. The content of Pernar's page was extremely eclectic, exhibitionistic and resembled a page of a social media influencer rather than a politician. This is why Pernar could be classified as a *populist celebrity,* a populist politician who adopts a celebrity strategy to construct himself as a political reality star.

Miroslav Škoro: the people's president

Miroslav Škoro campaigned with the slogan, "Let's give Croatia back to the people – It's now or never!". Facebook was his main digital marketing tool (Mikašinović Komšo 2020) where he published 69 posts in the analyzed period. He mentioned the people in 28 posts, either neutrally (eight posts) or positively (twenty posts). Elites were mentioned in eight posts, all of them with a negative slant, while eleven posts contained explicit attacks on mainstream politicians, mostly on the frontrunners Grabar Kitarović. Milanović. Škoro sees the people as his allies and as a source of strength in his crusade against corrupt elites: "This is unstoppable! The people have decided, and God is helping us!" (Facebook 13 December 2019). Škoro insisted that he was "responsible solely to his people" (Facebook 09 December 2019), and as president, he would ensure that people play a greater role in decision making through referenda. He mostly used the terms "the people" or "Croatian people". Škoro mentioned "dangerous others" in six posts (from the media to "mighty financial interests"), but he did not systematically target any particular group. Although Škoro entered the political arena as an extremely popular singer, he did not explicitly use his celebrity capital to appeal to the people. To the contrary, it seems Škoro tried to distance himself from his celebrity background. He made only one reference to his singing career when he posted a link that was announcing his television interview, featuring a glamourous photo of himself holding a microphone (Facebook 16 December 2019). Škoro also made mention of pop culture three times but solely to promote his slogan and his number on the list (11). For instance, he posted a link to Elvis Presley's *It's Now or Never* and wrote "Jacques Houdek [a fellow singer] sent me one great song this morning. I listen to it for the 11th time in a row" (Facebook 22 December 2019). On the other hand, Škoro briefly mentioned that he is a successful entrepreneur, challenging the incompetency of the political elite: "Not a single entrepreneur, including me, wouldn't hire this ruling clique to work in their company" (Facebook 10 December 2019). Škoro made no reference to his personal life whatsoever.

The majority of the Facebook posts contained photos, mostly of Škoro (22) or somebody else, such as other candidates (4). Videos were also prevalent. Most videos were announcements from rallies and other campaign events (13), five were segments from television shows that hosted Škoro, and four were classic video ads. Škoro was featured in all videos except for the ads. Links to articles were detected in four posts, a graphic in one and six posts contained only text.

Škoro's campaign narrative was clearly populist with a right-wing slant. It was mainly built around his alliance with "Croatian people", and, to a lesser degree, on criticism of elites as a collective enemy or scolding of specific politicians who were often used as a proxy for the Croatian political establishment. Although various elements of celebrity discourse were present through Škoro's identity as a singer, i.e., through his "sphere of origin" (Marsh, 't Hart, and Tindall 2010), they were entirely ignored in his campaign communication. We can only hypothesize that this strategic decision was based on an understanding that his celebrity background would make him appear less serious and less credible in the political arena. Apart from his clearly populist narrative, the overall impression is that Škoro ran a professional, rather traditional-style, election campaign on Facebook.

Discussion

The preceding analysis points to four main conclusions. First, we established that both *celebrity populism* and *populist celebritism* were present in the 2019–2020 presidential election. Škoro is a *celebrity populist* who ran the most traditional campaign of all analyzed candidates. Paradoxically, he tried to distance himself from his celebrity background and boasted about his entrepreneurial accomplishments instead. Škoro was reluctant to refer to elements from his entertainment career, possibly out of fear that this would trivialize his image and diminish his electoral prospects. However, it is quite unlikely that Škoro would have risen from a political outsider into one of the frontrunners if he had not already been famous and if people had not related to his celebrity persona. Pernar is a *populist celebrity* who used social media to harness an image of a *political reality star*. He branded himself as a showman whose career as a populist star started fading as he fell out with his political project, *Živi zid*. Kolakušić has no obvious connections to the celebrity world, and he did not explicitly integrate celebrity cues into his campaign communication. However, Kolakušić's campaign was designed exclusively to promote his messianic role and generate admiration by his supporters, that is, fans, which makes him, conditionally, a populist celebrity in his own right.

Second, communication of the examined candidates was intensely personalized, vibrant and dramatic. Hypothetically, the rise of these politicians from political nobodies to political somebodies, in a relatively short period of time, may encourage mainstream politicians to succumb to campaign standards introduced by celebrity populists. Third, this analysis confirms previous findings about the potential of social media when it comes to disseminating personalized populist messages and constructing different types of celebrity personae. Finally, Giglioli and Baldini (2019, 590) argue that countries with "low levels of systemic trust and a destabilization of the political system favor the successful entry of outsider, celebrity politicians in the electoral arena". Since Croatia is a country with one of the lowest trusts in political institutions in the EU (Henjak 2017), it is plausible to assume that the 2019–2020 presidential election marks the advent of celebrity populism in Croatia.

Conclusion

The paper discussed the concept of *celebrity populism* as an amalgam between populism and celebrity politics and examined if and how it was present in the 2019–2020 Croatian presidential election. The relationship between populism and celebrity politics is too often taken as obvious or implicit because of their common reliance on performance and style, which is why we call for a more solid definition that would encapsulate the specifics of a celebrity-populist mix. Unlike the existing typologies of celebrity politicians that regard politics as one single sphere of origin, we introduce two political spheres of origin, mainstream politics and populist politics, and combine them with the celebrity sphere. A three-sphere approach generates four types of celebrity politicians: (1) celebrity politicians; (2) political celebrities; (3) celebrity populists; and (4) populist celebrities.

In the empirical section, we deconstruct the celebrity-populist mix in the 2019-2020 presidential election. A content analysis of Facebook posts from the three populist candidates, Mislav Kolakušić, Ivan Pernar and Miroslav Škoro, points to two main findings. First, we established that the analyzed candidates may be classified within the proposed categories. Škoro's celebrity background, combined with his populist messages, makes him a true *celebrity populist*. Unlike Zelensky in Ukraine, Škoro tried to distance himself from his career as a singer. One possible assumption for his reluctance to make the most of his celebrity capital is that he feared it would tarnish his political image and damage his electoral chances. However, Škoro's rise from a political nobody to a political somebody can be attributed to his celebrity charisma. On the other hand, Pernar and Kolakušić may both be classified as *populist celebrities,* albeit of a very different kind. Pernar is a self-proclaimed "clown" who strategically uses elements from the celebrity world to construct himself as a controversial *populist reality star*. However, Pernar's political stardom has deflated since he broke away from his party basis. Kolakušić is an outright populist who has no explicit connections to the celebrity world. Nevertheless, we argue that Kolakušić may be conditionally categorized as a populist celebrity because of his communication strategy based on fandom and idolization of his persona.

Secondly, the analyzed candidates ran highly personalized, performative and dynamic Facebook campaigns that were characterized by inventive uses of different digital styles and formats. This, along with the lessons learned from previous elections, may inspire mainstream political parties and candidates to match populists' know-how and increasingly re-direct their campaign resources from traditional channels to digital marketing.

Finally, what implications may this have for the future of political marketing? Personalization and spectacularization of politics have already been identified as distinctive features of populist politics. Yet, the celebrity factor makes it even more performative and potentially more appealing. The seductiveness of populist messages has been pushed to new levels. Celebrity appeal and a populist narrative create a potent mix that may boost politicians' visibility and amplify their popularity. This is especially true in countries with low trust in political institutions, such as Croatia. The full marketing potential of the celebrity-populist fusion is yet to be discovered. However, in a celebritized world of cynical and disenchanted voters, it seems plausible to assume that celebrity populism is here to stay.

Notes

1. https://www.youtube.com/watch?v=wLsxywQpNpI&t=2s.
2. Miroslav Škoro: https://www.facebook.com/MiroslavSkoroofficial/; Mislav Kolakušić: https://www.facebook.com/sudacmislavkolakusic/; Ivan Pernar: https://www.facebook.com/PernarMP.

ORCID

Marijana Grbeša http://orcid.org/0000-0003-0050-9694
Berto Šalaj http://orcid.org/0000-0002-9913-8477

References

Aalberg, Toril, Frank Esser, Carsten Reinemann, Jesper Stromback, and Clas H. de Vreese. 2017. *Populist Political Communication in Europe.* New York: Routledge.
Albertini, Alessandro, and Dina Vozab. 2017. "Are 'United Left' and 'Human Blockade' Populist on Facebook. A Comparative Analysis of Electoral Campaigns." *Contemporary Southeastern Europe* 4 (2):1–19. doi: 10.25364/02.4:2017.2.1.
Alomes, Stephen, and Bruno Mascitelli. 2021. "Celebrity Meets Populism in Europe: The Political Performances of Nicolas Sarkozy and Silvio Berlusconi." *Australian and New Zealand Journal of European Studies* 2012-2013 5 (1):30–43. doi: 10.30722/anzjes.vol5.iss1.15133.
Barišić, Branimir. 2020. *Populizam u Hrvatskoj: populistički Elementi u Političkoj Komunikaciji Ivana Pernara. Zbornik radova.* Zagreb: Fakultet političkih znanosti Sveučilišta u Zagrebu.
Bartoszewicz, Monika G. 2019. "Celebrity Populism: A Look at Poland and Czech Republic." *European Politics and Society* 20 (4):470–85. doi: 10.1080/23745118.2019.1569342.
Biberović, Mia. 2015. "Društvene mreže tik pred izbore: HDZ moćan, SDP popularan, Živi zid aktivan." *Netokracija*, November 5. https://www.netokracija.com/drustvene-mreze-izbori-hdz-sdp-zivi-zid-109639
Biberović, Mia. 2019a. "Kako je Mislav Kolakušić uz Facebook i Google oglase postao najveće iznenađenje izbora za EP." *Netokracija*, May 27. https://www.netokracija.com/mislav-kolakusic-drustvene-mreze-izbori-157555
Biberović, Mia. 2019b. "Velika analiza kampanje kandidata za predsjednika 2019: Tko najbolje plovi digitalnim vodama?" *Netokracija*, December 22. https://www.netokracija.com/izbori-predsjednik-2019-drustvene-mreze-163222
Blassnig, Sina, Nicole Ernst, Sven Engesser, and Frank Esser. 2019. "Populism and Social Media Popularity: how Populist Communication Benefits Political Leaders on Facebook and Twitter." In *Power Shift? Political Leadership and Social Media*, edited by Richard Davis and David Taras, 97–111. New York: Routledge.
Bodo, Balasz, Natali Helberger, and Clas H. de Vreese. 2017. "Political Micro-Targeting: A Manchurian Candidate or Just a Dark Horse?" *Internet Policy Review* 6 (4). doi: 10.14763/2017.4.776.
Borge Bravo, Rosa, and Eduardo Santamarina Sáez. 2016. "From Protest to Political Parties: Online Deliberation in New Parties in Spain." *Medijske Studije* 7 (14):104–22. doi: 10.20901/ms.7.14.8.
Cooper, Andrew F. 2008. *Celebrity Diplomacy.* New York: Routledge.
Corner, John, and Dick Pels. 2003. "Re-Styling of Politics." In *Media and the Restyling of Politics*, edited by John Corner and Dick Pels, 1–18. London: SAGE Publishing.
Čular, Goran, and Marijana Grbeša. 2020. "Croatia." In *The European Parliament Election of 2019 in East-Central Europe. Second-Order Euroscepticism*, edited by Vit Hloušek and Petr Kaniok, 39–60. London: Palgrave.

Danas. 2019. "Analitičar žestoko uzvratio Kolakušiću, svašta je izgovorio: On je Hitler iz našeg sokaka koji bi htio udarati sjekirom..." *Danas*, Decembar 10. https://net.hr/danas/hrvatska/analiticar-zestoko-uzvratio-kolaku sicu-svasta-je-izgovorio-on-je-hitler-iz-naseg-sokaka-koji-bi-htio-udarati-sjekirom/#.

Driessens, Oliver. 2013. "The Celebritization of Society and Culture: Understanding the Structural Dynamics of Celebrity Culture." *International Journal of Cultural Studies* 16 (6):641–57. doi: 10.1177/1367877912459140.

EEMC Report. 2019. *Croatia* https://www.electionsmonitoringcenter.eu/article/b8948aed-67b6-4575-bb9c-df29ae08538.

Eurobarometer. 2019. *Croatia* https://ec.europa.eu/commfrontoffice/publicopinionmobile/index.cfm/Survey/getSurveyDetail/surveyKy/2255.

Enli, Gunn. 2017. "Twitter as Arena for the Authentic Outsider: Exploring the Social Media Campaigns of Trump and Clinton in the 2016 US Presidential Election." *European Journal of Communication* 32 (1):50–61. doi: 10.1177/0267323116682802.

Esser, Frank and Jesper Stromback, eds. 2014. *Mediatization of Politics: Understanding the Transformation of Western Democracies*. Basingstoke: Palgrave Macmillan.

Freeden, Michael. 1996. *Ideologies and Political Theory: A Conceptual Approach*. Oxford: Clarendon Press.

Freeden, Michael. 2003. *Ideology*. Oxford: Oxford University Press.

Giglioli, Matteo, and Gianfranco Baldini. 2019. "Kings, Jesters, or Kingmakers? European Populist Parties as a Microcosm for Celebrity Politics." *The British Journal of Politics and International Relations* 21 (3):576–93. doi: 10.1177/1369148119844494.

Glavinić, Iva. 2016. "Stranke na društvenim mrežama: Živi zid najpopularniji na Facebooku, SDP na Twitteru." *Mediatoolkit*, September 7. https://www.mediatoolkit.com/blog/hr/politicari-na-drustvenim-mrezama-tko-pobjed uje-u-kampanji-na-drustvenim-mrezama/.

Grbeša, Marijana. 2009. "Politika Osebnosti na Hrvaškem: analiza Volilnih Kampanj na Parlamentarnih Volitvah 2003 in 2007." *Teorija in Praksa* 45 (6):788–816.

Grbeša, Marijana, and Berto Šalaj. 2016. "Textual Analysis of Populist Discourse in 2014/2015 Presidential Election in Croatia." *Contemporary Southeastern Europe* 3 (1):106–27.

Grbeša, Marijana, and Berto Šalaj. 2018a. *Dobar, Loš Ili Zao? Populizam u Hrvatskoj*. Zagreb: Tim Press.

Grbeša, Marijana, and Berto Šalaj, Faculty of Political Science, University of Zagreb, Croatia. 2018b. "Populism in Croatia: The Curious Case of the Bridge (Most)." *Anali Hrvatskog Politološkog Društva: časopis za Politologiju* 14 (1):7–30. doi: 10.20901/an.14.01.

Grbeša, Marijana, and Berto Šalaj. 2019. "Croatia." In *Thirty Years of Political Campaigning in Central and Eastern Europe*, edited by Otto Eibl and Milos Gregor, 237–54. London: Palgrave.

Groshek, Jacob, and Karolina Koc-Michalska. 2017. "Helping Populism Win? Social Media Use, Filter Bubbles, and Support for Populist Presidential Candidates in the 2016 US Election Campaign." *Information, Communication & Society* 20 (9):1389–407. doi: 10.1080/1369118X.2017.1329334.

Hašić, Jasmin. 2020. "'Deviating' Party Leadership Strategies in Bosnia And Herzegovina: A Comparison of Milorad Dodik and Dragan Čović." In *Party Leaders in Eastern Europe: Personality, Behavior and Consequences*, edited by Sergiu Gherghina, 17–41. Basingstoke: Palgrave Macmillan.

Henjak, Andrija. 2017. "Institutional Trust and Democracy Satisfaction in Croatia: Partisanship versus Outcome Driven Evaluations." *Hrvatska i Komparativna Javna Uprava* 17 (3):343–63. doi: 10.31297/hkju.17.3.1.

Homolar, Alexandra, and Ronny Scholz. 2019. "The Power of Trump-Speak: populist Crisis Narratives and Ontological Security." *Cambridge Review of International Affairs* 32 (3):344–64. doi: 10.1080/09557571.2019.1575796.

Index. 2019. "Crobarometar: Evo za koga bi Hrvati glasali da su izbori za EU parlament danas." *Index*, April, 27. https://www.index.hr/vijesti/clanak/crobarometar-evo-za-koga-bi-hrvati-glasali-da-su-izbori-za-eu-parlament-danas/2081471.aspx.

Kaltwasser, Rovira Cristobal. 2014. "The Responses of Populism to Dahl's Democratic Dilemma." *Political Studies* 62 (3):470–87. doi: 10.1111/1467-9248.12038.

Klauški, Tomislav. 2016. "Politički trash: Živi zid je tek karikatura hrvatske politike." *24sata.hr*, October, 6. https://www.24sata.hr/kolumne/politicki-trash-zivi-zid-je-tek-karikatura-hrvatske-politike-494068.

Kunac, Suzana, Dražen Lalić, and Martina Andrijević. 2013. "Tihi Glas, Ujutro u Americi: izborna Kampanja 2011. u Hrvatskoj." *Politička Misao* 50 (2):75–97.

Langer, Ana I. 2012. *Personalisation of Politics in the UK. Mediated Leadership from Attlee to Cameron*. Manchester: Manchester University Press.

Lyman, Rick. 2017. "The Trump-Like Figures Popping Up in Central Europe." *New York Times*, February 24. https://www.nytimes.com/2017/02/24/world/europe/zbigniew-stonoga-andrej-babis.html.

Manning, Nathan, Ruth Penfold-Mounce, Brian D. Loader, Ariadne Vromen, and Michael Xenos. 2017. "Politicians, Celebrities and Social Media: A Case of Informalisation?" *Journal of Youth Studies* 20 (2):127–44. doi: 10.1080/13676261.2016.1206867.

Manucci, Luca. 2017. "Populism and Media." In *The Oxford Handbook of Populism*, edited by Rovira Cristobal Kaltwasser, Paul Taggart, Paulina Ochoa Espejo and Pierre Ostiguy, 467–88. Oxford: Oxford University Press.

Marsh, David, Paul 't Hart, and Karen Tindall. 2010. "Celebrity Politics: The Politics of Late Modernity?" *Political Studies Review* 8 (3):322–40. doi: 10.1111/j.1478-9302.2010.00215.x.

Marshall, David P. 1997. *Celebrity and Power: Fame in Contemporary Culture*. Minneapolis: University of Minnesota Press.
Mazzoleni, Gianpietro. 2008. "Populism and the Media." In *Twenty-First Century Populism: The Spectre of Western European Democracy*, edited by Daniele Albertazzi and Duncan McDonnell, 49–64. New York: Palgrave.
Mazzoleni, Gianpietro. 2016. "Did the Media Create Trump?" In *US Election Analysis 2016: Media, Voters and the Campaign* edited by Darren Lilleker, Daniel Jackson, Einar Thorsen, and Anastasia Veneti, 21. Poole: Bournemouth University.
Mazzoleni, Gianpietro, and Roberta Bracciale. 2018. "Socially Mediated Populism: The Communicative Strategies of Political Leaders on Facebook." *Palgrave Communications* 4 (1). doi: 10.1057/s41599-018-0104-x.
Miconi, Andrea. 2015. "Italy's 'Five Stars' Movement and the Role of a Leader: Or, How Charismatic Power Can Resurface through the Web." *New Media & Society* 17 (7):1043–58. doi: 10.1177/1461444814520872.
Mikašinović Komšo, Matej. 2020. "Izbori su završili, vrijeme je i za konačnu ocjenu digitalnih kampanja vodećih kandidata." *Jutarnji list*, January 6. https://www.jutarnji.hr/naslovnica/izbori-su-zavrsili-vrijeme-je-i-za-konacnu-ocjenu-digitalnih-kampanja-vodecih-kandidata-tjednima-smo-ih-pratili-na-mrezama-a-ovo-su-zakljucci-9824818
Moffitt, Benjamin. 2016. *The Global Rise of Populism: Performance, Political Style, and Representation*. Stanford: Stanford University Press.
Mudde, Cas. 2004. "The Populist Zeitgiest." *Government and Opposition* 39 (4):541–63. doi: 10.1111/j.1477-7053.2004.00135.x.
Mustapić, Marko, and Ivan Hrstić. 2016. "Populizam u Hrvatskoj Između Ideologije i Političkog Stila – Temeljne Odrednice Predizborne Retorike Predsjedničkog Kandidata Ivana Vilibora Sinčića." In *Jezik, Ideologija i Sjećanje u Suvremenom Kontekstu*, edited by Ivica Šarac, 63–82. Mostar: Filozofski fakultet Sveučilišta u Mostaru.
Pels, Dick. 2003. "Aesthetic Representation and Political Style: Re-Balancing Identity and Difference in Media Democracy." In *Media and the Restyling of Politics*, edited by John Corner and Dick Pels, 41–63. London: SAGE Publishing.
Petrovova, Iva, and Otto Eibl. 2019. "Celebrities in Czech Politics in 1996-2013." *European Journal of Communication* 34 (1):3–19. doi: 10.1177/0267323118790163.
Reuters Institute for the Study of Journalism. 2020. *The Reuters Institute Digital News Report*. https://reutersinstitute.politics.ox.ac.uk/sites/default/files/2020-06/DNR_2020_FINAL.pdf.
Romić, Tea. 2019. "Kolakušić: Bit ću šef države, pravosuđa, MUP-a i premijer." *Večernji list*, May 27. https://www.vecernji.hr/vijesti/kolakusic-se-u-13-sati-obraca-javnosti-najavljuje-predstojece-korake-protiv-korupcije-1321985.
Schneiker, Andrea. 2019. "Telling the Story of the Superhero and the anti-Politician as President: Donald Trump's Branding on Twitter." *Political Studies Review* 17 (3):210–23. doi: 10.1177/1478929918807712.
Schroeder, Ralph. 2018. *Social Theory after the Internet: Media, Techonology and Globalization*. London: UCL Press.
Street, John. 2004. "Celebrity Politicians: Popular Culture and Political Representation." *British Journal of Politics and International Relations* 6 (4):435–52. doi: 10.1111/j.1467-856X.2004.00149.x.
Street, John. 2019. "What is Donald Trump? Forms of 'Celebrity' in Celebrity Politics." *Political Studies Review* 17 (1):3–13. doi: 10.1177/1478929918772995.
't Hart, Paul, and Karen Tindall. 2009. "Leadership by the Famous: Celebrity as Political Capital." In *Dispersed Democratic Leadership: Origins, Dynamics, and Implications*, edited by John Kane, Haig Patapan, and Paul 't Hart, 255–78. Oxford: Oxford University Press.
Tsaliki, Liza, Christos A. Frangonikolopoulos, and Asteris Huliaras. 2011. *Transnational Celebrity Activism in Global Politics. Changing the World?* Chicago: The University of Chicago Press.
Vuković, Silvija. 2019. "Celebrity Populizam u Hrvatskoj na Primjeru Ivana Pernara i Miroslava Škore." Master thesis, Faculty of Political Sciences, University of Zagreb.
Waisboard, Silvio. 2018. "The Elective Affinity between Post-Truth Communication and Populist Politics." *Communication Research and Practice* 4 (1):17–34.
West, Darrell M., and John M. Orman. 2003. *Celebrity Politics*. Englewood Cliffs: Prentice Hall.
Wheeler, Mark. 2013. *Celebrity Politics – Image and Identity in Contemporary Communications*. Cambridge: Polity.
Wirz, Dominique S. 2018. "Persuasion through Emotion? An Experimental Test of the Emotion-Eliciting Nature of Populist Communication." *International Journal of Communication* 12:1114–38.
Wood Matthew, Jack Corbett, and Matthew Flinders. 2016. "Just like Us: Everyday Celebrity Politicians and the Pursuit of Popularity in an Age of anti-Politics." *The British Journal of Politics and International Relations* 18 (3):581–98. doi: 10.1177/1369148116632182.
van Zoonen, Liesbet. 2005. *Entertaining the Citizen: When Politics and Popular Culture Converge*. Oxford: Rowman and Littlefield.
van Zoonen, Liesbet. 2006. "The Personal, the Political and the Popular: A Women's Guide to Celebrity Politics." *European Journal of Cultural Studies* 9 (3):287–301.
24sata.hr. 2016. "*Pernar: Ako će mediji raditi show, spreman sam biti klaun*". 24sata.hr, October, 6. https://www.24sata.hr/news/pernar-ako-ce-mediji-raditishowspreman-sam-biti-klaun-494030.

A Rumbling from Below? Opposition Party Rebranding, Regional Elections, and Transforming the Regime in Russia

John Ishiyama and Mikhail Rybalko

ABSTRACT
In this paper we examine whether opposition parties, particularly the Communist Party of the Russian Federation (CPRF), can promote transition in the electoral authoritarian regime in Russia. We use the example of the National Action Party's (PAN) evolution as an "official opposition" party in Mexico and discuss how its campaign strategy and party identity evolved. Using a framework derived from the political marketing literature on party branding and rebranding, we argue that the PAN successfully rebranded itself *via* the electoral opportunities afforded by structure of Mexican federalism, which ultimately led to the democratic transition in 1999. We then address the possibility of a similar evolution occurring in Russia, by examining how the CPRF altered its national campaign message between 2015–2018. Finally, we speculate whether local opposition victories will spark the kind of transition in Russia that occurred in other electoral authoritarian regimes, such as Mexico.

Introduction

Although there has been growing interest in campaigning in electoral authoritarian regimes (Ishiyama 2020; Hutcheson and McAllister 2017; Langston and Morgenstern 2009) research on how the political opposition campaigns in such regimes is limited. Opposition parties under such conditions are very circumscribed, and their ability to campaign is limited. However, as Langston and Morgenstern (2009, 165) note, if winning votes is fundamental to autocratic regimes then campaigning to win these votes should be of central concern. Nonetheless, the extant literature on such regimes only focuses at the national level, and usually on the campaign activities of the governing party (Hutcheson and McAllister 2017). What is absent is a focus on campaigning at the regional level and how the opposition campaigns in localities.

Some scholars suggest that in Russia (Golosov 2011; Ross 2011) the roots of electoral authoritarianism were built from below, in the regions. Yet the *unraveling* of electoral authoritarianism can also begin in the regions, as illustrated by the case of Mexico. In that country, the opposition gradually built up a power base in state level elections, which eventually led themto winning power nationally in 1999. Thus, how the opposition campaigns (and wins) at the local and regional level is critical to understanding transformation processes in electoral authoritarian regimes. In this paper we examine how the main opposition party (particularly the Communist Party of the Russian Federation–CPRF) campaigned in regional elections since electoral authoritarianism began in 2004, with a particular focus on the regional elections in Eastern Siberia since 2015. We also examine how the CPRF has changed its message to present to the electorate a new face for the party and investigate whether it can really emerge as a force for change in the Russian Federation.

In this paper we adopt a political marketing frame in order to understand that the process of democratization in electoral authoritarian regimes (Steger, Kelly, and Wrighton 2006). We use the concept of branding developed in the political marketing literature (Perloff 1999; Scammell 2015, 2007; Lees-Marshment 2009, 7) and the idea of imaging in the literature on political parties, to explain how formerly coopted oppositions can be transformed and lead the way to democratic transition. In particular we argue that this involves, as illustrated by the Mexican case, that one of the established official opposition parties rebrands itself to offer a credible alternative to the governing dominant party. Such a successful rebranding occurs when issue opportunities arise upon which the opposition party can refashion its message (such as the belief that the incumbent authoritarian party is incompetent and corrupt). However, we also argue that such opportunities for rebranding occur first in local areas (particularly in federal systems) and it is from these regional bases that the major opposition parties build their new image (which involves developing a party image for competent government and an anti-corruption stance).

We use the example of the National Action Party's (PAN) evolution as an "official opposition" party in the Mexican electoral authoritarian regime and discuss how party rebranding evolves. This evolution coupled with the electoral opportunities afforded by structure of Mexican federalism, which provided PAN with an opportunity to establish a track record of governance that burnished the party's reputation and brand, ultimately led to the democratic transition in 1999. We then address the possibility of a similar evolution occurring in Russia, by examining how the CPRF altered its national campaign message in 2018 and how it campaigns at the regional level, particularly in Eastern Siberia. Finally, we speculate whether that local opposition victories will spark the kind of transition in Russia that occurred in other electoral authoritarian regimes like Mexico. Although there appears to be a potentially similar process occurring now in the Russian Federation, with the CPRF scoring some regional electoral victories in relatively wealthy parts of the country, the CPRF currently appears to be incapable of "rebranding" itself in a way similar to the PAN in Mexico.

Branding and Rebranding Party Image

As part of the framing for this article, we turn to the political marketing literature that deals with the concept of party branding and rebranding. Indeed, much of the literature on branding in the political marketing field has focused on political parties. This is because, like corporate actors, political parties compete for political market, and offer their brand to attract consumers (or in the case voters). Thus, as Scammell (2015) notes political parties are communicative institutions that seek to create an image to connect with voters in order to gain greater share of the political market (see also Hallin and Mancini 2004, 8). For Scammell (2015, 15) political image is conceived as a reputation where parties seek to convey their competence, strength of leadership, and their credibility. Ultimately political parties (like firms) begin with an image they portray, which may (or may not) turn into a brand. Brands are defined as the psychological representation of a product or service or organization, providing symbolic, rather than tangible value to consumers. A successful brand is where an emotional connection is established with consumers beyond the product itself (for instance Coca-Cola). Thus, the brand operates as a marker of quality and a shortcut for consumers when making choices (Kornberger 2010). However, ultimately, the brand emerges not simply because the firm creates an image but also shaped by the experiences and perceptions of consumers that arise out of multiple encounters with the product (Clifton and Simmons 2003).

There is also the literature on rebranding. In the marketing literature corporate rebranding is difference from corporate branding in as much as rebranding refers to changing from one corporate brand to another (Merrilees and Miller 2008). Corporations often rebrand in order to respond to both changes in an external market and/or internal factors, or changes in corporate management who seek to explore new market opportunities, set themselves ahead of the competition (Tevi and Otubanjo 2013). Although there has been a good deal of literature on corporate rebranding, scholars studying political party rebranding have noted that it is far more difficult to change party's brand and image (Kim and Solt 2017; Ishiyama and Marshall 2017; Harmel and Janda 1994). As Marland and Flanagan (2013) note, for instance, that rebranding of the Canadian Conservative Party from the ashes of the 2003 election demonstrated the difficulty of rebranding. The newly rebranded Canadian Alliance Party faced great resistance particularly because of intense emotional attachment by partisans to old party symbols (such as the color of the Canadian Maple Leaf). This extreme emotional attachment to partisan symbols makes parties different from corporations. However, this does not mean rebranding cannot take place, only that is much more difficult to do so than it is for corporations.

Indeed, much of the political science scholarship on party image change (or rebranding) suggests that changes only occur after political catastrophes, such as losing elections (Harmel and Janda 1994; Janda et al. 1995). From this perspective, parties are assumed to be conservative organizations that are unlikely to change unless forced (Harmel and Janda 1994). Janda et al. (1995) that generally calamitous or disappointing elections were associated with the greatest degree of party image change, indicating that parties only try to change their images when voters reject the policy face they had presented in the previous election.

Although the predominant view is that parties will only rebrand if they face electoral catastrophe, other scholars have argued that there are internal factors that also cause party image change. For instance Ishiyama and Marshall (2017), when examining former rebel parties as they transform from armed groups to political parties after civil wars, argue that image change is often the result of a political leadership that sees longer term opportunities by refashioning the image of the party (see also Ishiyama 2019). This is not dissimilar to corporate efforts at rebranding, where corporate leaders see opportunities to exploit future markets (Tevi and Otubanjo 2013).

However, as noted with the branding literature above, an opposition party, particularly one that has been branded as the "coopted opposition" in an authoritarian regime, must develop a track record of performance to have a rebranded identity take root with voters. This means that the party must have a track record of good governance, economic success, and incorruptibility in office in order to take advantage of opportunities to challenge the ruling party. This is especially useful to take advantage of growing citizen disgust with the ruling party's inefficient governance and corruption. One way to do this is to build a reputation of effectiveness and incorruptibility in regional or state governments and build up a new brand from this foundation. This provides an opportunity to convince voters that the new brand represents a credible symbol for reform. In many ways this was how the PAN in Mexico was able to rebrand itself so that it could more effectively challenge the dominance of the Institutional Revolutionary Party (PRI) in the 1990s.

The Transformation of Political Oppositions in Electoral Authoritarian Regimes: The Case of PAN in Mexico

To understand party campaigns in Russia, at any level, it is important to examine the nature of the system, and the institutional context, (both the nature of the regime and the party system). Some like Ross (2011, 2014) has characterized Russia as akin to what Andreas Schedler has referred to as an "electoral authoritarian" regime (Schedler 2006, 2). In such a regime there are regularly held elections which are, "*broadly inclusive* (they are held under universal suffrage), *minimally pluralistic* (opposition parties are permitted to run), *minimally competitive* (parties and candidates outside the ruling coalition, while denied victory, are allowed to win votes and seats), and *minimally open* (dissidence is not subject to massive, but often to selective and intermittent repression)." Elections in such regimes, however, are not minimally democratic in as much they are subject to many forms of "manipulation that violate the liberal–democratic principles of freedom, fairness, and integrity" (Schedler 2006, 2). Such manipulations include "barriers to opposition parties' ability to campaign; generate a pro-government media bias; stack electoral commissions and courts with their supporters; or resort to stuffing ballot boxes and manipulating vote tabulations" (Donno 2013, 704). As Ross (2011, 2014) points out all these forms of electoral malpractice have been widely practiced in regional elections in Russia.

Can democratic transitions occur in electoral authoritarian regimes, and what role do the "official" opposition parties play in promoting that transition? In this respect the case of Mexico is informative. Mexico under the PRI was the archetype of electoral authoritarianism according the Schedler (2006, 3). Although not the "party state" that existed under the Soviet Union, Mexico was certainly a dominant party regime where elections were seen as largely ceremonious, "a mere legitimizing ritual" (Smith 1979, 271). Elections before the democratic transition were, Daniel Levy, Kathleen Bruhn, and Emilio Zebadua (2006) suggest, eminently "safe and predictable." Further the scholarship on Mexican authoritarianism generally concluded that "Mexican voters had invariably faced overwhelming institutional and informal, often violent impediments" (Gillingham 2012, 54).

Although at the national level there was no denying that dominance of the PRI, Gillingham (2012) suggest that there were "unseen" elections at the local level that suggested a very different path of electoral evolution. He contends that closer examination of local elections indicated many more opportunities for the opposition parties than has been assumed. For instance, as early as the 1940s, the PRI "frequently lost control of local elections; that popular protests vetoed the accession of mayors and governors, or toppled them once in power; and that key presidential policies, such as conscription and literacy campaigns, were successfully flouted or reversed by massive civil disobedience" (Gillingham 2012, 64). Even though the PRI won most elections, the opposition made significant inroads at the local level even at the height of the electoral authoritarian regimes. From 1962 to 1978 the National Action Party (PAN) won 26 of the 236 largest *municipios* in Mexico. By the 1990s the opposition parties governed about *half* of all Mexicans. As Gillingham (2012, 68) notes, this pattern of competition helped generate and maintain an "electoral culture" and "that culture was highly salient in structuring Mexico's transition to democracy."

The actions of the opposition parties, particularly PAN, "the loyal opposition" according to Gillingham (2012, 60–61), took the "the strategic decision early in its existence to build power gradually and from the bottom up". PAN was *not* a created opposition (in many ways similar to the CPRF), but it was also not a genuine opposition party. It was like a cooperative party in the authoritarian party cartel and it sought the limited sharing of power, particularly at the local level in Northern Mexico. The PRI itself encouraged the inclusion of PAN (as part of the party cartel) to broaden the legitimacy of the existing regime by allow PAN isolated victories—a handful of federal deputies, a minority of *municipios* and, later, expanded inclusion with the introduction of a proportional representation into Mexican legislative and local elections (Camp 2012).

PAN itself also underwent a major transformation of its image. The party, which had been rooted in pro-Catholic politicians early in its history, underwent an ideological transformation in the 1970s, jettisoning much of its pro-Catholic agenda and adopting an increasingly secular stance. Further, one of the main platforms of the party, the privatization of communal landownership and privatization of the land, was in effect coopted by the PRI in 1992, when PRI Salinas administration introduced radical reforms to the land tenure law that allowed for the sale of land and privatization. This led to a convergence of both the PRI's and PAN's economic programs, prompting the PAN to alter its campaign strategy. After that the PAN sought to distinguish itself from PRI, by focusing on political issues such as the need for democratization, the elimination of government corruption, and further electoral reforms. By the 1994 presidential election, PAN campaigned on the slogan "por un México sin mentiras" ("for a Mexico without lies") and won a comfortable second place. The second-place win consolidated the PAN's role as the primary opposition political force in the country (Merrill and Miro 1996). These developments set the stage for PAN to challenge PRI dominance in the 1990s, leading ultimately to the victory of PAN's presidential candidate, Vincente Fox, in the election of 1999, thus ending the PRI electoral authoritarian regime.

In short, the rise of PAN and its role in the democratization of the electoral authoritarian regime in Mexico was premised on two different dynamics. First, the nature of Mexican federalism created openings at the regional level for the opposition to gain political access and a foothold in local elections, upon which they could expand its appeal. Thus, the less "policed" (in the sense of close regime oversight) areas of Northern Mexico (but economically well off states that bordered the United States) afforded the PAN and opportunity to gain a foothold in governance at the local level. Second the PAN reinvented itself from a conservative Catholic party defending traditional values, to a secular, anti-corruption, and pro-democracy party that was able to capitalize on growing discontent with PRI rule. By doing so, it was able to transform itself from a "symbolic" opposition party to a real opposition party in the 1990s, challenging for national power. Rather than a party representing a narrow set of religious dissidents, it became a party that appealed well beyond its original political roots. This was a remarkable transformation of a party that had been coopted as part of the cartel party system under electoral authoritarianism to help legitimize the PRI regime.

Can we expect that the main opposition party in Russia, the CPRF, will play a similar role in Russia as PAN did in Mexico? Again, as we argue below, much of this depends on the changing context in Russia as well as the CPRF's ability to "re-image" itself in future campaigns. In the section below we examine both the changing dynamics in the country from 2015–2019 and the extent to which the party has altered its campaign message to attract voters.

The Institutional Context in Russia: The Regime and the Party System

Although there is little debate over the characterization of Russia as an electoral authoritarian regime, there is less consensus about the nature of the party system. In the 1990s, several scholars labeled the Russian party system as a "floating" system (Rose et al. 2001). This system was characterized by the frequent appearance and disappearance of political parties, and weak connections between the parties and voting constituencies. However, by the twenty first century the party system had consolidated around four very stable parties: UR, CPRF, LDPR and AJR.

The CPRF and the LDPR have been active and represented in every Duma election since 1993. Moreover, they have had continuous leadership under Gennady Zyuganov (CPRF) and Vladimir Zhirinovsky (LDPR). The CPRF is the organizational successor to the Communist Party of the Soviet Union, founded in 1993 after the ban on the Communist Party was lifted. It has generally followed a program that promotes the adoption of a modernized form of socialism in Russia, which would include the nationalization of ownership of strategic natural resources, land and large industries while maintaining a mixed economy and private ownership of some of the means of production, particularly for small and medium consumer industries. The party also has under Gennady Zyuganov, emphasized a left-wing nationalist ideology, that has emphasized the transformation of class struggle into a civilizational struggle, pitting East against West (March 2002).

The LDPR was founded in 1989 and is headed by Vladimir Zhirinovsky. It is a statist, ultra-nationalist party that is based on Zhirinovsky's ideas of a renewed "Greater Russia" (Hanson 2011; Hale 2010) The party official opposes both communism and neoliberal market developmental solutions, and prefers a mixed economy with strong state direction, making its core principles similar to that of the CPRF (although they differ on state ownership). The core of the party's ideology is that there is a clash of civilizations with the West as the principal external threat to Russia and the Pan Slavic community (Hale 2010). Although it often promotes itself as an opposition to the governing UR, the party overwhelmingly votes with UR (unlike the CPRF) (Hutcheson and McAllister 2017, 458)

AJR was formed on October 2006 as a merger of the Rodina (Motherland) Party, the Russian Party of Life and Russian Pensioners party as well as six other minor parties. Scholars, such as Sakwa (2011) and March (2009) have suggested that AJR was created by Putin and the "siloviki" (or power men)[1] to siphon off support from the CPRF in preparation for the 2007 Legislative elections. Indeed, Luke March (2011, 505) "certainly, Just Russia can be understood as a regime created "parastatal party" aimed at providing limited competition for the main "party of power" (United Russia)" The Party's program is loosely social democratic and calls for a "new socialism" that protects freedoms but also the creation of a welfare state (March 2011). It has, at times, expressed open opposition to the Putin regime, but not often (Hutcheson and McAllister 2017).

United Russia was founded in 2001 as unification of the Unity Party, which was created prior to the 1999 Duma elections to support Yeltsin in holding off a challenge from Yuri Luzhkov, the Mayor of Moscow and his Fatherland-All Russia party. In July 2001, the two parties merged to form UR. The focus UR has been the maintenance of stability and unity, and the restoration of Russian "greatness". It positions itself as a "centrist" party that seeks to balance left and right. It favors a strong regulatory state, with expanded welfare programs, but also the promotion of market freedoms (Roberts 2012). The UR is the core of the Russian party system as the "Party of Power", and as such is the primary party supporter of President Putin. The UR has won the largest number of seats in the State Duma since 2003 and dominates most of the regional legislative assemblies (Hutcheson and McAllister 2017).

Many scholars currently characterize the Russian party system as a "hegemonic" or "dominant" party system (Smyth, Lowry, and Wilkening 2007; Reuter and Remington 2009). The key feature of such a party system is one where a single party dominates but there exists "official opposition" parties which "afford the appearance but surely does not afford the substance of competitive politics" (Sartori 2005, 205). In such party systems official oppositions are created to provide official channels for some limited power sharing (Maglioni 2008; Gillingham 2012).

Reuter (2010, 294) argues that the UR has emerged as a dominant party and this has been "one of the most important developments in Russian politics since the end of the Soviet Union." For Reuter the UR has established itself in "the leading role in determining access to most political offices. It is the site of coordination for a winning coalition of elite actors. It is an institution that successfully supplies certain goods to rulers, elites and voters (...) and the distribution of spoils gives elites incentives to remain loyal to the regime" (Reuter 2010, 295). Gel'man also claims that after the 2007 State Duma elections UR emerged as a dominant party that "established and closely tied the rulers of (the) authoritarian regime" and employs "state power and resources to maintain its dominance and uses extra-constitutional means to control the outcomes of politics during elections and beyond" (Gel'man 2008, 915).

However, Hutcheson (2010) suggests that the claim the UR is a dominant party is quite exaggerated. Unlike the predominant "hegemonic" view of the Russian party system, Hutcheson (2013) argues that the system resembles more of a party "cartel." Katz and Mair (1995) contend that cartel party systems are systems in which parties, rather than compete with one another, collude to extract subventions from the state and to keep out competitors who might challenge the parties' access to state patronage resources. Using the idea of the party cartel, Hutcheson (2013) argues that the relationship between UR, CPRF, LDPR and AJR is cooperative rather than the UR opposition merely being an "official opposition" (see also Oversloot and Verheul 2006). In other words, the opposition parties, especially the CPRF and LDPR are independent from the UR, and not merely a "symbolic opposition" but cooperate with the "party of power."

However, unlike other cartel party systems in the West (where there is collusion between relatively equally matched parties), in Russia there is clearly a dominant partner (UR) which controls a supermajority of seats in parliament. In this sense, the Russian system is a *dominated cartel party system* where UR is the central actor.

The features of the party system affect how politicians' campaign in Russia. First, unlike in hegemonic party systems, campaigns *do* matter; and like a cartel party system, election results count (affecting the share of the "pie" the individual parties receive). Second, given the nature of the dominated cartel party system, the campaign messages of the competing parties in the cartel must define their positions (either for or against) the positions taken by UR. However, because UR portrays itself as the party of stability, without much in the way of taking hard positions on any issues, this provides openings for parties like the CPRF and LDPR (and to a much lesser extent AJR) to define themselves very differently from UR during campaigns (but colluding with UR once the election is over).

Most of the literature on the Russian party system has tended to only focus on the national level. However, as Panov and Ross (2013) rightly point out, this focus on national level politics belies the great deal of regional diversity in Russia. As one of the most ethnically diverse multinational federations in the world is highly incongruent and asymmetric. Although the constitution enshrines regional autonomy, there has been a growing concentration of power in the president's hands since Vladimir Putin became president of the Russian Federation in 2000. Furthermore, UR's dominance in regional parliaments and executives has greatly limited regional autonomy. Thus, like the Soviet Union, federalism is hollowed out, with most all power concentrated in the hands of the political center (Chuman 2011).

Nonetheless, given the existing diversity in the Russian Federation, this creates "openings" for the opposition in local election. The 83 federal subjects vary greatly in term of economics and ethnicity, and for Panov and Ross (2013, 739) this makes it much more "difficult for parties to nationalize and create strong unified structures than in a unitary state". Thus, there remain important variations within Russia leading to a variety of electoral politics and types of regimes that vary across these regions. Indeed, like other federations Russia has a variety of regional party systems "with patterns of competition that are unique to them and that are shaped by the local institutional context in which they operate" (Gibson and Suarez-Cao 2010, 512).

Further, control over governorships is still important, and the political parties compete for these offices. Governors were directly elected from 1995 to 2005. Later, from 2005 to 2012 under Putin, governors were nominated by the federal president and confirmed by the legislatures of subjects of the Russian Federation (although the presidents/heads of two republics, Tatarstan and Bashkortostan, continued to be directly elected during this period) (Chuman 2011). In June 2012, direct elections of governors were reintroduced. The reintroduction of direct elections has provided another level of competition for the political parties, as well as opportunities for the opposition. For instance, the CPRF in 2019 controlled two governorships and a republic head (in Oryol and Irkutsk, and Khakassia), the LDPR controls three (Khabarovsk, Smolensk, Vladimir), and AJR, one (in Omsk).

This diversity, as Panov and Ross (2013, 739) note, has limited UR's ability to establish dominance at the local level–although "UR undoubtedly has an 'electoral domination' of Russia's regional assemblies, this does not mean that it should be considered to be a 'dominant party' at this level." Indeed as Slider points out, although UR has been able to establish hegemony at the national level, in part *via* control over patronage, in the regions its "patronage potential appears to be meager. Patronage systems in most regions are largely under the control of regional leaders, independent of United Russia's national or regional party organizations" (Slider 2010, 263). Thus, in many ways the nature of the Russian federal system, as with the case of federalism in Mexico, creates opportunities for opposition parties, to campaign and win elections.

Beyond the political opportunities created by the structure of federalism, events since 2011 have also created opportunities for the opposition, and particularly the CPRF. In 2011, the obvious manipulation of the Duma results in favor of UR led to the largest anti-government rallies since Soviet times. The CPRF has since sharpened its attacks on UR, with Zyuganov saying a "moment of truth" had arrived for the "popular patriotic forces" to unite against the

Kremlin elite (Galeotti 2016). In 2018, another wave of mass protests swept Russia, this time over the Putin administration's decision to significantly increase the retirement age for pensions. The protests were led largely by CPRF and was the largest nation-wide protest since the dissolution of the Soviet Union. The protests continued for months, and in the end the government had to partially retreat, but discontent carried over into the local elections of the following year.

In response to the demonstrations that followed the 2011 Duma elections, the Kremlin reintroduced direct election of governors (which had been suspended since 2004). However, this change was rather limited. Elected or not, Governors were primarily responsible to the Putin. As Slider (2019, 124) notes there was a winnowing process included in the legislation reintroducing gubernatorial competition, what he calls a "municipal filter" at the candidate registration phase. To qualify as governor, candidates had to demonstrate support of between 5-10% of municipal council members (this varied from region to region) and had to be from at least 75% of the municipal councils in the region. Many regions required that gubernatorial candidates had to be from a registered political party (further reducing the scope to mainly candidates from the four recognized parties in the party cartel). These restrictions ensured that only acceptable gubernatorial candidates ran for election.

Despite these limitations, the largest opposition party, the CPRF, began to challenge UR dominance in the regions. Bolstered by the mass demonstrations in 2011 and in 2018, the CPRF campaigners embraced talking points that emphasized government corruption and incompetence. The Communists also pushed for real policy changes, such as increasing taxes on the rich (who only pay the thirteen percent flat income tax), rather than on simply calling for the restoration of the Soviet Union. By focusing their campaigns after the 2016 election on real issues, the CPRF reshaped the national conversation, onto sensitive issues relating to poverty, corruption, and maladministration. This has helped the party more at the regional level than nationally. CPRF candidates at the local level tried to portray an image of incorruptibility and competence, while also hinting at nostalgia for a more ordered past. This certainly appeared to be the basis of the political appeal of communist candidates in the regional elections.

A Rumbling in the East? The 2015 Election in Irkutsk

In many ways Eastern Siberia and the Russian Far East share some features in common with Northern Mexico, where PAN scored its first electoral successes. First, these areas are fairly remote from the political center but have extensive economic ties and investment from its neighbors. The distance from the political center provides opportunities to evade control and are often areas considered by the state as politically less important than regions around the capital. However, on the other hand, extensive economic ties with foreign investors (historically the United States in the case of Mexico, and China, Japan, and Korea in the case of Russia) and the existence natural resources (which generates hard currency revenues) provides a good degree of economic independence from the political center. Thus, one might surmise that if there were rumblings of change from below in the electoral authoritarian regime in Russia, they would first occur in areas like Eastern Siberia.

Since 2011, which was marked by widespread protests over the results of the State Duma election, there has been an effort for the opposition overall to vote tactically in order to support the most viable candidate in opposition to United Russia.[2] This often benefited the communist candidate. The CPRF's first major electoral success in Eastern Siberia, was the victory of Sergei Levchenko, a long time regional communist leader in the first contested gubernatorial election in the Irkutsk since the reintroduction of gubernatorial elections in 2012.

In many ways, the fact that the Communists were able to break through in Irkutsk is not surprising. Since the end of the Soviet times, Irkutsk oblast politics was different when compared to other regions. In the 1990s, the oblast was under the leadership of a popular independent governor Yuri Nozhikov (1991-1997) who attempted to keep some sectors of regions' economy (hydroelectric gridwork) in regional hands. He was a symbol of the regional control and some economic autonomy from the Kremlin and there is a monument to him in the center of the city. The region has also kept a strong affinity for both the communist and imperial legacies. In Irkutsk city one can find intact monuments from the Soviet period-the statue of Lenin in the city center is located only two city blocks from the reestablished monument to Emperor Alexander III, the constructor of the Trans-Siberian railway.

In addition, the Putin regime was also intent on broadening its legitimacy, which created an opening for the opposition. As Richard Sakwa (2020) suggests that the 2015 election in Irkutsk was really part of a concerted effort on the part of the Kremlin to "deconcentrate" authority and allow greater electoral competition to help legitimate the regime (Sakwa 2020, 88). "The new overseer of political matters, (Vyacheslav) Volodin, sought to introduce greater competition into a managed political system as part of his relegitimation strategy. (…) The fear of being swept from office through some sort of popular movement prompted concessions, although accompanied by new forms of control. This was deconcentration rather than liberalization."

Whatever the reason, an opportunity emerged for the communists in Irkutsk, Levchenko, the communist gubernatorial candidate who defeated the UR incumbent in 2015, was also a veteran of several campaigns. He had run in 2001, against the "Party of Power" candidate, Boris Govorin, and lost a close election. In 2015 three years after the restoration of direct elections for governors, Levchenko ran again against the "acting" UR governor, Sergei Yeroshenko. Yereshenko had been appointed as governor by President Putin but had voluntarily resigned to pave the way for new gubernatorial elections. In the first round Sergey Levchenko gained 36.61% but Yeroshenko was just short of an absolute majority of the vote (at 49.6%). In the second round, the several high ranking CPRF politicians, including Zyuganov, campaigned for Levchenko, whereas Yeroshenko held no major campaign events for the second round. In the second round Levchenko won 56.39% of the vote and was elected as governor, the first non-UR governor since direct elections were reinstituted in 2012 (Komsomolskaya Pravda 2019).

Although Levchenko campaigned against corruption and had support from mine workers and other workers from other depressed industries in the region, by most local accounts, Levchenko achieved his victory by capitalizing on general discontent in the region with UR governance. Voters were angry with the high cost of living and wanted to send a message to Moscow (Tsvetkova 2015). Indeed, Levchenko's victory was not seen as a vote for change, but an opportunity to express discontent with UR rule. However, Levchenko's election was not only regarded as a reaction to UR's complacency and a stagnant local economy, but that as one voter put it "Our city is not a priority for United Russia, so they don't campaign as much here. And there's also much less rigging" (Hoad 2018, 1). Also, there a number of observers of Irkutsk politics suggested Levchenko's election was not an "unacceptable" outcome for the Kremlin (Tsvetkova 2015, 1). However Levchenko was not the preferred choice by the Kremlin, and, according to Sharafutdinova (2016, 33) since "Levchenko stayed accountable to the coalition that brought him to power" this resulted in a "municipal 'revolt' as the mayors of cities in Irkutsk oblast affiliated with United Russia started a coordinated campaign criticizing the regional authorities."

Because of this, according to Kara-Murza (2018) Levchenko "toed the line where it mattered", and ultimately was removed by President Putin in 2019, after being blamed for the mishandling of massive flooding in the region in 2019. To replace him the Kremlin dispatched a *Varyag* (Viking—or a person from outside of the region) Igor Kobzev who came from Voronezh. There was little in the way of protest by the local communists and Kobzev has been able to secure federal funding for a number of local public works projects. With these advantages, in the rescheduled election in September 2020 Kobzev won a full term as governor with 70% of the vote.

Remaking the Image of the CPRF and the 2018 Presidential Election

Although Levchenko may have won less because of the effectiveness of his campaign message, and more because of protest vote in the region (along with him being deemed not "unacceptable" by the Kremlin), his election was in many ways a significant event for the CPRF. Indeed, the CPRF as a whole has sought to remake its image since 2011 in part to capitalize on the growing discontent in the country with UR. Although the party remains headed by its aging Soviet era leader Zyuganov, who has been resistant to changing the party's communist identity (March 2002; Ishiyama 1996), in 2018, the party nominated Pavel Grudinin, not Zyuganov who had been the party's nominee every election except for the 2004 presidential contest. Grudinin was a manager of a Sovkhoz (a former Soviet state farm) who had transformed it into a very profitable enterprise. Like many successful businessmen of the period Grudinin also entered politics. He was elected to the Moscow Oblast Duma in 1997 and joined UR when it came into existence in 2001. In 2011, however, UR replaced his candidacy with someone else, forcing him out—he then gravitated toward the CPRF.

Grudinin rose to prominence in 2015 when at a meeting of the 2015 Moscow Economic Forum, Grudinin railed against corruption and stated that some of the participants "definitely should be serving time" (Gershkovich 2018, 1). This speech was widely broadcast on social media, and Grudinin appeared to be a new kind of Communist entrepreneur, unafraid to speak his mind. The CPRF nominated Grudinin as the party's presidential candidate in December 2017, with Zyuganov named as his campaign head. Although seen as an attempt by the party appeal to younger and reform minded voters, the nomination was criticized by many in the left wing of the party. This was largely because Grudinin represented the "bourgeois class" to which Communism is ideologically opposed, and that he was also a previous member of UR and held foreign accounts (Muromski 2018; Rudenko 2018; Isaichenko 2018). To many in the party Grudinin's nomination represented an ideological "sell-out".

In Grudinin's campaign for the presidency, the CPRF deemphasized its connection with the Soviet Union, and emphasized its anti-graft credentials and its managerial competence. Grudinin's campaign, which had no chance for electoral success, nonetheless emphasized the candidate's connection to European style socialism, denounced Russia's "imperial ambitions," particularly given how pensioners lived in poverty at home. Grudinin campaigned on ending corruption and end to the rich's offshore accounts (although as it turned out Grudinin held foreign accounts as well). The communist campaign pointed to the benefits of "socialist enterprise," and that his campaigned wanted to turn Russia into an "even better version of China" (Gershkovich 2018, 1). Although, as expected President Putin overwhelmingly won reelection in March 2018 (Grudinin won only 11.8% of the vote) Grudinin's campaign represented a significant shift in the remaking of the party's image—a deemphasizing of ties to the Soviet past, an embrace of market enterprise (with socialist protection) and a more direct attack on corruption. All of these represented a significant remaking of the CPRF's image to voters.

After the election, Grudinin remained a rather high-profile figure in the CPRF. Nobel Laureate, Zhores Alferov, dies on March 1, 2020. Alferov had been on the CPRF party list and held a Duma seat. On March 19, 2019, the Communist party decided to replace Alferov with Pavel Grudinin (Blinov 2019). However, on March 21, the CEC refused Grudinin because of uncovered foreign accounts (Mukhmetschina and Korzhova 2019). This decision caused a negative reaction from the Communist party. On March 23, communist protests took place across the country (Radio Svoboda 2019). In November, Grudinin announced he would seek the CPRF's nomination for the presidency again in 2024.

The 2018 Regional Elections in Khakassia and Primorskii Krai

Shortly after Putin's reelection, a key event that provided an opportunity and major campaign issue for the CPRF was the June 14, 2018 announcement of a major overhaul of the pension system. The reform increased the retirement age for men from 60 to 65, and for women from 55 to 63. Since the average life expectancy in Russia is around 71 years (66 for men and around 77 for women), this reform meant that an average Russian had to work for almost the entirety of their adult life to be eligible for pension.

Between July and September and again from November 5-7, Russia was swept by waves of protests against the Putin administration's decision to increase the retirement age for pensions. The protests were led largely by CPRF, with the support of other leftist parties. It was the longest and possibly largest nation-wide agitations since the dissolution of the Soviet Union. The communists organized large demonstrations and sustained the movement for over two months. In the end, the government had to retreat, bringing down the retirement age for women from 63 to 60.

Being at the forefront of the movement, the CPRF was one of the major beneficiaries in the local elections that followed. While the LPDR was not actively involved in the protests, its political platform has been that of economic protectionism and it too opposed the pension reforms. Thus, some portion of the anti-United Russia vote seems to have gone to the LDPR as well, particularly in the gubernatorial election in Khabarovsk where the LDPR candidate Sergei Furgal won.

One of the first tests for the CPRF was the Presidential election in the Republic of Khakassia, one of the ethnic republics that are among the 83 subjects of the Russian Federation. Khakassia, also in Eastern Siberia, is in many ways like other regions in the area, poverty stricken, with abundant mineral deposits and timber, and an aging industrial base, although it is not as much a target for Chinese investment as is Irkutsk and neighboring Krasnoyarsk Krai. In September 2018 there were elections for the regional executives (in the case of the ethnic republics like Khakassia, the presidency). The incumbent, Viktor Zimin of the UR, was widely expected to win—the communist challenger was 30-year-old Valentin Konovalov, a regional CPRF leader who had served as deputy in the Abakan City assembly and was nominated as the party's candidate for president in June 2018. Konovalov was widely seen as a "technical candidate", one who was nominated just to lose, and to offer no more than a token challenge to the incumbent (Roth 2018). Further, UR invested heavily in campaigning for Zimin in this election. The Kremlin dispatched heavyweight political figures to campaign for Zimin, held musical performances and even an air show to Khakassia before the elections to raise public support for the UR candidate The Red Army military choir performed also performed at a Zimin event and numerous public forums were held under the hashtag #What'sNotRight? In support of Zimin (Roth 2018). Yet in the end Konovalov won the most votes in the first round of the election, despite after much maneuvering by political establishment to block Konovalov's ascendency. In the second round there was an attempt to replace Zimin with a new UR candidate and to remove Konovalov from the ballot (due to a technicality). Nonetheless, Konovalov won the second round with over 57% of the vote in November 2018.

To a large extent Konovalov's victory was not so much a result of a popular preference for the communist candidate but resulted from voter disgust with the incumbent governor and the UR. Konovalov had the support of the local Communist Party organization, but not nearly the resources that Zimin's campaign machine possessed. Indeed, he really did not present himself as a "reform communist" as had Grudinin had during the presidential election. He portrayed himself as an ardent Communist, born to engineer parents in the factory town of Norilsk, who joined the party in his second year of college. He referred to Lenin as his personal idol in an interview, describing him as "a man who could unite people of different views."[3] He also referred to Stalin as a "great state actor" who had made "mistakes as a leader" a very traditional position taken by Zyuganov as well. However, Konovalov was a young new face for the CPRF, and more than anything else he represented something different than the status quo.

Another very contentious election in September 2018 involving a CPRF candidate was held in Primorskii Krai, the eastern-most region of Russia, is where the fallout of the protests became most apparent. In the gubernatorial election the CPRF nominated Andrei Ischenko, a construction executive and a member of the regional assembly, and a leader in the pension protests in the region. Again, as with the election in Khakassia, Ishchenko was not expected to win. In the first round, neither Andrei Tarasenko, the UR incumbent, nor Andrei Ischenko of the CPRF won a majority of the vote. Tarasenko led 46.6% of the vote and Ishcenko came in second with 26.6%–neither candidate won an absolute majority, which required a second round (Kara-Murza 2018).

In the second round, a considerable proportion of the opposition votes went to Ischenko, who was among the leaders of the protests in the region. However, the final results were deeply controversial. Ischenko had between a one to two perecent lead over the UR candidate Tarasenko with 99% of the vote counted. However, when the last one percent was counted, Tarasenko emerged as the victor, which meant that that he had won almost all of the remaining votes. The CPRF contested the results, alleging electoral manipulation and fraud. They were supported by many other opposition figures, including Alexei Navalny, who wrote from his jail cell calling on the residents of Primorskii Krai to go to the streets to defend their votes and called on other people in surround regions to support them. "Let us forget about ideological differences, it doesn't matter which party Ishchenko represents. (…) The blatant and brazen election fraud in Primorye is an insult to the whole country" (quote in Kara-Murza 2018). There were also widespread protests in Vladivostok in front of the governor's office (Mikhailov 2018).

After reviewing the complaints, the Central Election Commission invalidated the results and scheduled fresh elections on December 16. However, UR replaced Tarasenko (who resigned as acting governor after the second round) with the veteran politician Oleg Kozhemyako as their candidate and he also took over from Tarasenko as acting governor of the region. The regional party leadership of the CPRF decided to boycott the repeated vote in protest, and Ischenko failed to gather the required signatures for an independent bid for governor. He was then removed from the ballot. As a result, Kozhemyako won the rescheduled election easily. However, many in the region felt the election had been stolen by UR (Kozlov and Snegovaya 2019).

Conclusion

Above we posed the question: Can we expect that the main opposition party in Russia, the CPRF, will play a role in Russia similar to the role played by PAN in Mexico? As we noted above, in many ways contemporary Russia is similar to the features of Mexican electoral authoritarianism under the PRI. Both fit Schedler's (2006) classic definition of electoral authoritarianism and both fit the kind of authoritarian cartel party system identified by Hutcheson (2013). Further both the PAN and CPRF represent examples of originally "symbolic oppositions" largely coopted by the dominant party.

In addition, institutionally, both Mexico and Russia are large federal systems, although Russia's is more complex and asymmetric. This means that there are "remote" areas that can avoid central government scrutiny that provides for opportunities for coopeted opposition parties to win office. Further, the relative economic independence of the regions of the East in Russia (like the northern states in Mexico) also means more immunity from the economic pressures from the political center. In both cases, as time passed, there was growing popular discontent with the dominant party rule and rampant corruption. In Russia, the pension reform crisis certainly exacerbated voter disgust with the ruling UR party. This created a window of opportunity for the CPRF, particularly in Eastern Siberia and the Far Eastern regions of the Russian Federation.

But as we noted above, a key development in Mexico was the transformation and reimaging of the PAN into a real opposition party that could represent a governing alternative to the PRI for Mexican voters. This is where differences exist between the CPRF and PAN. Although it is true that the CPRF tried to present a "reformed" image of itself with the presidential campaign of Pavel Grudinin, the reality has been that the party has been unable to transform its image to represent a real alternative to UR. The party's program still emphasizes an embrace of Marxist Leninism, a transition to socialism in stages, and the goal of building "twenty first century socialism" and a rejection of bourgeois liberal democracy (as well as the corruption of the West).[4] This emphasis on national communism has been part of the CPRF ideology since the 1990s and has not really changed. Indeed the principal architect of that ideology, Zyuganov, remains head of the CPRF, and as long as the CPRF remains the "party of Zyuganov" there is little chance of it transforming into a European style social democratic or even a socialist party (and hence an acceptable alternative to the majority of Russian voters).

In addition, the CPRF is still widely seen as a "loyal" opposition, that does little to challenge UR rule (Sakwa 2011). Unlike the PAN which was able to transform its image away from the role of "symbolic opposition" the CPRF does little to challenge the UR, even in the regions. Indeed, the party under Zyuganov seems content to play the role of "loyal opposition" rather than really compete with UR. If the CPRF has enjoyed some electoral success in regional elections recently, this is due to more to voter disgust with United Russia, and not support of communism. Given the inability to transform, the CPRF is unlikely to be continued beneficiary of growing voter discontent with the regime as PAN had been in Mexico.

Of course, there are other opposition parties in Russia, such as the LDPR and AJR, but neither has much in the way of the organization at the local level and the network of supporters that the CPRF has. Although certainly the LDPR has benefited from protest voting, and the recent mass demonstrations in Khabarovsk that have protested the removal of the LDPR governor Sergei Furgal there illustrates the power of such protests, the LDPR does not have the organizational resources for sustained action that the CPRF does (as indicated by the massive country wide pension demonstrations in 2018). The AJR has little in the way of organizational resources and is even more tainted than CPRF and LDPR because it was a creation of the regime.

Recent developments, however, may point to some changes. There has been some hope in opposition circles (and for some observers in the West) that the actions of the dissident leader Alexei Navalny, and the symbol of resistance he represents, may effect changes in Russia (Weiss 2021). Although it certainly is the case that Navalny and his movement can mobilize opposition to the current regime, his movement cannot offer voters a demonstrated and credible governing alternative. Moreover, his movement does not possess the organizational resources to sustain political action beyond street protest. Organizations like the PAN and CPRF do. However, Navalny's movement *has* affected the internal dynamic within the CPRF with many younger and regional leaders (including Sergei Levchenko) supporting Navalny and calling for his release and senior leaders like Zyuganov condemning Navalny and supporting the Kremlin.

Thus, the only opposition party that has the potential to evolve as a challenger to the electoral authoritarian regime, in a way PAN did in Mexico, is the CPRF. However as long as it clings to a discredited past it will be unable play that role as an agent for change. Judging from its campaign appeals its current leadership appears either unwilling or unable to make such a transformation. However, recent developments suggest that there is some hope for the CPRF, particularly if the more progressive, faction, opposed to the Zyuganov line, is able to gain greater influence in the party in the run up to the State Duma elections this year. This remains, nonetheless, a remote possibility at best. Thus, despite the growing discontent with the current Putin regime, currently, there appears to be no viable alternatives to continued UR dominance, and as such, it is unlikely Russia will follow the same path that led to the demise of the electoral authoritarian regime in Mexico.

Notes

1. *Siloviki* refers to the elite associated with security agencies (who are aligned with Putin).
2. Alexei Navalny later, in November 2019, called for a "smart vote" campaign by improving strategic coordination among voters to oppose UR candidates. According to Turchenko and Golosov (2021) this effort did affect the outcomes of the regional elections in September 2019, and has the potential to affect future elections.

3. This is an interesting distinction within the CPRF. As Light (2021) notes "Leninists" in the KPRF are associated with the reform wing of the party and the "Stalinists" are associated with Zyuganov and the senior leadership. For Konovalov to associate himself with Lenin suggests he has more affinity for the reformist wing of the party.
4. Programma Partii KPRF (CPRF Party Program). Accessed June 24 2020. http://www.kprf.ru/party/program/

ORCID

John Ishiyama http://orcid.org/0000-0002-9934-6030
Mikhail Rybalko http://orcid.org/0000-0001-7816-8397

References

Blinov, Maksim. 2019. "КПРФ передаст Грудинину мандат депутата Госдумы" (CPRF will transfer the mandate of the State Duma deputy to Grudinin). *Novosti*, March 14, 2019. Accessed July 10, 2020. https://ria.ru/20190314/1551794347.html
Camp, Roderic Ai. 2012. "The Democratic Transformation of Mexican Politics." In *The Oxford Handbook of Mexican Politics*, edited by Roderic Ai Camp. New York: Oxford doi: 10.1093/oxfordhb/9780195377385.013.0001.
Clifton, Rita, and John Simmons. 2003. *Brands and Branding*. London: Profile Books.
Chuman, Mizuki. 2011. "The Rise and Fall of Power-Sharing Treaties between Center and Regions in Post-Soviet Russia." *Demockratizatsiya* 19:133–50.
Donno, Daniela. 2013. "Elections and Democratization in Authoritarian Regimes." *American Journal of Political Science* 57 (3):703–16. doi: 10.1111/ajps.12013.
Galeotti, Mark. 2016. "Russia's Communist Party is Making a Comeback—and It's Bad News for Putin." Accessed April 2019. https://www.vox.com/2016/3/8/11179332/russia-communist-party.
Gel'man, Vladimir. 2008. "Party Politics in Russia: From Competition to Hierarchy." *Europe-Asia Studies* 60 (6):913–30.
Gershkovich, Evan. 2018. "Under Grudinin, Russia's Communist Party Gets a Capitalist Makeover: The charismatic farm boss is the party's new presidential candidate." *Moscow Times*, January 26, 2018. Accessed July 20, 2020. https://www.themoscowtimes.com/2018/01/26/grudinin-russia-communist-party-gets-capitalist-makeover-lenin-sovkhoz-a60185
Gibson, Edward L., and Julieta Suarez-Cao. 2010. "Federalised Party Systems and Subnational Party Competition: Theory and an Empirical Application to Argentina." *Comparative Politics* 43 (1):21–39. doi: 10.5129/001041510X12911363510312.
Gillingham, Paul. 2012. "Mexican Elections, 1910-1994: Voters, Violence and Veto Power." In *The Oxford Handbook of Mexican Politics*, edited by Roderic Ai Camp. New York: Oxford University Press. doi: 10.1093/oxfordhb/9780195377385.013.0003.
Golosov, Grigorii. 2011. "The Regional Roots of Electoral Authoritarianism in Russia." *Comparative Politics* 63 (4):623–39. doi: 10.1080/09668136.2011.566427.
Hale, Henry. 2010. *Why Not Parties in Russia*. New York: Cambridge University Press.
Hallin, Daniel C., and Paolo Mancini. 2004. *Comparing Media Systems: Three Models of Media and Politics*. Cambridge: Cambridge University Press.
Hanson, Stephen E. 2011. *Post-Imperial Democracies: Ideology and Party Formation in Third Republic France, Weimar Germany, and Post-Soviet Russia*. New York: Cambridge University Press.
Harmel, Robert, and Kenneth Janda. 1994. "An Integrated Theory of Party Goals and Party Change." *Journal of Theoretical Politics* 6 (3):259–87. doi: 10.1177/0951692894006003001.
Hutcheson, Derek, and Ian McAllister. 2017. "Explaining Party Support in the 2016 State Duma Election." *Russian Politics* 2 (4):454–81. doi: 10.1163/2451-8921-00204004.
Hutcheson, Derek. 2010. "Russia: Electoral Campaigning in a 'Managed Democracy." In *Routledge Handbook of Political Management*, edited by D. Johnson. New York: Routledge.

Hutcheson, Derek. 2013. "Party Cartels beyond Western Europe: Evidence from Russia." *Party Politics* 19 (6):907–24. doi: 10.1177/1354068811436033.

Hutcheson, Derek S. 2017. "Contextualizing the 2016 State Duma Election." *Russian Politics* 2 (4):383–410. doi: 10.1163/2451-8921-00204001.

Hoad, Phil. 2018. "Irkutsk in the spotlight: the leak in Putin's watertight system?" *The Guardian*, March 16, 2018. Accessed July 20, 2020. https://www.theguardian.com/cities/2018/mar/16/irkutsk-in-the-spotlight-overlooked-leak-putin-united-russia-system.

Isaichenko, Oleg. 2018. "Политолог: Почему Грудинину пришлось лично ехать в Австрию, чтобы закрыть «транзитный счет»?" (Political Scientist: Why did Grudinin have to personally go to Austria to close the "transit account"?) *Vzglyad*, 14 January 2018. Accessed May 2020. https://vz.ru/news/2018/1/14/903441.html.

Ishiyama, John. 1996. "Red Phoenix?: the Communist Party in Post-Soviet Russian Politics." *Party Politics* 2 (2):147–75. doi: 10.1177/1354068896002002001.

Ishiyama, John. 2019. "Identity Change and Rebel Party Political Success." *Government and Opposition* 54 (3):454–84. doi: 10.1017/gov.2018.48.

Ishiyama, John. 2020. "Russia." In *Thirty Years of Political Campaigning in Central and Eastern Europe*, edited by O. Eibl and M. Gregor, 391–408. New York: Palgrave.

Ishiyama, John, and Michael Marshall. 2017. "What Explains Former Rebel Party Name Changes after a Civil Conflict Ends? External and Internal Factors and the Transition to Political Competition." *Party Politics* 23 (4):364–75. doi: 10.1177/1354068815600913.

Janda, Kenneth, Robert Harmel, Christine Edens, and Patricia Goff. 1995. "Changes in Party Identity: Evidence from Party Manifestos." *Party Politics* 1 (2):171–96. doi: 10.1177/1354068895001002001.

Kara-Murza, Vladimir. 2018. "Anyone but Putin: Russians are starting to look for an alternative." Washington Post, September 23, 2018. Accessed July 24, 2020. https://www.washingtonpost.com/news/democracy-post/wp/2018/09/20/anyone-but-putin-russians-are-starting-to-look-for-an-alternative/

Katz, Richard, and Peter Mair. 1995. "Changing Models of Party Organization and Party Democracy: The Emergence of the Cartel Party." *Party Politics* 1 (1):5–28. doi: 10.1177/1354068895001001001.

Kim, Mi-son, and Frederick Solt. 2017. "The Dynamics of Party Relabeling: Why Do Parties Change Names?" *Party Politics* 23 (4):437–47. doi: 10.1177/1354068815603240.

Komsomolskaya Pravda. 2019. 12/12. Accessed June 3, 2020. https://www.hab.kru/daily/27067.4/4136377/

Kornberger, Martin. 2010. *Brand Society: How Brands Transform Management and Lifestyle*. Cambridge: Cambridge University Press.

Kozlov, Vladimir, and Maria Snegovaya. 2019. "Factors of competitiveness in russian gubernatorial elections, 2012-2018." Washington DC: Free Russia Foundation. Accessed July 10, 2020. https://www.4freerussia.org/wp-content/uploads/sites/3/2019/05/Elections_web_eng.pdf.

Langston, Joy, and Scott Morgenstern. 2009. "Campaigning in Electoral Authoritarian Regimes: The Case of Mexico." *Comparative Politics* 41 (2):165–81. doi: 10.5129/001041509X12911362971954.

Lees-Marshment, Jennifer. 2009. *International Political Marketing: An Introduction*. London: Taylor & Francis.

Levy, Daniel C., Kathleen Bruhn, and Emilio Zebadúa. 2006. *Mexico: The Struggle for Democratic Development*. Berkeley: University of California Press.

Light, Felix. 2021. "Russia's Communists Are Split over Support for Navalny." *The Moscow Times*, February 12, 2021. Accessed February 14, 2021. https://www.themoscowtimes.com/2021/02/12/russias-communists-are-split-over-support-for-navalny-a72917

Magaloni, Beatriz. 2008. "Credible Power-Sharing and the Longevity of Authoritarian Rule." *Comparative Political Studies* 41 (4-5) :715–41. doi: 10.1177/0010414007313124.

March, Luke. 2002. *The Communist Party in Post-Soviet Russia*. Manchester: Manchester University Press.

March, Luke. 2011. "Just Russia—From "Second Leg" to "Footnote"?" *Russian Analytical Digest* 102:7–10.

Marland, Alex, and Tom Flanagan. 2013. "Brand New Party: Political Branding and the Conservative Party of Canada." *Canadian Journal of Political Science* 46 (4):951–72. doi: 10.1017/S0008423913001108.

Merrilees, Bill, and Dale Miller. 2008. "Principles of Corporate Re-Branding." *European Journal of Marketing* 42 (5/6):537–52. doi: 10.1108/03090560810862499.

Merrill, Tim L. and Ramón Miró, eds. 1996. *Mexico: A Country Study*. Washington: GPO for the Library of Congress.

Mikhailov, Andrei. 2018. Митинг сторонников КПРФ на площади Владивостока: как это было (The rally of supporters of the CPRF on Vladivostok Square: how it went). *VladNews*. Accessed July 18, 2020. https://vladnews.ru/2018-09-17/138210/miting_storonnikov.

Mukhmetschina, Elena, and Dariya Korzhova. 2019. "ЦИК отказался передать Грудинину мандат депутата Госдумы" (CEC refused to transfer the mandate of the State Duma deputy to Grudinin) Vedomosti, March 21, 2019. Accessed July 20, 2020. https://www.vedomosti.ru/politics/articles/2019/03/21/796949-grudinin

Muromski, Ilya. 2018. "КПРФ совершает огромную ошибку: Сурайкин о выдвижении Грудинина" (The CPRF is making a huge mistake: Suraykin on the nomination of Grudinin". Politika. https://riafan.ru/1013515-kprf-sovershaet-ogromnuyu-oshibku-suraikin-o-vydvizhenii-grudinina Accessed June 2020.

Perloff, Richard. 1999. "Elite, Popular, and Merchandised Politics: Historical Origins or Presidential Campaign Marketing." In *Handbook of Political Marketing*, edited by B. I. Newman, 19–40. Sage: Thousand Oaks.

Oversloot, Hans, and Ruben Verheul. 2006. "Managing Democracy: Political Parties and the State in Russia." *Journal of Communist Studies and Transition Politics* 22 (3):383–405. doi: 10.1080/13523270600855795.

Panov, Petr, and Cameron Ross. 2013. "Sub-National Elections in Russia: Variations in United Russia' Domination of Regional Assemblies." *Europe-Asia Studies* 65 (4):737–52. doi: 10.1080/09668136.2013.767581.

Radio Svoboda. "В Москве и других городах прошли акции коммунистов за права граждан." (In Moscow and other cities Communist take action for rights of citizens) Radio Svoboda, March 23, 2019. Accessed July 4, 2020. https://www.svoboda.org/a/29837824.html

Reuter Ora, J., and Thomas F. Remington. 2009. "Dominant Party Regimes and the Commitment Problem: The Case of United Russia." *Comparative Political Studies* 42 (4):501–26. doi: 10.1177/0010414008327426.

Reuter, Ora J. 2010. "The Politics of Dominant Party Formation: United Russia and Russia's Governors." *Europe-Asia Studies* 62 (2):293–327. doi: 10.1080/09668130903506847.

Roberts, Sean P. 2012. *Putin's United Russia Party*. London: Routledge.

Rose, Richard, Neil Munro, and Stephen White. 2001. "Voting in a Floating Party System: The 1999 Duma Election." *Europe-Asia Studies* 53 (3):419–43. doi: 10.1080/09668130120045870.

Ross, Cameron. 2018. "Regional Elections in Russia: Instruments of Authoritarian Legitimacy or Instability?" *Palgrave Communications* 4 (1) :641–61. doi: 10.1057/s41599-018-0137-1.

Ross, Cameron. 2011. "Regional Elections and Electoral Authoritarianism in Russia." *Europe-Asia Studies* 63 (4):641–61. doi: 10.1080/09668136.2011.566428.

Roth, Adam. 2018. "Communist challenger exposes cracks in Putin's grip on power." *The Guardian*, October 13, 2018. Accessed July 10, 2020. https://www.theguardian.com/world/2018/oct/13/communist-challenge-exposes-cracks-putins-power

Sakwa, Richard. 2011. *The Crisis of Russian Democracy: Dual State, Factionalism and the Medvedev Succession*. New York: Cambridge University Press.

Sakwa, Richard. 2020. *The Putin Paradox*. New York: Bloomsbury Publishing.

Sartori, Giovanni. 2005. *Parties and Party Systems: A Framework for Analysis*. Colchester, UK: ECPR Press.

Scammell, Margaret. 2015. "Politics and Image: The Conceptual Value of Branding." *Journal of Political Marketing* 14 (1-2):7–18. doi: 10.1080/15377857.2014.990829.

Scammell, Margaret. 2007. "Political Brands and Consumer Citizens: The Re-Branding of Tony Blair." *The Annals of the American Academy of Political and Social Science* 611 (1):176–92. doi: 10.1177/0002716206299149.

Schedler, Andreas. 2006. *Electoral Authoritarianism: The Dynamics of Unfree Competition*. London: Lynne Rienner.

Sharafutdinova, Gulnaz. 2016. "Regional Governors Navigating through Putin's Third Term: On the Wave of Patriotism through the Troubled Waters of the Economy." *Russian Politics* 1 (4):372–97. doi: 10.1163/2451-8921-00104003.

Slider, Darrell. 2010. "How United is United Russia? Regional Sources of Intra-Party Conflict." *Journal of Communist Studies and Transition Politics* 26 (2):257–75. doi: 10.1080/13523271003712617.

Slider, Darrell. 2019. "A Federal State?." In *Developments in Russian Politics 9*, edited by Richard Sakwa, Henry Hale, and Stephen White. Durham NC, USA: Duke University Press.

Smyth, Regina, Anna Lowry, and Brandon Wilkening. 2007. "Engineering Victory: Institutional Reform, Informal Institutions, and the Formation of a Hegemonic Regime in the Russian Federation." *Post Soviet Affairs* 23 (2) :118–37. doi: 10.2747/1060-586X.23.2.118.

Tevi, Alexander, and Olutayo Otubanjo. 2013. "Understanding Corporate Rebranding: An Evolution Theory Perspective." *International Journal of Marketing Studies* 5 (3) :87–93. doi: 10.5539/ijms.v5n3p87.

Tsvetkova, Maria. 2015. "When Kremlin candidate loses election, even voters are surprised." *Reuters World News*, September 29, 2015. Accessed July 4, 2020. https://www.reuters.com/article/us-russia-vote-irkutsk/when-kremlin-candidate-loses-election-even-voters-are-surprised-idUSKCN0RT0Z220150929.

Turchenko, Mikhail, and Grigorii Golosov. 2021. "Smart Enough to Make a Difference? An Empirical Test of the Efficacy of Strategic Voting in Russia's Authoritarian Elections." *Post-Soviet Affairs* 37 (1):65–79. doi: 10.1080/1060586X.2020.1796386.

Weiss, Michael. 2021. "Alexey Navalny Is Succeeding Where Putin's Other Opponents Have Failed. Why?" *Time*. January 27. Accessed February 1, 2021. https://time.com/5933718/alexey-navalny-putin-protests/.

Facebook as a Political Marketing Tool in an Illiberal Context. Mapping Political Advertising Activity on Facebook during the 2019 Hungarian European Parliament and Local Election Campaigns

Márton Bene, Márton Petrekanics and Mátyás Bene

ABSTRACT
The research examines political advertising on Facebook during the 2019 European and local election campaigns in Hungary. Previously, political advertising had been difficult to study due to a lack of publicly available data. However, since spring of 2019, information on political advertising on Facebook has been publicly accessible in European countries. The study collected all political ads during the two nationwide election campaigns in Hungary to map the political advertising sphere based on spending. The research tests theories regarding the political restructuring potential of social media, including the oppositional/democratizing role of social media, and the theses of normalization versus equalization. Additionally, the ad-specific thesis of 'stealth media' is tested, which argues that Facebook's ad platform can be employed to circumvent campaign-related regulations. Our findings suggest that the opposition remarkably dominates the political Facebook advertising sphere in the present illiberal context. Beyond this fact, the normalization theory seems to prevail, and there is no evidence that ads are used to increase the personalization of politics. In Hungary, Facebook's advertising platform is not a type of 'stealth media' as it is dominated by official political actors, but a few partisan media outlets were strongly involved in the advertising campaign.

Introduction

Over the last few years, the political advertising sphere, once largely dominated by television, has been remarkably transformed, and social media platforms, especially Facebook, have become the central field of political advertising (Chester and Montgomery 2017). Political actors have considerably extended the share of their advertising expenditure spent on Facebook during political campaigns (Barnard and Kreiss 2013). Nonetheless, political advertising has long been a "black box" of social media research (Kim 2016) because of the lack of publicly available data (but see Broockman and Green 2014; Kim et al. 2018; Hager 2019). However, due to the public and political pressure resulting from the so-called 'techlash' following the Brexit referendum and the 2016 US presidential election, since 2018 Facebook has been running the open Ad Library that offers some limited information on each political ad on the platform (Leerssen et al. 2019). As a result, for the first time ever, it has become possible to map in detail the entire political advertising sphere on Facebook. Our research is one of the first attempts in this direction. Our purpose is to map how the total expenditure on political Facebook ads is distributed across different types of political actors in the contexts of two nationwide election campaigns in Hungary: the European Parliament (EP) elections in May 2019, and the local elections in October 2019.

As argued by Körösényi, Illés, and Gyulai (2020), the current Orbán-regime in Hungary can be described as a Plebiscitary Leader Democracy (PLD), where the authoritarian rule is based on popular, electoral legitimation. Consequently, while European and local elections are often considered of second order (Heath et al. 1999), in the PLD-context all nationwide elections are crucial for maintaining the regime, irrespective of their actual institutional stakes. However, there are major inequalities in the offline political marketing conditions in these regimes (see Róka 2017) that make Facebook's advertisement options which are equally available to all actors especially relevant. Hungary is an excellent case as it highlights the role Facebook could play in a context where the information environment is controlled or influenced mostly by the incumbents. Also, it advances our knowledge about the role social media plays in the under-studied Central-Eastern European region (see Surowiec and Štětka 2017) as most findings about the effects of social media on politics originate from the US or from Western Europe.

In order to map the political advertising sphere in the specific Hungarian PLD context, we first downloaded all political Facebook ads circulated during the two election campaigns (3,675 ads from 565 pages for the EP election, and 21,143 ads from 2,265 pages for the local elections) with their available metadata, including a range with specific lower and upper ranges regarding the price of specific ads. Then, we aggregated these metadata on the level of pages that run ads during the campaigns as the unit of analysis. To our knowledge, this is the first study to investigate the entire political advertising sphere on Facebook based on spending. It is also the first comparative study to focus on ads in two different election campaigns, which increases the external validity of the findings.

Our mapping is guided by several more specific hypotheses and research questions derived from the literature. On the one hand, we have tested existing theories regarding the political restructuring potential of social media, such as the oppositional and democratizing role of social media (see Tucker et al. 2017) and the issues of normalization versus equalization (see Jacobs and Spierings 2016). These theories have been thoroughly tested in the case of organic social media communication, but the role of non-organic, sponsored communication is still untapped. Our results show that the Facebook advertising sphere is dominated by oppositional actors who, in the offline sphere, are in disadvantaged positions compared to incumbents. Further, while lower level political actors also use Facebook's advertisement options intensively, the normalization thesis, arguing that more powerful political actors benefit more from using social media, seems to prevail. On the other hand, we test the ad-specific thesis of 'stealth media' that argues that Facebook's ad platform can be easily employed to circumvent campaign-related regulations (Kim et al. 2018). While this theory has been confirmed in the context of the 2016 US presidential election (Kim et al. 2018), since then Facebook has implemented several measures to increase the transparency of political ads (Leerssen et al. 2019). Also, the European regulatory framework differs from that of the US, yet we do not know if the 'stealth media' hypothesis prevails in this context as well. Our findings suggest that the political advertising sphere is largely dominated by official political actors, while pages with obscure or unknown backgrounds are marginal in terms of the total expenditure. However, partisan media outlets play important roles in the political ad campaign on both sides of the political spectrum.

Political advertising on Facebook

Political actors' organic communication on Facebook can be regarded as advertising activities in themselves as they are under their own control (Kaid 2012). Nonetheless, by default, their content only reach a segment of their direct followers. A large part of these followers, however, tend to be highly engaged supporters of the given political actors (Fisher et al. 2019). Therefore, this type of organic social media communication has a 'preaching to the converted' character (Norris 2003). There are two common ways to reach users beyond direct followers on Facebook. The first strategy is 'preaching through the converted' (Vissers 2009): followers' engagement with political actors' posts (reactions, comments, and shares) can spread the message widely, as users can see the posts their friends engage with (Bene 2017). In this scenario, however, political actors lose control over the message as it is selected, filtered or even commented by followers. Another strategy is 'preaching through money' as Facebook enables page owners to display their messages beyond their direct followers *via* paid advertisements. From a marketing perspective, these strategies can transform Facebook communication from 'pull media' that are capable of reaching people opting in into 'push media' that target users regardless of whether or not they want to see political actors' messages (Nielsen and Vaccari 2013). This way undecided and uninterested voters are also easy to reach. On Facebook, a further incentive toward a push media strategy is that this platform applies the strongest algorithmic filtering, and the organic reach of individual posts may be extremely low even in the circle of direct followers (Bossetta 2018).

The attraction of Facebook as a political advertisement platform lies in its huge audience, low prices, fast and flexible opportunities for production, and especially in its extremely sophisticated targeting capacities. Thirty-seven per cent of the global population are now active Facebook-users[1], but in the European Union this ratio is around 50 per cent.[2] With 64 per cent of the total population being monthly users of Facebook, this proportion is even larger in Hungary.[3] As a result, an extremely large segment of the voter population can be approached *via* one platform. Facebook ads are comparatively cheap, and the production cost may also be extremely low, since any simple text or visual can be promoted. Moreover, it is highly cost-effective because the fee depends on the number of impressions or clicks the ad has generated, and pricing is incredibly flexible as it can be purchased for small increments of impressions or clicks (Edelson et al. 2019; Fowler et al. 2021). Due to their flexible format, ads can be created very quickly. Therefore, Facebook commercials can immediately react to current events. However, its most valued feature is that advertisers have unprecedentedly extensive micro-targeting options at their disposal. Facebook's business model is based on collecting exhaustive data from its users through registering all their activities within and beyond the platform, and in turn sharing this knowledge with advertisers. This way advertisers can target their audiences with carefully crafted messages (van Dijck 2013). Advertisers can identify their target groups based on tens of thousands of attributes, moreover they can use their own data to match Facebook users or use the 'lookalike' function to find users similar to their previously detected target groups. These micro-targeting options offered by Facebook are especially attractive in a European context. Due to stricter privacy and data-protection legal frameworks, in Europe opportunities for data-intensive campaigning that operates in the US at a highly advanced level are limited (Kruschinski and Haller 2017). However, in this case Facebook offers ample leeway, as data are not handled by parties. Therefore, highly sophisticated microtargeting campaigns can be run without violating strict data protection laws (Dobber et al. 2019).

These more general benefits can be supplemented with one context-specific aspect that makes Facebook's advertising platform especially attractive for oppositional actors in an illiberal context. While in illiberal regimes the offline information and advertising environment can be more effectively controlled by different soft measures (see Polyák 2019), global online communication platforms are beyond incumbents' immediate influence and could be regulated only by openly anti-democratic actions (i.e., banning, firewalls, etc.). While we will discuss this aspect in more detail below, it is important to note that in an illiberal context Facebook's uncontrolled advertising platform can be highly attractive for non-incumbent actors.

Though few studies have addressed the question of the effectiveness of Facebook ads, they have usually found subtle but existing effects on voters' mobilization (i.e., Broockman and Green 2014; Haenschen and Jennings 2019; Hager 2019). For instance, according to Hager's calculations

(2019), one vote costs approximately 3 to 7 EUR in the German electoral context. However, these studies do not involve the impacts of microtargeting; their results are for non-targeted or poorly-targeted ads. Overall, microtargeting may be a highly effective campaign tool that may significantly amplify the pure subtle effect of Facebook ads described in the literature. However, in short of any empirical evidence, it is also conceivable that the hype around it may be unfounded and may have no substantial contribution to the main effect (Baldwin-Philippi 2019). Nonetheless, existing research shows that political actors tend to exploit microtargeting options, but the less-resourced politicians have less sophisticated methods at their disposal (Dobber et al. 2017; Kruschinski and Haller 2017). This implies that differences in resources may have dual effects: parties spending more on Facebook can obtain more votes simply because they generate more impressions or clicks, but also because they are able to use more sophisticated targeting strategies, which may then result in further extra votes.

So far, however, there have been no reliable publicly available information about the total level and distribution of spending on political Facebook ads during campaigns. Due to this lack of transparency, advertising activity has been a 'black box' for social media research (Kim 2016). Although certain methodological innovations have produced incredibly valuable and truly revealing indirect insights into the world of Facebook political ads (see Kim et al. 2018), they could obtain information only on the number of ads, while the level of spending on ads remained unavailable. However, due to the so-called 'techlash' following the unexpected results of the Brexit referendum and the 2016 US presidential election, there has been increasing public attention to global tech companies and their advertisement policies. To avoid state regulation, Facebook has made significant steps toward larger transparency, and in May 2018 it created its Ad Library in the US, where the public can obtain limited information about all the ads that are registered as political (Leerssen et al. 2019). Initially, the service was available in only a few countries, but after the self-regulatory but European Commission-assisted Code of Practice on Online Disinformation (CoP) had been accepted, the Ad Library was launched in the EU countries in March 2019. For the first time ever since the existence of Facebook, the mapping of the entire political advertising sphere is possible. So far only a few studies have been conducted using the Facebook Ad Library (Edelson et al. 2019; Fowler et al. 2021; Silva et al. 2020), with none of them focusing on the European context. Moreover, most of them had obtained their data before the Ad Library was made available *via* API, therefore they could not capture the entire political advertising sphere (as an exception see Silva et al. 2020). In order to fill this gap, our research aims at describing in detail the composition of the Hungarian political ad sphere on Facebook.

RQ: How was expenditure on Facebook ads distributed across different types of actors during two election campaigns in Hungary in 2019?

Social media advertising in an illiberal context

In this study, political advertising is analyzed in the context of two nationwide election campaigns held in Hungary: the European Parliament election in May 2019, and the local elections in October 2019. Hungary is a specific context due to the recent transformation of the political regime, which may affect the role of Facebook in general, and the advertising on this platform in particular. In the following section, these specificities are briefly summarized.

Over the last few years, there has been a global retreat from the liberal type of democracy, which is especially evident in some countries in Central and Eastern Europe. These tendencies are particularly prominent in Hungary where Viktor Orbán has been building his regime for ten years. There are abundant public and academic interpretations about the nature of this transformation (for an overview see, Körösényi, Illés, and Gyulai 2020). One of the common points shared by both the regime's opponents and proponents (including Viktor Orbán himself) is that it involves a certain level of moving away from the liberal understanding of democracy.

In one of the most detailed analyses to date, Körösényi, Illés, and Gyulai (2020) define the Orbán-regime as a specific manifestation of the Weberian Plebiscitary Leader Democracy (PLD). The main feature of the system is that it is "democratic in form but authoritarian in substance" (Weber 1978, 266-278; ref. Körösényi, Illés, and Gyulai 2020, 22) as it is characterized by charismatic leadership with blank-checked authorization to rule, but this charismatic authority is legitimized and maintained by competitive elections and constant references to the "people's will". This plebiscitary aspect is especially relevant from a political marketing perspective because it implies that all elections are of crucial importance, irrespective of their true institutional significance, because they reinforce, maintain or even question charismatic leadership. Concerning their explicit stakes, the supranational EP election and the subnational local elections can be viewed as of second order (Heath et al. 1999), but due to the reasons discussed above, there are no lower-order elections in a PLD. On the one hand, incumbents must demonstrate in each election that they still enjoy popular support. On the other hand, this also means that each election is a chance for the opposition to break or at least significantly weaken the regime and its authority. This fact ensures that both elections are highly relevant and enjoy similar significance within the specific Hungarian context.

Nonetheless, beyond this common ground and context, the two specific elections under investigation can be regarded as most different cases. In the EP election, voters vote for party lists, therefore there is stronger emphasis on parties than on individual politicians. In contrast, in the local elections a mixed electoral system is at work, but mayors and most candidates are elected directly, therefore politicians are in the forefront rather than parties. *Fidesz* won the EP election with a vote share similar to all other national elections since 2006, ahead of the large number of minor opposition parties that ran separately. However, in the local elections, *Fidesz* suffered sensitive losses unprecedented since the regime's birth. While they received a similar vote share as in previous elections, the more strongly collaborating opposition managed to win in several larger cities, including the capital. If we can find some common patterns in political advertising across these two different cases, we can reasonably assume that they are independent from their specific electoral context.

While the local elections proved that elections are truly competitive in PLD, as *Fidesz* can be defeated, it is also widely demonstrated that in the campaign context the incumbent has a significant advantage over its opponents. A highly centralized extensive network of media outlets, including the entire public service media conglomerate, is associated with the incumbent party that transmits to the audience the governmental actors' messages uncritically (Merkovity and Stumpf 2021). While it is true that there are also a large number of anti-government media outlets, especially in the online sphere, these are often highly critical also of the oppositional actors (Polyák 2019). In addition, the opposition has increasingly limited access to the public billboard interfaces (Róka 2017) that are traditionally important in the European (see Kaid 2012) and Hungarian (Kiss and Szabó 2019) campaigns. Further, government parties are the most resourceful in the political sphere. It has made the opposition's position more precarious that over the last few years the State Audit Office has severely fined several of their parties[4]. This resource gap is deepened by the fact that the government is one the most active actors in the political advertisement market, constantly running TV-, radio- online- and billboard-campaigns to popularize government measures and attack opponents (Bátorfy and Urbán 2020).

Hypotheses

Our efforts to map the entire Hungarian Facebook ad sphere based on spending will be driven by hypotheses mostly derived from the more general literature of social media and politics but adopted them to the specific PLD context under investigation. Our hypotheses are based on several key characteristics of the pages that run ads, such as type (pages of party, politicians, media outlets, NGOs, movements, and non-official political Facebook pages, etc.), political leaning (pro-government, oppositional, and party affiliation) and political level (national, local, and European).

Facebook as a force restructuring the political landscape

There are several arguments in the social media and politics literature that Facebook has the potential to restructure or transform the political landscape. Two arguments are relevant here. The first is strongly related to the specific PLD context, as it highlights the potential of the opposition against illiberal or authoritarian incumbents to exploit the more accessible services Facebook offers. The second is associated with the more general political dynamics and stress Facebook's potential to transform or at least modify the logic of political competition by offering more opportunities for less resourced political actors (equalization). These arguments have been extensively tested in several areas of social media communication, but we have no information about the role advertisement may play in these processes.

It is an important question what the role Facebook as an advertisement tool plays in the highly unbalanced advertising context of a Plebiscitary Leader Democracy. The Internet has long been considered a 'liberation technology' (Diamond 2010) that can contribute to processes of democratization (Groshek 2009). These arguments have been applied to Facebook as well, especially after social media platforms played crucial roles during the Arab Spring (see Howard and Hussain 2013). However, these claims are often challenged, and several authors argue that these technologies can be exploited by powerful incumbents to reinforce their dominance and control in the political sphere (see Rød and Weidmann 2015; Spaiser et al. 2017).

When it comes to Facebook advertising in Hungary, there are arguments for both claims. On the one hand, it is a recurring claim in the literature that Facebook has a democratizing potential as it offers an easily available and unbiased platform to actors who are legally or practically disadvantaged in the offline communication context (see Tucker et al. 2017). Concerning advertising, one can argue that Facebook can mitigate the disadvantages of the opposition, as all political actors have equal access to its advertisement platform. Moreover, pro-government actors often argue that Facebook is biased toward the opposition and left-liberal political actors, and that its approval process actively hinders pro-government advertisements[5]. Further, as for pro-government actors it is easier to access other more expensive advertising tools, Facebook is only one of the multiple options for promoting messages. Last, previous findings suggest that oppositional actors in Hungary pay special attention to Facebook, as they can reach more people *via* this platform than offline (Bene and Farkas 2018). On the other hand, the contrary expectation, namely that pro-government actors and messages dominate the advertising sphere on Facebook, is also plausible. Advertising is the feature of Facebook where differences in the available resources are most relevant. As the incumbents are more resourceful than their opposition, it can be reasonably assumed that they spend more money on Facebook ads. Also, the relative disadvantages of pro-government actors in some areas of the political Facebook sphere can be counterweighed by intensive ad campaigns. Consequently, there are arguments for both scenarios. Therefore, two competing hypotheses are formulated at this point.

1. H1a. Oppositional actors (including politicians, parties, media outlets, civic actors, and non-official political pages) spent more on Facebook ads than pro-government actors.
2. H1b. Pro-government actors (including politicians, parties, media outlets, civic actors, and non-official political pages) spent more on Facebook ads than oppositional actors.

A related but more general theoretical question is associated with the longstanding debate on the equalizing versus normalizing potential of online communication tools. A central argument of the normalization thesis is that more resourceful political actors can build more sophisticated and effective online and social media presence, thereby these platforms reinforce existing political inequalities. In contrast, proponents of the equalization thesis suggest that the internet and social media can equalize political competition, as these options are more accessible to less resourced actors (for an overview, see Jacobs and Spierings 2016). It is easy to see that the usage of ads that enable individual actors to buy reach is a crucial aspect of this controversy. On the one hand, more resourceful actors can purchase more ads to increase their visibility on these platforms, but on the other hand, due to their cost-effective and flexible nature, advertising options on Facebook are more readily available to smaller political actors compared to other advertising platforms. However, while numerous studies have addressed this topic, the role of ads continues to be a largely 'black box' due to the inability to access information. Recently, a few analyses have shown that larger political actors can exploit microtargeting options more effectively than minor actors (i.e., Kruschinski and Haller 2017). However, even if in a less complex way, but minor actors can still apply microtargeting (Dobber et al. 2017), and the Facebook advertising sphere is a more even playing field than television (Fowler et al. 2021). Our research will investigate the degree of inequality in spending on Facebook ads during the overall campaigns at two levels.

First, at the level of the parties, we will uncover the differences across individual parties in both campaigns under investigation. The two competing hypotheses are as follows:

1. H2a. The differences between parties (including party pages, their politicians' pages and any other associated pages) in spending on Facebook ads are in line with the differences in their electoral share (normalization hypothesis 1).
2. H2b. Smaller parties (including party pages, their politicians' pages and any other associated pages) spend more on Facebook ads than it is expected based on their electoral share (equalization hypothesis 1).

Second, at the individual level, differences are interpreted across political positions. This will be investigated only in the context of the local election campaign where individual politicians from different political levels are at the forefront. During the local elections many politicians ran for lower level positions (i.e., mayor in smaller cities or villages or representative in local council), and few of them competed for the more important mayoral positions in larger cities. Also, while politicians in national positions (MPs, MEPs, etc.) did not run for any elected position in the local elections, they could also publish political ads to support their fellow party members.

1. H3a. National politicians and mayoral candidates from larger cities spend more on Facebook ads in total than local council representative candidates and mayoral candidates in smaller cities and villages (normalization hypothesis 2).
2. H3b. National politicians and mayoral candidates from larger cities spend less on Facebook ads in total than local council representative candidates and mayoral candidates in smaller cities and villages (equalization hypothesis 2).

Facebook as stealth media

Since the so-called 'techlash' following the Brexit referendum and the 2016 US presidential election, the political role of Facebook has been increasingly challenged and criticized in public discourses. One of the main targets of public scrutiny is Facebook's advertising service that has enabled foreign interference into these campaigns (Ribeiro et al. 2019). These incidents motivate researchers to move beyond the dominant topics of social media and politics research and argue the political role of Facebook advertising in itself. Drawing upon these insights, we will uncover if in the European context Facebook is 'stealth media' (Kim et al. 2018) after it had introduced several measures to make its political advertising platform more transparent.

Legally, political advertising on Facebook for the most part is still unregulated (Leerssen et al. 2019). It is a grey zone of national laws, as it generally falls outside the stricter regulation of offline political advertising all over the world, including most EU countries. Kim et al. (2018) argue that this legal loophole together with the less-transparent nature and microtargeting capacities of its advertisement platform makes Facebook a type of 'stealth media'. Stealth media "enables deliberate operations of political campaigns with undisclosed identities of sponsors/sources, furtive messaging of divisive issues, and imperceptible targeting" (Kim et al. 2018, 4). Silva and her coauthors stress that "the Facebook ads platform can also be used for slush funds" (2020, 1) because Facebook pages can spend unlimited amounts of undeclared money on shaping political agenda. Outsourcing certain elements of political campaigns is an old strategy in political marketing (see Kaid 2012), but on Facebook it is easier to implement in a more opaque and non-legal way.

Kim et al. (2018) collected a large number of political ads during the 2016 US presidential election and found that only 11 per cent of the ads were published by registered campaign organizations, while 42 per cent were sponsored by suspicious, unknown pages, including several ads with a Russian background, astroturf unregistered groups or 'questionable' news sites. By collecting data through the newly created Ad Library, Edelson et al. (2019) looked at the spending distribution rather than merely at the numbers of ads during the 2018 US midterm elections. Though they could not access the entire political advertising sphere due to the limitation of the Ad Library at the time, their sample shows that 37 per cent of the total ad spending belong to registered political pages (candidates, parties, and Political Action Committees), and 45 per cent to unknown pages, a share that is much higher than on Twitter or Google. While the concept was invented in the US context, the phenomenon is not limited to the US: the stealth media character may have been even more evident during the 2018 Brazilian elections when Silva et al. (2020) found that several ads were sponsored by NGOs, media outlets or other pages, even though according to Brazilian law only parties and politicians are allowed to launch political ads during election campaigns.

Following the 'techlash', Facebook introduced some self-regulatory measures to make its advertising platform more transparent and accountable, but it is still unclear if its 'stealth media' character could be mitigated. For instance, advertisers are required to authorize themselves before running political ads, but it appears that it is relatively easy to deceive this system (Leerssen et al. 2019; Edelson et al. 2019). At the same time, other measures may work more effectively. Facebook has also introduced the regulation that only in the country where they are authorized are sponsors allowed to run ads. Only with Facebook's specific temporary permission were European parties and institutions able to bypass this measure (see Dobber et al. 2019). Also, the pure fact that all political Facebook ads are registered and publicly available may have a moderating effect on stealth campaigning, as ads can no longer be concealed through carefully crafted microtargeting strategies.

While the few studies discussed above point out the 'stealth media' character of Facebook advertising, they were mostly conducted before the recent preventative measures, and no research has been conducted in the European context. The stricter offline political marketing regulations and data protection policy in European countries may yield stronger motives for political actors to exploit the 'stealth media' potential of the underregulated and less transparent advertising platform offered by Facebook. Also, due to the limitations of data access, none of these analyses have been able to cover the entire Facebook ad sphere. Our research aims at filling these gaps by investigating the distribution of ad spending between different page types during two election campaigns in Hungary.

The Hungarian context is especially suitable to investigate the 'stealth media' character of Facebook because the platform does not treat Hungarian news media outlets in the same way as in other countries. News media outlets are important actors in the political Facebook advertising sphere, and this is especially true for partisan media that may promote highly biased political content on the platform. Yet, in most countries Facebook does not treat news media outlets as political advertisers, and their ads are not registered in the Ad Library as political (Leerssen et al. 2019). However, Facebook made an exception for Hungary where the news media have been extremely polarized over the last few years, and decided that news media outlets' ads should be treated as political, therefore included in the Ad Library. This way we can examine the role news media play in the Hungarian Facebook ad sphere, which would be a 'black box' in any other context.

To sum up, in this research we test the following stealth media hypothesis:

1. H4 The Facebook political advertising sphere is dominated by unconventional political actors, such as media outlets, NGOs, astroturf groups and non-official political pages rather than parties and politicians.

Methods

Data

In the European countries, access to the Facebook Ad Library was granted in March 2019. The library contains all ads that are about social issues, elections and politics[6]. This dataset can be reached *via* API, which we used through a self-developed app to query all political ads in Hungary during the two campaigns.[7] In both campaigns, we focused on the last month (26th April – 26th May in the EP, and 13th September – 13th October in the local election). For the EP elections, we collected 5,433 ads from 1123 pages, while for the local elections 17,984 advertisements from 2,134 Facebook pages. The cost of individual ads is provided as a range in the form of lower and upper ranges as opposed to exact price.[8] While based on these data it is impossible to determine the exact level of spending, the range-based comparison can uncover important patterns. Therefore, our analytical strategy is to run analyses both on lower- and upper-range data separately. It is important to note that lower range data cannot be contrasted with upper range data, comparisons should be limited to the identical range. As our units of analysis are individual Facebook pages that run ads, we aggregated these ranges by pages. As there were a few ads paid in foreign currency, their fees were converted to HUF based on the exchange rate in the last day of the respective time frame.

Variables

In order to map the political advertising sphere, we categorized these pages from different perspectives. The first variable we used was the type of the page. The following categories were applied: party, politician, campaign page, media outlet, NGO/think tank/movement, governmental body, other (non-official) political FB page, for-profit corporation, other individual (journalists, celebrities, experts, public intellectuals) and other/non-identifiable. We also coded the geographical focus of the page as national, local, European or transnational, based on the audience the specific page appeared to address. The page name and/or the 'about' section usually refer to the target audience in geographical terms, especially when they address local (i.e., name of the domicile or county) or European groups (i.e., European Parliament). When a page clearly targets international audiences (i.e., communication in foreign language), but does not specify its European interest in its name or in its 'about' section, it is considered transnational-focused. When a page clearly addresses Hungarian audiences, and there is no reference in its name or in its 'about' section to its local focus, it is categorized as national-focused. In the local election campaign, we also differentiated between types of domicile for pages that have a local focus: the capital of Hungary, city with county rights[9], or another city and village. Perceived political leanings of the pages were also considered. First, we identified whether the particular page formally or informally supports or opposes the government, or it is politically neutral. Next, we also registered if the given page is formally or informally associated or sympathized with a particular party. Our coding decisions were mostly based on the name and the 'about' section of the page, but we often checked the posts and ads the pages published during the specific campaign to obtain accurate information about their type, focus or political leaning.

For both campaigns we had two coders to categorize the data[10]. As Facebook has a broad definition of politics (see Footnote 5), some pages entered our database from outside the political sphere, most typically for-profit corporations, as their ads had some connection with specific social issues, such as a reference to 'green' or environmentalist issues. Therefore, we checked the ads ran by each nonpolitical Facebook page and removed those that did not publish any explicit political ads. We also excluded pages that we could not categorize because they had been deleted or their identity was unclear. The final databases contain 890 Facebook pages (4,550 ads) for the EP campaign and 1799 pages (17,221 ads) for the local election campaign.

Findings

In the analysis, we will report two values for each calculation: the first is always based on the lower ranges, while the second is calculated for the upper ranges. To make it easier to distinguish the two values, lower ranges are signed with the 'V', while upper ranges with the '∧' visual shortcuts. Before testing our hypotheses, we will look at the overall political Facebook advertising sphere in the campaigns under investigation. Over the 31 days of the EP campaign 890 advertisers spent between HUF[11] ∨159 (= lower range) and ∧195 million (= upper range) on 4,550 ads. During the 31 days examined in the local campaign, the 1799 advertisers identified spent between HUF ∨276 and ∧367 million on the 17,221 recorded advertisements. During the EP campaign, 53 per cent of the advertisements were run on less than HUF 10,000, and only 9 per cent of the advertisements cost over HUF 100,000. During the local campaign, 65 per cent of the advertisements cost under HUF 10,000, 18 per cent were run on less than HUF 1000, and only 2 per cent on more than HUF 100,000. Consequently, the actors of the local campaign seem to have exploited the opportunity to campaign with micro-amounts. Although to different extents, but the advertising sphere is highly centralized in both campaigns: in the EP campaign, ∨75 per cent and ∧77 per cent of the money spent on all political advertisements can be attributed to the top ten advertisers, while these percentages in the local campaign were ∨47 per cent and ∧50 per cent, respectively. These 'super-advertisers' are shown in Tables 1 and 2.

Turning to the first hypothesis, most pages that published political ads clearly support or oppose the government. In the EP elections, ∨95 per cent and ∧94 per cent of the expenditure on ads belonged to actors with obvious political leaning, while the respective figures were ∨89 per cent and ∧89 per cent in the local elections. In both campaigns, there is significant opposition dominance in terms of both the lower and upper ranges. In the EP campaign, actors that leaned toward the opposition spent HUF ∨98-∧118 million, and the pro-government pages bought ads for HUF ∨54-∧64 million. In the local government campaign, opposition-related pages spent HUF ∨163 to ∧196 million, while the total expenditure of the government side was HUF ∨83 to ∧129 million (Figure 1). In other words, in the European campaign, pages affiliated with the opposition spent almost twice as much those who sympathized with the government,

Table 1. Top ten advertiser pages during the EP 2019 election (list based on the upper range).

	Lower range	Upper range	No. of ads	Identity
Fidesz	49.1M	57.7M	213	Incumbent party
Jobbik Magyarországért Mozgalom	16M	28.9M	68	Opposition party
MSZP	12.8M	14.4M	146	Opposition party
Momentum Mozgalom	11.8M	13.9M	343	Opposition party
LMP - Lehet Más a Politika	6.9M	7.6M	78	Opposition party
European Parliament	4.8M	6.7M	58	EU governmental body (categorized as 'non-affiliated')
Dobrev Klára	5.2M	6.3M	153	EP list leader of an opposition party (DK)
Demokratikus Koalíció	4.6M	5.7M	175	Opposition party
Kálmán Olga Hivatalos oldala	4.2M	5.1M	144	Opposition journalist (future politician)
Nemzeti Televízió	4M	4.8M	85	Opposition news site

Table 2. Top ten advertiser pages during the 2019 local elections (list based on the upper range).

	Lower range	Upper range	Number of ads	Identity
EzaLényeg.hu	49M	58M	1538	Newly founded opposition news site
Fidesz	16.7M	35.1M	47	Incumbent party
European Parliament	13M	17.4M	46	EU governmental body (non-affiliated)
Fidelitas	3M	15.7M	13	Youth division of the incumbent Fidesz party
Momentum Mozgalom	12.4M	14.8M	369	Opposition party
Karácsony Gergely	12.1M	14M	193	Joint mayoral candidate of opposition parties in Budapest
Veres Pál	7.1M	8.3M	82	Joint candidate of opposition in Miskolc (4th largest city)
Nemesi Pál	5.7M	6.7M	115	Mayoral candidate of Fidesz in Szeged (3rd largest city)
Jobbik Magyarországért Mozgalom	5.2M	6.2M	43	Opposition party
Alakszai Zoltán	4.9M	5.8M	74	Mayoral candidate of Fidesz in Miskolc (4th largest city)

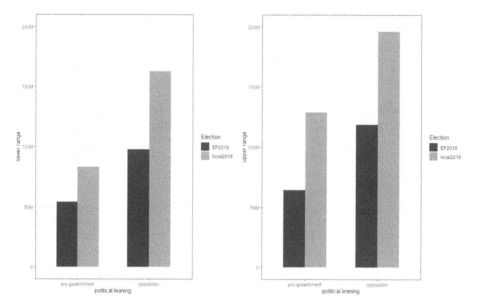

Figure 1. Distribution of ad spending based on political leaning during the EP 2019 and local 2019 elections (only pro-government and opposition pages are presented).

and in the local elections their dominance is also remarkable. These differences are smaller if only the official political pages (party, politician and campaign pages) are taken into account. They are still substantial during the EP campaign as pages officially related to the opposition spent ∨58 and ∧57 per cent more on ads than government-related pages, but these proportions were ∨41 and only ∧5 per cent respectively for the local campaign[12]. Overall, these findings support the H1a hypothesis, while they do not support its competing H1b hypothesis.

In the EP campaign, a similarly high proportion of advertising expenditure (∨91 and ∧89 per cent) could be attributed to pages with formal or informal affiliations to specific parties, but during the local campaign this proportion was much lower: only ∨55 and ∧57 per cent of advertising expenditure can be connected to specific parties. The reason behind this result is probably the fact that numerous political actors (candidates, and local parties) in the local campaign were members of opposition coalitions, therefore they could not be linked to specific parties.

In the EP elections, most parties' share in the total advertising expenditure is in line with their election results (Table 3). Nonetheless, *Fidesz* underperforms significantly, while Jobbik and *LMP* tend to have similar proportions to their share in the last parliamentary elections rather

Table 3. Distribution of ad spending based on formal or informal party affiliation during the EP 2019 and local 2019 elections and the electoral shares of parties.

	Lower range (EP 2019)	Upper range (EP 2019)	Lower range (local 2019)	Upper range (local 2019)	Electoral share (EP 2019)	Electoral share (national 2018)
Fidesz-KDNP	37%	37%	55%	61%	53%	50%
DK	9%	9%	8%	7%	16%	5%
Momentum	10%	10%	12%	11%	10%	3%
MSZP-P	14%	14%	14%	12%	7%	12%
Jobbik	20%	20%	7%	7%	6%	19%
Mi Hazánk	1%	1%	1%	1%	3%	–
MKKP	0.1%	0.1%	0.2%	0.1%	3%	2%
LMP	9%	9%	2%	2%	2%	7%

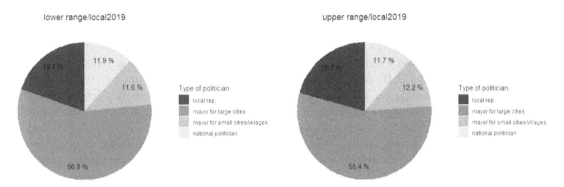

Figure 2. Distribution of ad spending based on individual politicians' political position during the local 2019 elections.

than in the EP election. Also, the smallest parties (*MKKP*, and *Mi Hazánk*) lag far behind their electoral performance in terms of their spending. Overall, in the context of the EP elections, we cannot see a significant equalization trend, although it is true that the largest party could not dominate to the same extent as in the ballot and in the offline campaign environment.

The results for the local campaign should be treated with more caution due to the reason given above: *Fidesz* takes a similar (or larger when it comes to the upper range) share in the parties' total spending to its electoral support, but this is due to the fact that more than half of the advertising expenditure (∨∧58 per cent) related to the opposition cannot be linked to specific parties. If we also consider spending related to opposition pages that are not associated with parties, we find a very similar share (∨34 per cent and ∧40 per cent) as in the EP campaign. Nonetheless, tendencies similar to those of the EP campaign are detected. The normalization hypothesis is also supported by the fact that *Jobbik* and *LMP* seem to align their advertising spending with the results of the EP campaign, but DK underperforms while *MSZP-P* overperforms it. Overall, the normalization hypothesis (H2a) has more support than the equalization thesis (H2b) on the party level, even though it is true that the largest party cannot dominate the advertisement sphere.

The second part of the normalization-equalization hypotheses examines the distribution of advertising expenditures according to the political positions of individual politicians. Since politicians competing at different levels only played a role in the local campaign, we examine these hypotheses only in that sample. The results clearly support the normalization hypothesis (H3a) (Figure 2). More than half of the advertising expenditure associated with politicians was spent by mayoral candidates in cities with county rights. The pages associated with these types of politicians make up only 5 per cent of all advertisers, and the ads they launched account for ∨23 per cent and ∧20 per cent of all advertising expenditure in the campaign. National politicians who did not even run personally in the local elections represent ∨∧12 per cent of the total advertising expenditure associated with individual politicians. Thus, roughly two-thirds of all the money that politicians spent on Facebook was related to higher-level politicians. However, it is important to note that Facebook advertising options have also been intensively used by lower-level politicians. More than half (52 per cent) of pages that ran ads during the campaign and a third (34 per cent) of all political ads were attributed to candidates for municipal council representatives or mayors in smaller towns, but these ads accounted only for ∨13 per cent and ∧12 per cent of the total advertising expenditure. In sum, while the normalization hypothesis is clearly confirmed, it is important to stress that Facebook's advertising platform is actively used by lower-level political actors circulating mainly low-cost ads, something which is hardly possible for them on other platforms.

The stealth media hypothesis is tested by examining the distribution of advertising expenditures according to page type (Table 4). In the EP campaign, ∨85 per cent and ∧82 per cent of all advertising expenditure, while in the local campaign ∨60 per cent and ∧63 per cent are related to official political actors, parties and politicians. These are 78 per cent (EP 2019) and 73 per cent (local 2019) of all ads running on the platform. Government bodies also account for a relatively larger slice of the total expenditures, but ∨∧99 per cent (EP 2019) and ∨∧98 per cent (local 2019) of these are related to European political institutions (European Parliament, European Commission, and Council of the European Union). Unlike in other advertising platforms (see Bátorfy and Urbán 2020), domestic government bodies did not participate in the Facebook advertising campaign. The media, on the other hand, play a relatively important role in the campaign, especially during local elections. However, a significant part of the outlets running ads are news sites or blogs with authentic publishing information. Only in the local campaign did we find a few media outlets publishing ads with unidentifiable or suspicious backgrounds, but their share within the total ad expenditure is barely ∨∧0.1 per cent. Similarly, ads from unofficial political Facebook pages are negligible, accounting for less than ∨∧0.1 per cent in the EP campaign, and ∨∧1 per cent in the local campaign. NGOs, think tanks and movements were more active in the EP campaign, but within them, party foundations and think tanks closely linked to parties played the prominent role.

It is also worth examining all of these based on political leaning (Figure 3). In the EP campaign, ∨∧97 per cent of pro-government spending came from official political pages with pro-government media outlets accounting for only ∨∧2 per cent, and affiliated NGOs for ∨∧1 per cent. Within opposition-leaning advertisers, only ∨84 per cent and ∧82 per cent of spending came from official political pages, ∨8 per cent and ∧9 per cent from opposition media, and ∨3 per cent and ∧5 per cent from opposition civic actors. Although there were several unofficial political pages on both sides in the political advertising market of the local campaign, again we find more non-official actors on the opposition side. In this context, ∨79 per cent and ∧84 per cent of advertising expenditure on the government side came from official political pages, the share of pro-government media was ∨17 per cent and ∧14 per cent, while the share of NGOs did not reach ∨∧1 per cent, but other unofficial political pages accounted for ∨∧2per cent. On the opposition side, ∨∧57 per cent of advertising spending came from official political pages, and the share of opposition media was ∨∧41 per cent. NGOs and other

Table 4. Distribution of ad spending based on page type during the EP 2019 and local 2019 elections.

	EP 2019			Local 2019		
	Lower range	Upper range	Number of ads	Lower range	Upper range	Number of ads
party	70%	67%	48%	20%	26%	19%
politician	15%	15%	30%	40%	37%	54%
campaign page	0	0	0	0.3%	0.3%	0.6%
media outlet	6%	6%	10%	30%	27%	18%
NGO/think tank/movement	3%	4%	4%	1%	2%	3%
governmental body	4%	4%	4%	6%	6%	0.6%
other (non-off.) pol. FB page	0	0	0%	1%	1%	3%
for-profit corporation	0	0	0	0	0	0%
other individual	3%	3%	4%	0.1%	0.1%	0.4%
other/non-identifiable	0	0	0	0.7%	1%	2%

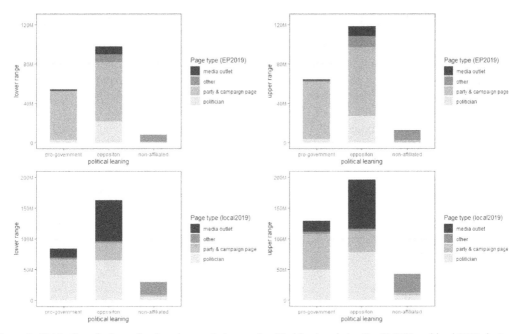

Figure 3. Distribution of ad spending based on party type and political leaning during the EP 2019 and local 2019 elections.

Table 5. Public expenditure of parties and their spending on Facebook ads (in HUF million).

Party	Total party exp. 2019[a]	Exp. on political activity[a]	Funded ads (lower range)[b]	Funded ads (upper range)[b]	% FB ads/ political activity exp. (lower range)	% FB ads/ political activity exp. (upper range)
Fidesz	2375	1618	65	93	4%	6%
MSZP	690	538	14	16	3%	3%
DK	268	48	20	24	42%	50%
Jobbik	605	141	25	30	18%	21%
Momentum	172	134	29	35	22%	26%
LMP	236	110	12	14	11%	13%
P	124	95	10	12	11%	13%

[a]Total and political expenditure data are from parties' official documents available on their websites.
[b]All ads are funded (not posted) by the party itself. They include ads from party, campaign, and politician pages. These data are available in the Ad Library.

unofficial political pages also account for ∨^1 per cent of the total opposition advertising expenditure.

As the share of media outlets' spending is substantial, especially during local campaigns, we take a closer look at their advertising activity. In both campaigns, the sphere of media ads is strongly dominated by opposition-leaning media outlets. In the EP campaigns oppositional media outlets spent seven times as much as the pro-government media expenditure, while in the local campaign this difference is almost fivefold. However, it is true for both campaigns that no more than one or two outlets accounted for these large differences by largely dominating the ad sphere. In the EP-campaign, two interlinked online media outlets owned by the party foundation of *Jobbik*, *Alfahír* and *N1TV* spent ∨69 per cent and ^65 per cent of the total media ad expenditure, i.e., HUF ∨6.5 – ^7.7 million. After the EP campaign, the two pages published no ad for ten months, and since then up to June 2020 they have spent only between HUF ∨270,000 and ^826,000. In the local campaign, a strongly oppositional blog family launched only few weeks before the election, *ezalenyeg.hu* and its local editions account for ∨^77 per cent of all media ads. Moreover, as they started to run ads only in the last month of the campaign, in 29 days they spent between HUF ∨63 million and ^75 million. This amount is even more than the combined sum that any party but Fidesz spent during the two campaigns (see Table 5).

After the election, the blog family consisting of one central and nine local pages published no ad for four months, and since then up to June 2020, they have bought ads for HUF ∨2.3 million – ∧2.9 million. These observations suggest that the particular media outlets pursued political rather than commercial goals with their political ads, as otherwise they would not have ceased their advertising activity following the campaigns. However, it is important to note that both media outlets are transparent in terms of their ownership and editorial board, therefore are not outlets with obscure backgrounds or without clear publishing information.

Overall, these findings suggest that Facebook's advertising platform seems less like stealth media, as most of the advertising expenditure is related to official political pages, and even political ads beyond them are predominantly from media outlets and NGO organizations with identifiable backgrounds. Therefore, these findings do not support our H4 hypothesis that the Facebook political advertising sphere is dominated by non-official political actors, such as media outlets, NGOs, astroturf groups and non-official political pages rather than parties and politicians. However, the prominent role of the media is important, especially as a few highly partisan outlets spent huge amounts of money during both campaigns.

Discussion

The aim of this study is to map the political advertising sphere on Facebook in two Hungarian nationwide elections, focusing on the distribution of ad spending. Because of the lack of available data, Facebook ads have long been a 'black box' of social media research. To our knowledge, this is the first research that has been able to collect all political ads during national campaigns, with the fees paid for them. As we have compared two nationwide elections, we have been able to draw conclusions beyond the specific election context.

Our results show that in the specific Hungarian Plebiscitary Leader Democracy (PLD) -context the advertising sphere on Facebook is largely dominated by the opposition, since actors related to it spent approximately twice as much money on ads as pro-government actors. This finding is surprising as numerous reports suggest that opposition political actors have major disadvantages over the incumbent *Fidesz* in the offline advertising sphere (see Bátorfy and Urbán 2020; Róka 2017).

However, it seems that the two wider political blocks follow different strategies. To illustrate this Table 5 summarizes parties' official total and political expenditure and the sums of money they spent on Facebook as official funders of ads collected *via* the Ad Library. It seems that while Facebook is marginal in *Fidesz*'s campaign in terms of its total political spending (∨4 per cent – ∧6 per cent), oppositional parties devote a significant part of their resources to Facebook's ads (∨10 per cent – ∧12 per cent combined). On the one hand, this way they could use Facebook's more open and equally available advertisement platform to countervail the disadvantages suffered in the offline context. On the other hand, a more general attitudinal difference may also be at play. Previous work demonstrates that left-liberal opposition actors view Facebook as one of their central campaign tools, and on this platform they perform better than *Fidesz* in such aspects of organic communication as the number of their followers, user engagement, and others (Bene and Farkas 2018). In contrast, *Fidesz* put more emphasis on billboard campaigns and direct marketing tools. (Kiss and Szabó 2019). Overall, these findings suggest that Facebook can be considered an oppositional campaign tool where the opposition of the illiberal regime are capable of reaching larger visibility than the incumbents, who largely dominate the offline communication sphere.

Beyond this specific issue, however, Facebook advertisements do not seem to have the potential to restructure political competition. As in the case of organic Facebook communication, normalization seems to be the rule in the ad sphere. The share of the main political forces in the total amount of advertising expenditure is similar to their electoral support with the exception of *Fidesz*, which somewhat underperforms in this aspect. Also, the advertising sphere is largely dominated by a small number of top politicians. However, it is also important that a large number of politicians from lower levels of the political sphere are able to boost their Facebook visibility by running cheap ads. This kind of small-scale ad campaign may be crucial in local-level campaigns where a significant share of the constituents can be reached by cheap ads. On Facebook ads running at a cost of HUF one thousand (EUR 3) may reach a thousand people based on the number of impressions reported by the Ad Library. Consequently, while the Facebook advertising sphere is rather uneven, by offering easy and cheap access to its platform (see Fowler et al. 2021) it still broadens the opportunities of lower-level political actors excluded from the offline advertising sphere.

One of the central topics in the evolving literature is the unregulated nature of Facebook ads, and the practical political consequences of this fact, such as campaign by astroturf pages or opportunities for 'slush funds', which can make Facebook a 'stealth media' (Kim et al. 2018; Silva et al. 2020). Even though the 'stealth media' character could be detected in previous non-European campaigns, our results show that it was not manifested in the two Hungarian nationwide elections in 2019. Non-official political actors play minor roles in the advertising sphere; in addition, a few of them have unknown backgrounds. It can be assumed that this marked change is due to the powerful self-regulatory measures implemented by Facebook. It is unclear, however, which specific steps are behind this clearer campaign. It is now impossible to run political ads on Facebook outside the countries where the sponsor is registered (see Dobber et al. 2019). This regulation may decrease the chance of such foreign interference *via* Facebook ads as was the case in the 2016 US presidential election (Ribeiro et al. 2018). Also, Facebook has implemented a stricter revision process: according to the report of the European Regulators Group for Audiovisual Media Service (ERGA) that monitored the implementation of the self-regulatory but European Commission-assisted Code of Practice on Online Disinformation (CoP), Facebook took action against 1.2 million ads for violating its policies during the EP election (ERGA 2019). However, it is also conceivable that more transparency has a deterring role in the stealth campaign in itself as the publicly available information may easily result in a backlash effect on the supported political actor.

Beyond official political actors, it is only the news media that are actively present in the political advertising sphere. This finding is especially important, because in most contexts Facebook does not register the ads of news media outlets as political, therefore it is impossible to assess the role they play in the political advertising sphere. The Hungarian case showed that in both campaigns there was one media outlet-family that spent a huge amount of money on political ads that after the election campaigns almost completely stopped their advertising activity. Both media outlet families had strong and clear political leanings toward the opposition. As they have a transparent background, they could not be labeled as stealth media. However, this evidence suggests that they pursue clear political goals with their advertising activity, which can be seen as a grey zone from the perspective of campaign financing.

The main limitation of this study is that we are forced to draw upon data collected, filtered, and published by Facebook but we do not have any information about the reliability and validity of this dataset. What we know is the specific definition of 'political' Facebook uses to categorize ads. Their definition is luckily quite wide to cover a wide range of content, including all ads from official political actors and ads that refer to official political actors, elections, campaigns or even social issues in the specific country. In practice, we experienced this rather wide definition of politics as our dataset contained numerous ads run by for-profit commercial pages only because they included a 'green' or environmentalist reference. Based on these observations, we suspect that the cover of the Ad Library is close to complete, but it is important to note that both Silva et al. (2020) in the 2018 Brazilian general election and the ERGA during the Hungarian local election campaign (ERGA 2020) have found some political ads that were not registered as such. From a research perspective, Facebook should enhance its collaboration with academics as suggested by the ERGA (2019) and be more transparent about the efficacy of its detecting mechanism.

Further, while the comparison of two nationwide elections strengthens the external validity of our findings, the single-country design still limits the ability to generalize the results. The Hungarian political advertising sphere may deviate from other contexts, especially due to the specific illiberal setting. However, the single-country focus is not unique in the field, as all previous work on Facebook ads were conducted in one particular country. Future studies should bridge this gap, especially as the Ad Library being available in many countries by now, makes it possible to conduct comparative, cross-country investigations. Also, there are several other important aspects of the advertising campaign on Facebook that are worth investigating. Primarily, examining the content of ads, and especially their relationship with spending would be an important step further to advancing our knowledge about Facebook advertising. The timing of Facebook advertising campaigns may also be an important factor to analyze.

Nonetheless, this study is an important step forward opening the 'black box' of social media and politics research. The investigation of ads could reinforce such established theories as the normalization hypothesis and the democratizing potential of social media, and nuance others, such as the stealth media thesis.

Notes

1. https://www.statista.com/statistics/264810/number-of-monthly-active-facebook-users-worldwide/
2. see https://www.internetworldstats.com/stats9.htm
3. see https://www.statista.com/statistics/568794/forecast-of-facebook-user-numbers-in-hungary/
4. https://www.reuters.com/article/us-hungary-opposition-fine/hungarys-jobbik-party-says-might-disband-after-second-audit-fine-idUSKCN1PQ58Z
5. https://www.france24.com/en/20190516-hungary-blasts-facebook-censorship-pro-government-media-group
6. Facebook: About Ads About Social Issues, Elections or Politics. https://www.facebook.com/business/help/167836590566506?id=288762101909005
7. Data were first collected right after the respective Election Days. However, as later the Ad Library included narrower ranges for the prices, we re-collected ads in September 2020.
8. Our scraping left empty the upper ranges for ads sponsored by more than HUF 1 million. We found 10 ads during the EP 2019 and 15 ads in local 2019 elections that were paid over HUF 1 million. As the Ad Library gives the accurate spending for each page since March 2019 to the actual date, in order to estimate the exact upper ranges for our missing cases, we scraped all ads published by these pages from March 2019 to 1st May 2020. We summed their total expenditure on the upper ranges and contrasted it with the accurate value. In this way we could determine conservative estimations for the missing cases by making the two aggregated values equal. However, it is important to note that this is a conservative estimation as we know that the sum of upper ranges should be higher than the accurate value.
9. They are typically the largest cities in Hungary with a population of over 31,000 inhabitants: 23 out of the 346 Hungarian cities.
10. We conducted inter-coder reliability tests on 100 pages for each of the two campaigns. For the EP campaign the values of Krippendorf's alpha are 0.98 for page type, 0.87 for geography, 0.90 for political leaning, and 0.97 for party support. For the local campaign, these values are 0.82 for page type, 0.81 for geography, 0.96 for type of domicile, 0.77 for political leaning, and 0.79 for party support.
11. In 2019, based on the average exchange rate EUR 1 = HUF 325
12. The large difference between the lower and upper ranges is due to the fact that pro-government pages ran more ads with extremely large prices while the maximum value of the lower range is 1 million HUF; therefore these ads caused a wider gap between the two ranges than usual.

Funding

This work was supported by National Research, Development and Innovation Office of Hungary (NKFIH) under the Grant Agreement no. FK-135189 (Networked locality: A multimethod approach to investigate the role of social media in local politics) and Bolyai János Research Fellowship of the Hungarian Academy of Sciences (BO/334_20).

ORCID

Márton Bene http://orcid.org/0000-0003-0177-9717
Mátyás Bene http://orcid.org/0000-0002-5611-9567

References

Baldwin-Philippi, Jessica. 2019. "Data Campaigning: Between Empirics and Assumptions." *Internet Policy Review* 8 (4):1–18. https://doi.org/10.14763/2019.4.1437
Barnard, Lisa, and Daniel Kreiss. 2013. "A Research Agenda for Online Advertising: Surveying Campaign Practices, 2000-2012." *International Journal of Communication* 7:2046–66.
Bátorfy, Attila, and Ágnes Urbán. 2020. "State Advertising as an Instrument of Transformation of the Media Market in Hungary." *East European Politics* 36 (1):44–65. https://doi.org/10.1080/21599165.2019.1662398
Bene, Márton. 2017. "Go Viral on the Facebook! Interactions between Candidates and Followers on Facebook during the Hungarian General Election Campaign of 2014." *Information, Communication & Society* 20 (4):513–29. https://doi.org/10.1080/1369118X.2016.1198411
Bene, Márton, and Xénia Farkas. 2018. "Kövess, Reagálj, Oszd Meg! a Közösségi Média a 2018-as Országgyűlési Választási Kampányban." In *Várakozások És Valóságok. Parlamenti Választás 2018*, edited by Balázs Böcskei and Andrea Szabó, 410–37. Budapest: Napvilág Kiadó, MTA TK PTI.
Bossetta, Michael. 2018. "The Digital Architectures of Social Media: Comparing Political Campaigning on Facebook, Twitter, Instagram, and Snapchat in the 2016 U.S. Election." *Journalism & Mass Communication Quarterly* 95 (2):471–96. https://doi.org/10.1177/1077699018763307
Broockman, David E., and Donald P. Green. 2014. "Do Online Advertisements Increase Political Candidates' Name Recognition or Favorability? Evidence from Randomized Field Experiments." *Political Behavior* 36 (2):263–89. https://doi.org/10.1007/s11109-013-9239-z
Chester, Jeff, and Kathryn C. Montgomery. 2017. "The Role of Digital Marketing in Political Campaigns." *Internet Policy Review* 6 (4):1–20. https://doi.org/10.14763/2017.4.773
Dijck, Jose van. 2013. *The Culture of Connectivity: A Critical History of Social Media*. 1 ed. New York: Oxford University Press.
Diamond, Larry. 2010. "Liberation Technology." *Journal of Democracy* 21 (3):69–83. https://doi.org/10.1353/jod.0.0190
Dobber, Tom, Damian Trilling, Natali Helberger, and Claes H. de Vreese. 2017. "Two Crates of Beer and 40 Pizzas: The Adoption of Innovative Political Behavioural Targeting Techniques." *Internet Policy Review* 6 (4):1–25. https://doi.org/10.14763/2017.4.777
Dobber, Tom, Ó Fathaigh Ronan, and Zuiderveen Borgesius Frederik. 2019. "The regulation of online political microtargeting in Europe." *Internet Policy Review* 8 (4):1–20.
Edelson, Laura, Shikhar Sakhuja, Ratan Dey, and Damon McCoy. 2019. "An Analysis of United States Online Political Advertising Transparency." *ArXiv:1902.04385* [Cs], February. http://arxiv.org/abs/1902.04385.
ERGA. 2019. "Report on the Implementation of the Action Plan Against Disinformation." https://eur-lex.europa.eu/legal-content/EN/TXT/PDF/?uri=CELEX:52019JC0012&from=EN.
ERGA. 2020. "ERGA Report on Disinformation: Assessment of the Implementation of the Code of Practice." https://erga-online.eu/wp-content/uploads/2020/05/ERGA-2019-report-published-2020-LQ.pdf.
Fisher, Caroline, Eileen Culloty, Jee Young Lee, and Sora Park. 2019. "Regaining Control Citizens Who Follow Politicians on Social Media and Their Perceptions of Journalism." *Digital Journalism* 7 (2):230–50. https://doi.org/10.1080/21670811.2018.1519375
Fowler, Erika Franklin, Michael M. Franz, Gregory J. Martin, Zahary Peskowitz, and Travis N. Ridout. 2021. "Political Advertising Online and Offline." *American Political Science Review* 115 (1):130–49. https://doi.org/10.1017/S0003055420000696
Groshek, Jacob. 2009. "The Democratic Effects of the Internet, 1994–2003: A Cross-National Inquiry of 152 Countries." *International Communication Gazette* 71 (3):115–36. https://doi.org/10.1177/1748048508100909
Haenschen, Katherine, and Jay Jennings. 2019. "Mobilizing Millennial Voters with Targeted Internet Advertisements: A Field Experiment." *Political Communication* 36 (3):357–75. https://doi.org/10.1080/10584609.2018.1548530
Hager, Anselm. 2019. "Do Online Ads Influence Vote Choice?" *Political Communication* 36 (3):376–93. https://doi.org/10.1080/10584609.2018.1548529
Heath, Anthony, Iain McLean, Bridget Taylor, and John Curtice. 1999. "Between First and Second Order: A Comparison of Voting Behaviour in European and Local Elections in Britain." *European Journal of Political Research* 35 (3):389–414. https://doi.org/10.1023/A:1006924510899
Howard, Philip N., and Muzammil M. Hussain. 2013. *Democracy's Fourth Wave?: Digital Media and the Arab Spring*. Oxford, Oxford University Press.
Jacobs, Kristof, and Niels Spierings. 2016. *Social Media, Parties, and Political Inequalities*. 1st ed. 2016 edition. London, Palgrave Macmillan.

Kaid, Lynda Lee. 2012. "Political Advertising as Political Marketing: A Retro-Forward Perspective." *Journal of Political Marketing* 11 (1–2):29–53. https://doi.org/10.1080/15377857.2012.642731

Kim, Young Mie. 2016. "Algorithmic Opportunity: Digital Advertising and Inequality in Political Involvement." *The Forum* 14 (4):471–84. https://doi.org/10.1515/for-2016-0034

Kim, Young Mie., Jordan Hsu, David Neiman, Colin Kou, Levi Bankston, Soo Yun Kim, Richard Heinrich, Robyn Baragwanath, and Garvesh Raskutti. 2018. "The Stealth Media? Groups and Targets behind Divisive Issue Campaigns on Facebook." *Political Communication* 35 (4):515–41. https://doi.org/10.1080/10584609.2018.1476425

Kiss, Balázs, and Gabriella Szabó. 2019. "Hungary." In *Thirty Years of Political Campaigning in Central and Eastern Europe*, edited by Otto Eibl and Gregor Miloš, London, 115–30. Palgrave Macmillan.

Körösényi, András, Gábor Illés, and Attila Gyulai. 2020. *The Orbán Regime: Plebiscitary Leader Democracy in the Making*. 1 ed. London, Routledge.

Kruschinski, Simon, and André Haller. 2017. "Restrictions on Data-Driven Political Micro-Targeting in Germany." *Internet Policy Review* 6 (4):1–23. https://policyreview.info/articles/analysis/restrictions-data-driven-political-micro-targeting-germany. https://doi.org/10.14763/2017.4.780

Leerssen, Paddy, Jef Ausloos, Brahim Zarouali, Natali Helberger, and Claes H. de Vreese. 2019. "Platform Ad Archives: Promises and Pitfalls." *Internet Policy Review* 8 (4):1–21. https://doi.org/10.14763/2019.4.1421

Merkovity, Norbert, and Peter Bence Stumpf. 2021. "Migrants during Halftime: The Framing of Hungarian Political News during the FIFA World Cup." *East European Politics* 37 (2):292–310. https://doi.org/10.1080/21599165.2020.1781095

Nielsen, Rasmus Kleis, and Cristian Vaccari. 2013. "Do People 'Like' Politicians on Facebook? Not Really. Large-Scale Direct Candidate-to-Voter Online Communication as an Outlier Phenomenon." *International Journal of Communication* 7 (0):24.

Norris, Pippa. 2003. "Preaching to the Converted?: Pluralism, Participation and Party Websites." *Party Politics* 9 (1):21–45. https://doi.org/10.1177/135406880391003

Polyák, Gábor. 2019. "Media in Hungary: Three Pillars of an Illiberal Democracy." In *Public Service Broadcasting and Media Systems in Troubled European Democracies*, edited by Eva Połońska and Charlie Beckett, 279–303. Cham: Palgrave Macmillan.

Ribeiro, Filipe N., Koustuv Saha, Mahmoudreza Babaei, Lucas Henrique, Johnnatan Messias, Fabricio Benevenuto, Oana Goga, Krishna P. Gummadi, and Elissa M. Redmiles. 2019. "On Microtargeting Socially Divisive Ads: A Case Study of Russia-Linked Ad Campaigns on Facebook." Paper presented at the Proceedings of the Conference on Fairness, Accountability, and Transparency – FAT* '19, 140–9. https://doi.org/10.1145/3287560.3287580

Rød, Espen Geelmuyden, and Nils B. Weidmann. 2015. "Empowering Activists or Autocrats? The Internet in Authoritarian Regimes." *Journal of Peace Research* 52 (3):338–51. https://doi.org/10.1177/0022343314555782

Róka, Jolán. 2017. "Does Political Advertising Still Have an Impact on the Outcome of Election Campaigns? Political Advertising in Hungary." In *Routledge Handbook of Political Advertising*, edited by Christina Holtz-Bacha and Marion R. Just, 2017th ed., 139–51. New York: Routledge.

Silva, Márcio, Lucas Santos de Oliveira, Athanasios Andreou, Pedro Olmo Vaz de Melo, Oana Goga, and Fabrício Benevenuto. 2020. "Facebook Ads Monitor: An Independent Auditing System for Political Ads on Facebook." *ArXiv:2001.10581 [Cs]*, January. http://arxiv.org/abs/2001.10581.

Spaiser, Viktoria, Thomas Chadefaux, Karsten Donnay, Fabian Russmann, and Dirk Helbing. 2017. "Communication Power Struggles on Social Media: A Case Study of the 2011–12 Russian Protests." *Journal of Information Technology & Politics* 14 (2):132–53. https://doi.org/10.1080/19331681.2017.1308288

Surowiec, Paweł and Václav Štětka, eds. 2017. *Social Media and Politics in Central and Eastern Europe*. New York: Routledge.

Tucker, Joshua A., Yannis Theocharis, Margaret E. Roberts, and Pablo Barberá. 2017. "From Liberation to Turmoil: Social Media and Democracy." *Journal of Democracy* 28 (4):46–59. https://doi.org/10.1353/jod.2017.0064

Vissers, Sara. 2009. "From Preaching to the Converted to Preaching through the Converted." Paper presented for the ECPR Joint Sessions of Workshops 2009, Workshop 20 Parliaments, Parties, and Politicians in Cyberspace, April 14–19, 2009, Lisbon."

Weber, Max. 1978. *Economy and Society*. 1st ed. Two Volume Set, with A New Foreword by Guenther Roth edition. Berkeley: University of California Press.

Electoral Political Communication in the Post-Communist Hybrid Regime – The Case of Serbia 2020

Dušan Vučićević and Siniša Atlagić

ABSTRACT
This study analyzes the 2020 Serbian election campaign in the context of institutional conditions of competition in a hybrid regime, comparing it to the regime of Slobodan Milosevic. The authors explore how electoral communication articulates social problems and solutions, and examine the impact of new information and communication technologies on political communication in hybrid regime. Taking into account the specific configuration of the public sphere inherited from the period of Milosević's rule and the comprehensive application of persuasive techniques, the authors come to several findings regarding electoral communication in Serbia: first, the election campaigns have not reified as a platform for addressing key political and identity issues; second, the development of new information and communication technologies and new means of promotion widen opportunities for propaganda, making hybrid regimes more resilient to internal pressures for democratization; and, third, given the institutional context in which electoral communication takes place, the question arises as to whether, in the institutional context of hybrid communication, one can speak of political marketing as opposed to merely a commercialized variant of political propaganda. The study is based on in-depth interviews with experts, public polls, researchers, and campaign managers.

Introduction

The results of previous research on the impact of election campaigns on the electoral decision of voters have shown that it has been rather limited in developed democracies and has manifested itself primarily as a consolidation of the electoral decision of a large part of the electorate as the crystallization of the electoral decision of the undecided (Lazarsfeld, Berelson, and Gaudet 1948; Campbell et al. 1960; Greene 2019, 164). On the other hand, there has been an increase in the importance of election campaigns in situations where the role of political parties had been declining due to the party tissue becoming atrophied and party activities waning (Kaid and Holtz-Bacha 1995, 9); this trend has also been observed in developing democracies (Greene 2019, 164). These case studies have demonstrated that significant changes in the mood of voters are possible if the election campaign is part of a pre-designed long-term strategy to promote the political entity, because in that case it enhances the effects of previous investments in its promotion (Slavujević 2009, 159; Box-Steffensmeier, Darmofal and Farrell 2009, 309; Jacobson 2015; Strömbäck 2017, 239). In hybrid regimes, however, this long-term plan for communication between opposition political entities and citizens has been thwarted and the campaign has barely been able to fulfill its basic function. Why?

While in democracies elections tend to be free and fair and in authoritarian countries multi-party elections either do not exist or are uncompetitive, hybrid regimes fall into the "political grey zone" category (Carothers 2002, 9). Their elections are competitive but often not free and almost always unfair. Practically, in most regimes of competitive authoritarianism "unequal access to finance and the media as well as incumbent abuse of state institutions make elections unfair even in the absence of violence and fraud" (Levitsky and Way 2010, 8). At the same time, civil liberties are nominally guaranteed but frequently violated as opposition politicians and other government critics become subject to harassment, arrests and violent attacks. Independent media exist but journalists and media outlets are frequently threatened, defamated, attacked and in some cases closed. Finally, high degree of incumbent advantage is based on uneven playing field when it comes to access to law, resources and media. In competitive authoritarian regimes "umpires" (state prosecutors, judiciary, electoral commissions, control bodies) are biased and designed to act systematically in favor of the ruling party, incumbents directly use state resources and monopolize private-sector finance while opposition parties and politicians and all government critics lack access to national media outlets, public as well as private, crucial to reaching most of the population (Levitsky and Way 2010, 9–12). One of the hallmarks of elections in the regimes of competitive authoritarianism is the struggle between the government and the opposition on two levels. While in democracies, the electoral strategy revolves only around gaining the trust of voters, in competitive authoritarianism one must engage on another playing field where rules of the game itself can be called into question. Aspiration of the authoritarian rulers is always to transfer competition completely to the electoral arena, where the rules are set to ensure their victory. In this nested game, different strategies are available to the opposition, with the most important ones falling within the scope of the dilemma between boycotting and participating in biased elections (Schedler 2002, 112–118).

Less than 30 years after declaration of liberal democracy's eternal dominance the decline of democratic regimes and third wave of autocratization are unfolding (Luhrmann and Lindberg 2019). Recent democratic setbacks in diverse range of countries sparked a new generation of studies on autocratization (Bermeo 2016; Coppedge 2017; Perez-Liñan and Altman 2017; Cassani and Tomini 2018; Levitsky and Ziblatt 2018; Luhrmann et al. 2018; Tomini and Wagemann 2018; Waldner and Lust 2018). However, most studies ignore the way new autocrats communicate with the public, "their own" and that of the opposition, as well as the question of whether the development of new information and communication technologies make it easier for authoritarian leaders to maintain control.

In this research, we deal with political persuasion as a function of political communication. We understand it as forming, consolidating and changing people's attitudes about various political phenomena, events and actors, as well as encouraging people to take part in political life in accordance with the intentions of the persuaders. It is a set of complex and lasting communication processes that are undertaken with the aim of convincing people of the correctness, usefulness, acceptability of political content and are directly focused on the attitude structure of an individual, i. e. on the relationship that an individual should have with a political object. In doing so, political persuasion targets all three elements of the attitude structure: the cognitive, affective and motivational component (Slavujević 2009, 10). Such an understanding of political persuasion is the result of an analysis of various concepts that can be subsumed under the broader notion of political communication – from early definitions of political propaganda as managing people's collective attitudes by manipulating significant symbols (Lasswell 1971, 28), through strategic communication as a form of imperative influence on people's consciousness (Habermas 1988), and those making connection between political persuasion and political marketing as well as" psychological coercion "and political propaganda (Bobin 1988, 82) to differentiation between coercive (analysis of crowd behavior and monopolistic control of the media) and manipulative (research on individual motivation) persuasion (Scammell 1995, 20).

We have selected Serbia as a highly relevant case in this respect. Serbia was a hybrid regime during 1990s, it was democratized after the fall of Milošević in 2000 but witnessed gradual erosion of democracy after 2012. Since their first electoral triumph the Serbian Progressive Party (SNS) has gradually been taking over the government both vertically and horizontally, which led to the Freedom House and V-Dem Institute reclassifying Serbia as a hybrid regime (Freedom House 2020) and "electoral autocracy" (V-Dem 2019), respectively. In recent years, several studies have also noted a significant rise in authoritarian practices, describing the regime as hybrid or competitive authoritarian (Bieber 2018; Keil 2018; Pavlović 2019).

Our main argument is that there is a considerable difference between Slobodan Milošević's and current president Aleksandar Vučić's hybrid regimes. While the former was more repressive, including the use of "legal "(i.e., defamation laws against journalists, editors and media outlets) and overt repression (arrests and assassination attempts of opposition leaders, widespread harassment and bullying of opposition activists and violent repression of popular protests), the latter is more persuasive. Its persuasiveness is enhanced by the use of modern information and communication technologies with which it conquers not only the center but also the periphery of the public sphere, frequent public polls and messages testing as well as spreading of false and semi-false information with the intention of introducing confusion among opposition voters. Change of tactics to sporadic repression and a permanent, almost everyday propaganda campaign helps the regime to be more resilient to internal pressures for democratization. Consequentially, after a series of popular protests during the 2016–2019 period the regime's support among the voters increased. Empirical evidence of our argument is based on interviews with key people who run election campaigns and shape communication strategies of key political actors – both government and opposition – and also on evidence from local surveys, media sources and reports.[1]

Our paper is divided into three sections. The first one focuses on the institutional context, the characteristics of Aleksandar Vučić's hybrid regime and the ways in which it resembles or differs from Slobodan Milošević's rule during the 1990s. The second section of the paper is dedicated to the development of electoral communication in Serbia from the renewal of the multiparty system in 1990 to the modern period. It gives an overview of the communication of political actors with voters and basic elements in the campaigns of the ruling and opposition parties during the thirty years of multi-party system. Special attention is paid to the differences in the electoral communication of the two hybrid regimes. The third part of the paper describes the specific persuasive activities of the representatives of the hybrid regime in the election campaign in Serbia in the spring of 2020 – the campaign for the first parliamentary elections in Europe since the outbreak of the coronavirus epidemic.

Lesson Not Learned: Death and Rebirth of Competitive Authoritarianism in Serbia

Transition from loosely decentralized socialist one-party system to competitive authoritarian multi-party regime in Serbia concludes with the 1990 elections. Milošević and the Socialist Party of Serbia (SPS) were successful at neutralizing their competition thanks to the high asymmetry of power between the "reformed" post-communist ruling elite and the disjointed and fragmented opposition. That asymmetry was achieved after the SPS had taken over the organizational, financial and personnel resources of the League of Communists of Serbia and with the help of majoritarian electoral system and uneven playing field which had undermined the opposition's ability to effectively organize and confront the government during electoral campaign, especially in the state-owned media. Unequal access to media, finance and state resources during 1990s made it extremely difficult for the opposition to defeat Milošević and the ruling party. Until the mid-1990s, Milošević was in control of almost all elements of power – army and police, extensive party patronage networks in economy, money and media (Dolenec 2013, 161–176). After Milošević, under pressure from the West, admitted electoral defeat in local elections in

Belgrade and major Serbian cities in 1996 (Vladisavljević 2016), equilibrium of power was gradually altered. As the regime entered the neo-patrimonial phase, pressure on media outlets, opposition politicians and journalists increased (including closing of media outlets, assassination attempts and murders). However, at the same time the control over the local media had slipped into the hands of the opposition which helped them to disseminate anti-regime messages to a larger portion of the electorate.

Milošević lost power following the September 2000 presidential election (Bujošević and Radovanović 2003). NATO bombing in 1999, loss of control over Kosovo territory, economic deprivation and poverty had eroded public support for the government and shifted it toward the opposition. Defection of a number of erstwhile loyal comrades coincided with organizational strengthening of the opposition forces with the backing, including financial assistance, of the West.

The early post-Milošević regime was ridden by crisis and inherited problems and marked by the rivalry of the key political figures of the victorious coalition of 2000 (DOS) up until its disintegration. However since the 2003 elections were free and fair and produced a reasonably even political playing-field (Vučićević 2010). After the overthrow of Milošević, Serbia started its processes of economic and political liberalization, European integration and regional cooperation, and introduced new democratic institutions, control and regulatory bodies. At the same time problems of transitional justice (extradition of war criminals to the ICTY), disputes over Kosovo's sovereignty and the province's de-facto authorities' unilateral declaration of independence in 2008 had a major impact on the political narrative during 2000s generating division and creating two blocks of parties made up of former DOS allies. Internal conflicts over identity issues and conditionality policies of key international actors diverted attention from strengthening democratic institutions necessary for the long-term survival of democracy, yet key political conflicts and problems were resolved democratically, in the elections and within the political institutions. The government was reorganized within the democratic bloc, as a result of elections, several times (2003, 2007, 2008, 2012) without any major exogenous objections to the quality of the election process (Listhaug, Ramet, and Dulić 2011; Gordy 2013, Vladisavljević 2019a).

During the 2000s Serbia may not have been high on the democratic scale but it did nevertheless exhibit some characteristics of a delegative democracy (O'Donnell 1994). The executive power in the form of the Government or the President of the Republic often ignored other branches of the state and regulatory bodies and generally dominated the political scene. Democracy backsliding started with a gradual and informal restriction of media freedoms in the years prior to the return to power of the rejuvenated old-regime parties. The gradual transformation of democratic parties into government parties, increasing clientelism and corruption, numerous privileges and misuse of public resources caused dissatisfaction among some sections of civil society and the public. The spillover of the 2007–2008 global financial crisis into Serbia, along with the collapse of the credibility of democratic parties, thus opened the way for a new rise of undemocratic challenges and a rebirth of competitive authoritarianism. It would be safe to say that 2012 – the year of the Serbian parliamentary and presidential elections was the pivotal year. The newly appointed leader of the main party in the coalition (Serbian Progressive Party – SNS), as well as the future prime minister and president Aleksandar Vučić, set out to bring the personalization of politics and the privatization of the public sphere in the country to its limits.

With the convincing victory of the SNS in the 2014 elections,[2] Aleksandar Vučić and the ruling party gradually increased pressure on the judiciary and control bodies. The latter were under particular pressure from the authorities because, in the absence of a consolidated opposition, they represented the most significant criticism of the regime. The campaign against the control bodies, and especially against the Protector of Citizens (Vladisavljević 2019b, 289–296), was followed by the campaign for the new parliamentary elections of 2016, which seemed to have been called in order to strengthen the position of the ruling coalition on the political scene. The 2016 parliamentary elections are significant not only because of another convincing victory of the SNS, but also because they represent the beginning of the resistance against the undemocratic government.[3] Following the election night, when the opposition representatives accused the government of electoral fraud and demanded a recount of votes, a series of protests organized by local and civic initiatives and opposition parties ensued and lasted in various forms until the 2020 elections. (Vladisavljević 2019b, 11–14).

The next stage of the government's campaign was the 2017 presidential election, which resulted in a convincing victory for Aleksandar Vučić.[4] Despite the remarks of the OSCE and domestic observation missions regarding the irregularities – unbalanced media coverage and pressure on voters above all (Birodi (Biro za društvena istraživanja) 2017; CRTA 2017; OSCE/ODIHR 2017) – responses from the international community and the European Union were weak. The government had taken control of all regulatory bodies and completely closed the center of the public sphere to representatives of the opposition in order to prevent any critical assessment of their work. The issue of free access to the public service and other key media, reminiscent of Milosević's rule, served as a pretext for the opposition to intensify protest actionin 2018–2019, as well as leave the parliament, which by then had lost its basic, deliberative function (Vladisavljević 2019b, 319–324).

The transition of the opposition to an extra-institutional struggle brought the government to the negotiating table. However, no agreement was reached. The government sought to shift the focus of the negotiations to the technical aspect of the election and not to the issue of media coverage of opposition activities. After the second round table talks most opposition parties left the negotiations and declared a boycott six months before the elections were held. They also confirmed their commitment to the boycott a few months later by refusing to take part in the talks organized by a group of representatives of the European Parliament. The strategies of the internal actors for the 2020 elections fully corresponded to the known theoretical models of hybrid regimes. Namely, the struggle between the government and the opposition can be observed on two levels: for votes and for rules of the game itself. However, the Serbian opposition had lost both battles across all arenas– at home, abroad and in the media.

The regime of hybrid institutions and relations that have been gradually established in Serbia with the coming to power of Aleksandar Vučić in 2012, and which were pointed out by domestic (Antonić 2016; CRTA 2016) and foreign researchers (Bieber 2015; Günay and Dzihic 2016), is characterized by a significant difference in relation to the Milošević's regime. Unlike Milošević's hybrid regime, that of Vučić has proven to be much more persuasive. In other words, of the two mechanisms by which the authorities ensure and maintain dominance – the use of force and engineering of consent (Louw 2010, 128–129), Vučić sticks to the latter. He was supported by the inherited structure of the public sphere, and widely used political marketing in the period after 2000, as well as the development of information and communication technologies, tacit support from the West (Richter and Wunsch 2019) and personal image characteristics (Slavujević 2017) to his advantage. All this has made Vučić's regime resilient to internal pressures compared to the 1990s and has been described as "stabilitocracy" (Bieber 2020). In such a context, the 2020 election campaign was only the final propaganda blow in the regime's permanent campaign that has been ongoing since 2012.

Lesson Learned: The New Hybrid Regime is More Persuasive than the Previous One

The rise of Milošević and the SPS to power and its sustainability during the 1990s is, to some extent, a consequence of a planned political persuasion. Despite the fact that political marketing had not yet been developed and that there was resistance to researching and taking into account public opinion, the persuasive action of the SPS as the ruling party and its regime during the 1990s was continuous, comprehensive and, complex, from the standpoint of the psychology of political communication (Atlagić and Vučićević 2019, 328–331). The main characteristic of this persuasion, which began in the late 1980s within the Communist Party that the SPS would succeed, was to connect a whole series of campaigns into a single, intensive permanent campaign with unambiguous-intentional messages, through orchestration of all techniques, means of propaganda and forms of promotion.

This permanent campaign was conducted through the concentrated action of state-party propaganda, which was accepted by the mass media as a distinct political-propaganda organ. The media was one of the central social mechanisms through which dominant political forces sought to mobilize majority of public support for their views on society, its key problems, and the solutions offered. The most important role in this was played by the public broadcaster, particularly their news programs, over which the ruling party would intensify its control, striving to homogenize the public around its own view of the world whenever the consensus on its program was threatened. By favoring the ruling party/coalition and discriminating against its opponents on the political and electoral scenes, the former was enabled to gain notoriety, as well as more sympathy from the voters and thus a chance of an electoral victory (Matić 2007, 252). The intention to form a positive image of the ruling political entities in the minds of the citizens and, when necessary, to form a negative image of the opposition, was the basis of this approach to the media presentation of the elections. Similar to other post-communist societies, a public space of a specific configuration had been formed. It distinguished the center, represented by television, more specifically the state television channel, and the periphery, which consisted of several local television channels, radio stations and print media. There are two consequences of this circumstance: First, the chance for a particular discourse to become "popular" depended on how much it was represented in the center of the public sphere. Second, in order to manage the social "agenda", it was sufficient to control the biggest channels of mass communication. The social arenas that made up the periphery of public space were few and could not make a significant impact. In the 1990s, the government's strategy for communication was to exclude, within reasonable limits of expediency (legal decisions, financial pressures, editorial decisions), any discourses that did not support it (Atlagić 2020, 33; Малинова 2013).

The change of government in 2000 proved to be crucial from the standpoint of understanding the manner of conducting election campaigns. The election actors understood the importance of public opinion research for modeling their image, choosing the type of campaign, designing and testing key messages, researching voters' communication habits, correcting some elements of the campaign, etc. (Atlagić and Vučićević 2019, 331–332). However, the new standards for election campaigns, which were recognized in Serbia after 2003, did not help the democratic parties survive the global economic crisis that gripped Serbia in 2009. The change of the global context, the crisis and the collapse of the policies of the parties of the democratic bloc had thus opened the way for Aleksandar Vučić to act simultaneously on both the domestic and foreign policy plans after the 2012 elections, uniting all activities, just as Milošević's SPS did in the first decade of the multi-party system, into a permanent campaign that continues to this day.[5]

In relation to the period of Milošević's rule, the main difference is that the mobilizing role of "traditional" media has now been transferred from public broadcasting to national-frequency commercial televisions and to cheap daily newspapers. Weekly magazines have been able to protect their freedom more than the television has. They are, along with one cable channel, social networks and a few local TV stations, the periphery of the public sphere. Therefore, it would be wrong to talk about the ban on free speech in Serbia. It has simply been pushed out to the periphery of public space (Atlagić 2020, 34).[6] However, unlike Milošević's, the current government in Serbia is determined to conquer the periphery of the public sphere. The reason for this is clear – although television is still the main source of information and the most credible source for most Serbian citizens, the Internet, which occupies the second place is dominant among the younger population (under 29) and is coming to pose significant competition to television for the under-39 age group (Ninković Slavnić 2016; Atlagić 2020). One of the indicators of the efforts to conquer the periphery of the public sphere are the intensive activities on Twitter that the ruling party undertook in order to oppose the aforementioned anti-Vučić protests during 2018 and 2019.[7] These activities were part of Vučić's campaign "Future of Serbia", conducted with the primary goal of diminishing the significance of these protests but also to promote the economic policy of Vučić and the Government of Serbia. It was a typical example of a so-called functionary campaign or state marketing in which officials use public functions to promote party and personal political goals and receive media attention.

The instrumentalization of the public sphere and the so-called state marketing are places of key differences and similarities between Milošević and Vučić and they are largely related to the issue of image – one of the most important factors of electoral motivation in Serbian politics (Slavujević and Atlagić 2015, 165–166). Both leaders belong to the group of "masters of the organization" – their leadership is built on authoritarian management of a strong party organization, strict discipline, arbitrary decisions and strong personal loyalty of other members of the organization, as well as the intensively created image of a charismatic leader. However, Milosevic's public relations were kept to a minimum. His promotion was based on the oversized publicity given to him by his presidency. He has never participated in official promotions and debates of presidential candidates, nor has he held daily discussions with opposition leaders and dissidents. Milošević's promotion strategy was based on the political, institutional and protocol advantages of his function and on the precise timing of rare public appearances that gave each of his appearances the impression of special significance (Slavujević 2017, 85–87). On the other hand, as a former employee of a PR agency, the current president has done a lot to modernize the promotion of the former party and the party he now heads. Vučić, with the advantages of the prime minister's and presidential functions, has monopolized the communication of his institutions by announcing their activities, evaluating them and speaking all the time on their behalf and for his own account (Slavujević 2017, 203). This has been accompanied by a new style of communication, emotionally very charged and populist. Vučić expresses empathy with the people and workers, promotes himself as a determined fighter against corruption, a fighter for media freedom, etc. Both Milosevic's and Vucić's public relations had become the "spirit" of their party organizations and were passed on to other members of the party leadership. However, unlike Milošević, whose shortcomings in communication with the public were not compensated by the inclusion of other party leaders in it (Slavujević 2017, 85), Vučić's personal engagement in everyday communication with the public acts at the level of personal example as a propaganda form, that is, an intention to influence the attitudes and behavior of party colleagues. This is especially pronounced in the above-mentioned communication through social networks. It is difficult to assess how Milosevic would have communicated in the age of modern communication technologies, but the general characteristics of his communication with the public do not provide grounds for concluding that his personal example would have been a stimulus for significant engagement of party activists in this field.

The current opposition to Vučić, which is marginalized in public, failed to get the support of the West, unlike the opposition to Milošević. The EU's and the United States' attitudes seem to be central to answering the question of why the boycott by the opposition parties had failed to generate a mass following. Their messages as far as the boycott was concerned were unambiguous and clear – the EU and the US do not support the boycott of the elections. The lack of Western support is a significant, though not the only, difference in relation to the boycotts of the opposition against Milošević through 1990s. The opposition opts for a boycott as a form of political action in a society that is significantly apathetic, in which the citizens' distrust of politics and politicians is noticeable. The problem with the opposition's boycott strategy in Serbia, however, is that the citizens who do not support the regime of Aleksandar Vučić do not trust opposition politicians either (Vučićević and Jović 2020).[8] On the one hand, it is a consequence of the continuous negative campaign led against them *via* almost all communication channels. On the other hand, the opposition bloc Alliance for Serbia (SzS) was an alliance of ideologically different parties and movements that could not even agree on practical issues such as whether to participate in the elections or boycott them.

An additional difference from the protests against Milošević, notwithstanding the same demands of free and fair elections, was the regime's response. Unlike in the 1990s, when the regime often responded to protests with repressions, by using the police to break up the demonstrations, Vučić has opted for removing the police from the streets and leaving the citizens to walk freely through Serbian cities. Repression was replaced by media manipulation. Protest organizers from the ranks of nonpolitical actors and public figures who were connected with opposition politicians found themselves dragged through media slander campaigns. After some of them had withdrawn and the opposition leaders had "taken over" the protest, the demands for free and fair elections and the threat of a boycott in the media were regularly presented as attempts by the fascist opposition to come to power "by lynching, rape and violence" even though they had no program and the people did not want them. Simultaneously with the creation of a violent narrative about the opposition in the center of the public sphere, organized activity on social networks took place. SNS internet teams received instructions and tasks through the Castle bot platform on when and how to attack the opposition politicians, as well as other public figures. These tweets would later be broadcast on prime-time news and talk shows. Information about the "bot "activitiesincluding the names of the people within the teams, most of whom had been employed in the public sector and engaged in those activities during the working hours, were posted on Twitter by @XudRobin, a member of the team of developers who had entered the SNS Castle system and monitored the ruling party's online operations for two years (Milivojević 2020).

Successful defamation of the protests in the public put the organizers in an awkward position and caused uncertainty as to whether the protests should be radicalized or not. Short-term radicalization, the invasion of the public broadcasting service building and the blockade of the presidency building were used by the media against the opposition. When the protests stopped, in the summer of 2019, and the opposition declared a boycott of the elections, additional internet teams were formed, which had the online task of making the act of boycott meaningless for the undecided and opposition voters. Stopping the protests and indecisiveness regarding the boycott strategy and its effects have not only disoriented the citizens, but also some local and regional opposition leaders who then decided to participate in the elections. In the short time since its constitution, the opposition movement, which had always faced media blockade and negative publicity, has failed to develop communication with the general public. Unrealistic assessment of the mood of the citizens, lack of Western support, lack of a clear strategy of political struggle, lack of consensus on the boycott, reliance on the Internet and social networks as the only channel of communication with the citizens, a low-intensity field campaign due to the pandemic and a strong counter-campaign of the government led to the opposition losing the battle in terms of political communication before the scheduled elections in early 2020.[9] Diversity at the level of value orientation of key parties and movements that participated in the boycott and drawing citizens' attention to the images of their leaders as a key offer in this campaign, contributed, in terms of communication, to the fragmentation of the periphery of the public sphere. It was reduced to several like-minded audiences that were supposed to fight, on a symbolic level, with the government's propaganda machine. Their symbolically diverse communication practices, simply, could not contribute to the aggregation of public opinion, which, on the other hand, contributed to the failure of the campaign.

In the end the government "crowned" their victory by lowering the electoral threshold for entering the parliament from 5% to 3% (Vučićević 2020), by involving part of the opposition parties in the election race, and even by creating electoral lists of individuals from different parties (i.e., the United Democratic Serbia (UDS) list had representatives from 14 organizations).

Serbian 2020 General Election Campaign: Campaign Without the Basic Function

On March 4, parliamentary elections were scheduled for April 26. However, just 11 days after the elections were scheduled, due to the outbreak of the Covid-19 epidemic and the imposition of a state of emergency, the election campaigns were suspended. After the end of the state of emergency, the election process continued, a new election date was scheduled (June 21), but the rules on collecting signatures had been changed. Public opinion polls in 2019 showed that, without the parties that declared the boycott, only two ruling parties – SNS and SPS – would cross the old electoral threshold. However, the lowering of the electoral threshold and the "liberalization" of the candidacy process led to the fact that as many as 21 electoral lists participated in the elections. Many of them were accused by the public of representing only SNS satellites in order to create the illusion of pluralism and increase the election offer. In addition, the introduction of a state of emergency and a curfew enabled the regime representatives to occupy communication channels to an even greater extent. During the state of emergency, in extended prime time (4:30 pm until midnight), 91% of the national media reports were about the state and government officials. Reports were biased in favor of the officials, while those who had decided to boycott the election had little airtime (4%) and were treated in negatively (Nedeljkov 2020). It is therefore not surprising that the support for the regime has grown further since the state of emergency ended.[10]

Shortly after the declaration of the state of emergency, the representatives of the authorities, with their persuasive activities, in the changed thematic framework, complemented the campaign they had led during 2018 and 2019. In a situation where the measures of the authorities in the fight against the virus had received great media publicity, the behavior of the president of the country, also the holder of the electoral list which was announced under number 1 at the beginning of the official campaign, has been completely determined by the logic of political promotion. The principle of personalization of politics, as one of the key principles of political persuasion, was taken to the extreme. Coping with complex social change had been reduced to virtues as elements of the image of the leading man in the country in whose actions numerous persuasive techniques could easily be identified – from personal example as a form of POTD (propaganda of the deed), through propaganda of transfer and repetition of messages to even shocking the audience.[11] Audience segmentation in the campaign was precise. Vučić meticulously adapts the messages to the characteristics of the target groups, and especially to the pensioners as the most endangered category of the population but also as a very large target group in the electorate. The publicity that the government had received in performing its function in the state of emergency activated a whole set of psychological mechanisms of individuals – identification, mechanisms of causal and social attribution, stereotyping, etc. Identification with the community embodied in the leader was provoked. For the sake of identification with the community perceived as "we", the essential ones are "they" – others, different ones. These are representatives of the opposition parties who had announced a boycott and criticized the severity of the measures taken by the government.[12]

This simplification of the image of the world, which comes down to the polarization of "good-bad", in a period of uncertainty and fear, was a subtext in which the campaign that had begun with the proclamation of victory over the virus would continue. In choosing the main themes of the campaign, in the way of shaping, arguing and placing marketing content, the campaign of the ruling party and the parties gathered around it in the pre-election coalition was a mixture of program and leadership, rational and irrational, constructive and capricious campaigns. Although he addresses human reason and experience, thematizes certain specific issues, sets closer goals, does not deepen ideological divisions in the electorate and insists on national unity, the party leader (and president) remains the dominant element of the election offer.[13] The ruling party, viewed from the standpoint of the psychology of political communication, uses persuasion, provides logically based argumentation, relies on empirical evidence and the so-called soft-sell persuasion, leading the recipient of the message to the appropriate conclusion.[14] However, all election messages are placed in the tone of emotional-affective attitude toward the personality of the party leader and belief in his readiness to lead people to a better life. In an atmosphere of uncertainty and fear in which the elections are taking place, a "reformer", a "savior" and a "firm hand" are being called for, and voters are encouraged to vote "FOR" the incumbent and "AGAINST" the representative of the previous government. Prosperity remains the terminal value on which the ruling coalition's electoral communication is based, just as it has been in all campaigns in Serbia since the establishment of the multi-party system (Slavujević and Atlagić 2015). However, accession to the European Union, in the context of international changes at the time of the COVID-19 pandemic, is not recognized as an instrumental value toward reaching the terminal value; nor is a solution to the Kosovo issue that had almost been forgotten in the course of the campaign. These two issues were the focus of only two minor opposition parties. Other opposition parties addressed other specific topics, such as changes in the form of government, changes in the electoral system, the issue of democracy and minority issues. Simply, in the thematic backbone of the campaign imposed by the ruling party, there was no room for discussion of the two key political problems in Serbian society in the last two decades, so as such the campaign had failed to fully fulfill its basic function.

Gaining voters based on the personal characteristics of the leader could be observed in most forms of promotion used not only by the ruling party, but also by most opposition parties. The names of most of the electoral lists included the names of the party leaders. In the case of the ruling party, this directly affected the emotional component of the voters' attitude. The name of the SNS electoral list "For our children – Aleksandar Vučić" is the result of a pre-election survey according to the results of which citizens see emigration from Serbia as one of the main problems that the society is facing. The intention was for the campaign to show that the president of the country and the leader of the party is capable of tackling this issue in the future (Anonymous2 2020). This basic slogan was varied in the campaign with additions such as "To build the future…" which makes a connection with the name of the campaign from 2018 and 2019 – The Future of Serbia.

When it comes to means and forms of promotion, the election campaign in Serbia was fairly standard. Electoral entities used free forms of promotion, such as representing parties and candidates on the public broadcasting service, and media debates and duels organized by private television stations in addition to the public broadcasting service. They paid for advertisements on the Internet, in the print and electronic media. The ruling party's television adverts made a remarkable difference in the number and quality of production compared to the few TV commercials of the opposition parties.[15] The poster campaign was not particularly intense, nor was the field campaign. Although at the end of the campaign he denied that it was a so-called state marketing or functionary campaign, Aleksandar Vučić had received a lot of publicity in the field, opening factories in the election campaign. Thus, the issue of the functionary campaign remained "the weakest link in the regulation of media behavior in campaigns" (Slavujević 2017, 20).[16]

There were almost no large promotional rallies as the ruling party had made the decision not to hold them, guided by the alleged concern for public health.[17] The campaign, however, did not pass without novelties in terms of promotion. An online rally was held in Serbia for the first time. Two such events were held, organized by the ruling party, *via* Facebook, the Instagram account "Aleksandar Vučić" and the Zoom application. The first of these two events announced the start of the campaign and the second its continuation. The speech was followed by thousands of citizens live, in a conference broadcast. This gathering was organized, to a significant extent, similar to an outdoor gathering – in the form of a spectacle. By showing the strength of the organization, legitimacy and success of the leader and through the presence of the audience, as to demonstrate that the organizer of the gathering and his policy are accepted, the basic function of the election spectacle – idealization of reality – had been realized.

Conclusion

The rule of Aleksandar Vučić to some extent resembles that of Milošević. His leadership is built on authoritarian management of the party and the state, on strict discipline, strong loyalty of associates and on intensive building of the image of a charismatic leader. However, unlike

Milošević, in selling this political offer to the citizens of Serbia, Vučić uses primarily political persuasion. Its effectiveness is based on the significant characteristics of the context in which it takes place. Firstly, Vučić acts in the changed international circumstances and has the tacit support of the West. Secondly, he exploits the weaknesses of the institutional context in Serbia and, in that sense, the structure of the inherited public sphere. Finally, Vučić does not have the personal shortcomings in communication with the public that Milošević had. Unlike Milošević, he is personally interested in political persuasion.

All this was reflected in the 2020 election campaign. This campaign showed that the media issue has not ceased to be an area of political conflict even thirty years after the country's first multi-party elections were held. The election campaign functioned as a "democratic" mechanism for opposing different political options, but it was democratic only from the standpoint of those who had the means of political promotion at their disposal. In addition, in the thematic backbone of the campaign, imposed by the dominant party, there was no room to discuss two political and identity issues – the issue of Kosovo and related European integration issues – on which the strongest rift in Serbian society rests. Bearing in mind that there was neither a plurality of mindsets in the inter-election periodnor the media as impartial information channels in place, and considering the nature of a hybrid regime, the question remains as to whether this was a matter of political marketing or rather a commercialized version of political propaganda. Furthermore, with the development of new ICTs and new means of promotion, the possibilities and effects of propaganda are expanding, which makes hybrid regimes even more resistant to internal pressures for democratization. Not only is the regime capable of closing the center of the public sphere to criticism and critics, but it has also been successful at employing this strategy in the periphery. Unlike Milošević, Vučić has won both the center and the periphery of the public sphere in Serbia. In the latter, primarily through the use of modern information and communication technologies, he prevented the aggregation of opposition opinions and the transformation of opposition ideas into collective action. Thus, the system is maintained not by the use of force but by persuasion.

Hence, the election results are not a big surprise. Apart from a few minority parties, for which an effective threshold applies, only the ruling parties managed to rise above the 3% threshold – two lists gathered around the parties that made up the republican government until 2020 (SNS – around 61% of votes; SPS – around 10.5%) and a new party formed by the president of Serbia's largest municipality, Novi Beograd (SPAS – around 4%). All opposition parties that had violated the boycott agreement and still decided to go to the polls failed to win even 3% of the vote.

Notes

1. One of the authors of the paper was a member of the expert team that led the protest "1 of 5 million" in 2019 and the owner of the research hub Sprint Insight which had contacts with different opposition leaders during that and the following year.
2. The SNS list won 48.35% of the votes and 63.2% of the seats, while only two lists from the ranks of politicians who participated in the government in the period 2000–2012 passed the 5% threshold (6.03% and 5.70%).
3. The SNS list won 48.25% of the votes and 52.4% of the mandate, the coalition partner SPS 10.95% of the votes, but five more lists managed to cross the 5% threshold.
4. Aleksandar Vučić won 55.06% of the votes, while the second-placed candidate and former Protector of Citizens Janković had 16.35%.
5. At the international level, concessions in the negotiations between Belgrade and Priština on the normalization of relations and the signing of the agreement in Brussels, which integrated the remaining Serbian institutions into the legal system of Kosovo, provided support to key international actors. Internally, a broad anti-corruption campaign was launched with lots of publicity, which included the arrests of prominent businessmen and the initiation of court proceedings against ministers and politicians of the former government.
6. Of the five television channels with a national frequency, over time all were brought under control through informal proxy arrangements. At the same time, the ownership transformation of local media, in the process of privatization, enabled their purchase by individuals close to the regime. In so doing, their financing, as well as the financing of all tabloids, is done through public competitions with money provided from the budget.

7. On March 26, 2020 Twitter announced a takedown of accounts targeting Serbian Twitter users. Twitter reported that this network worked steadily to legitimate Vučić's policies and undercut public support for his opponents, including those involved in the "1 of 5 Million" movement. This network was extensive: 8,558 accounts tweeted more than 43 million times (Bush 2020, 4).
8. The opposition is made up of ideologically diverse parties that cannot gather a significant number of supporters. It is not possible to "extract" from such parties the personality of a leader who is able to cover the ideological differences of opposition voters and develop the notion that he is capable of implementing promises (in this case and in others below, the content comes from personal communication with the interviewee for the purposes of writing this paper - Uljarević 2020).
9. In an interview with the leader of the polling and consultancy company Sprint Insight, who had contacts with part of the opposition Alliance for Serbia in the summer of 2019, we were told that a detailed boycott campaign strategy had been devised, aimed primarily at the periphery of the public sphere and youth, that control of its implementation and testing of effects through research and focus groups had been prepared, but the cooperation did not come to fruition (Anonymous1 2020 - The interviewee insisted on anonymity due to his business obligation of secrecy).
10. According to Ipsos Strategic Marketing, in February 2020, half of the citizens claimed that the government did not meet their expectations, while after the end of the state of emergency, the share of dissatisfied people was reduced to 40% (Uljarević 2020).
11. Thus, the President formally manages the Crisis Staff for the Economics, participates in regular press conferences with doctors and in special shows dedicated to the epidemiological situation (in which, among other things, he presents shocking messages about the possible consequences of the epidemic), welcomes help arriving from abroad at the airport (kissing, among other things, the Chinese flag), visits the works on equipping Covid hospitals, etc.
12. This aspect of the campaign was pronounced on social networks. Starting from the knowledge that the previous system of bots had limited effects, since the messages sent in this way were mostly generic and could not enter the ecosystem of opposition voters, a year before the elections in the ruling party, a team was formed whose task was to get to the opposition supporters and start communication there, which is basically neutral. Team members were tasked with asking opposition politicians about policies and plans for which they had no answer. During the state of emergency and epidemic, the team was tasked with defending the doctors who made up the Crisis Staff gathered around President Vučić, but the central task was to question the meaning of the boycott. Team members did this as citizens who were allegedly neutral by repeatedly asking opposition politicians what they would do the day after the boycott, what their plans were and whether the boycott made sense.The goal was to question the used logic and argumentation in order to show its weaknesses (Anonymous2 2020).
13. The campaign emphasized the achieved economic results, but also strengthened the emotional relationship with the leader (Uljarević 2020)
14. Thus, they talk about heroic deeds in extraordinary circumstances, timely and appropriate reaction of the state at the time of the virus, planned state aid for economic recovery, successes of the reform course undertaken in 2012 with the SNS coming to power, large investments in infrastructure, health care systems and military defense of the country and the project Serbia 2020–2025, which plans the highest economic growth in Europe (SNS 2020).
15. These are top production videos, dominated by talking-head adverts in which the party leader directly addresses the audience and slice of life political adverts in which various "ordinary" people, doing everyday work, speak positively about the president and his merits in respect of improving people's lives. It is a combination of transfer technique and personal example as a type of persuasive POTD technique.
16. Despite improvements to these issues resulting from the above-mentioned negotiations between the government and the opposition at the Faculty of Political Sciences in 2019, Article 29 of the Anti-Corruption Law states that a public official may participate in the activities of parties or other political entities if he does not jeopardize the performance of public office and if it is not prohibited by law (paragraph 1) but that he is "obliged to always unambiguously inform his interlocutors and the public whether he expresses the position of the body in which he performs a public function or the position of a political party, i.e. a political subject" (paragraph 4). However, the same article states that the provision of the latter paragraph does not apply to officials elected directly by citizens, i.e. to the President (Minić and Nenadić 2017; Atlagić 2019, 17).
17. The largest promotional gathering was held by the Socialist Party of Serbia (SPS) at the city stadium in the Serbian capital.

ORCID

Dušan Vučićević http://orcid.org/0000-0002-2836-9630
Siniša Atlagić http://orcid.org/0000-0001-5112-3682

References

Anonymous 1. 2020. Interview with the leader of the domestic research hub Sprint Insight by authors. June 21.
Anonymous 2. 2020. Interview with the member of Asaf Eisin's campaign team. June 5.
Antonić, Slobodan. 2016. "Izbori pod sumnjom: Kako je došlo do izbora 2016. i šta se tada zbilo." In *Izbori u Srbiji 2016. godine: Istorijska ili pirova pobeda*, edited by Milan Jovanović and Dušan Vučićević, 9–45. Belgrade: Institut za političke studije.
Atlagić, Siniša. 2019. "Državni marketing u izbornim kampanjama u Srbiji: Kako regulisati medijsko pokrivanje zloupotrebe jacnih resursa." *Kultura Polisa* 40:11–21.
Atlagić, Siniša. 2020. "The Public Sphere and Hybrid Regimes in the Digital Environment: The Case of Contemporary Serbia." In *Digitalne medijske tehnologije i društveno-obrazovne promene 9*, edited by Dejan Pralica and Stefan Janjić, 29–40. Novi Sad: Filozofski fakultet.
Atlagić, Siniša, and Dušan Vučićević. 2019. "Serbia." In *Thirty Years of Political Campaigning in Central and Eastern Europe*, edited by Otto Eibl and Milos Gregor, 325–42. London: Palgrave Macmillan.
Bermeo, Nancy. 2016. "On Democratic Backsliding." *Journal of Democracy* 27 (1):5–19. doi: 10.1353/jod.2016.0012.
Bieber, Florian. 2015. "Ten rules by a 21st-century Machiavelli for the Balkan Prince. "LSE Blogs, February 7, 2015. https://blogs.lse.ac.uk/lsee/2015/02/07/ten-rules-by-a-21st-century-machiavelli-for-the-balkan-prince/.
Bieber, Florian. 2018. "Patterns of Competitive Authoritarianism in the Western Balkans." *East European Politics* 34 (3):337–54. doi: 10.1080/21599165.2018.1490272.
Bieber, Florian. 2020. *The Rise of Authoritarianism in the Western Balkans*. London: Palgrave Macmillan.
Birodi (Biro za društvena istraživanja). 2017. *Mediji, javnost i izbori 2017*. Belgrade: Birodi. http://www.birodi.rs/wp-content/uploads/2017/08/Medijijavnost-izbori-2017.pdf.
Bobin, Jean- Paul. 1988. *La Marketing Politique*. Paris: Milan Midia.
Box-Steffensmeier, Janet M., David Darmofal, and Christian A. Farrel. 2009. "The Aggregate Dynamics of Campaigns." *The Journal of Politics* 71 (1):309–23. doi: 10.1017/S0022381608090208.
Bujošević, Dragan, and Ivan Radovanović. 2003. *The Fall of Milošević: The October 5th Revolution*. New York: Palgrave Macmillan.
Bush, Daniel. 2020. *Fighting Lika a Lion for Serbia: An Analysis of Government-Linked Influence Operations in Serbia*. Stanford: Stanford Internet Observatory.
Campbell, Angus, Philipp Converse, Warren Miller, and Donald Stokes. 1960. *The American Voter*. Chicago: University of Chicago Press.
Carothers, Thomas. 2002. "The End of the Transition Paradigm." *Journal of Democracy* 13 (1):5–21. doi: 10.1353/jod.2002.0003.
Cassani, Andrea, and Luca Tomini. 2018. "Reversing Regimes and Concepts: From Democratization to Autocratization." *European Political Science* 57 (3):687–716.
Coppedge, M. 2017. "Eroding Regimes: What, Where, and When?" Varieties of Democracy (V-Dem). Institute Working Paper No. 57.
CRTA. 2016. *Izveštaj Posmatračke Misije CRTA – Građani na Straži*. Belgrade: CRTA. https://crta.rs/finalni-izvestaj-2016/.
CRTA. 2017. *Izveštaj CRTA posmatračke misije – građani na straži*. Belgrade: CRTA. https://crta.rs/predsednicki-izbori-2017-finalni-izvestaj-sazetak-i-preporuke/.
Dolenec, Danijela. 2013. *Democratic Institutions and Authoritarian Rule in Southeast Europe*. Colchester: ECPR Press.
Freedom House. 2020. Freedom in the World 2020. https://freedomhouse.org/report/freedom-world/2020/leaderless-struggle-democracy.
Gordy, Eric. 2013. *Guilt, Responsibility, and Denial: The Past at Stake in post-Milošević Serbia*. Philadelphia: University of Pennsylvania Press.
Greene, Kenneth. 2019. "Dealigning Campaign Effects in Argentina in Comparative Perspective." In *Campaigns and Voters in Developing Democracies: Argentina in Comparative Perspective*, edited by Noam Lupu, Virginia Oliveros and Luis Schiumerini, 162–86. Ann Arbor: University of Michigan Press.

Günay, Cengiz, and Vedran Dzihic. 2016. "Decoding the Authoritarian Code: exercising 'Legitimate' Power Politics through the Ruling Parties in Turkey, Macedonia and Serbia." *Southeast European and Black Sea Studies* 16 (4): 529–49. doi: 10.1080/14683857.2016.1242872.

Habermas, Jürgen. 1988. *Nachmetaphisisches. Philosophische Aufsätze*. Frankfurt am Main: Suhrkamp.

Jacobson, Gary C. 2015. "How Do Campaigns Matter?" *Annual Review of Political Science* 18 (1):31–47. doi: 10.1146/annurev-polisci-072012-113556.

Kaid, Lynda Lee, and Christina Holtz-Bacha. 1995. *Political Advertizing in Western Democracies: Parties and Candidates on Television*. London: Sage.

Keil, Soeren. 2018. "The Business of State Capture and the Rise of Authoritarianism in Kosovo, Macedonia, Montenegro and Serbia." *Southeastern Europe* 42 (1):59–82. doi: 10.1163/18763332-04201004.

Lasswell, Harold D. 1971. *Propaganda Technique in the World War*. The M.I.T. Press.

Lazarsfeld, Paul, Bernard Berelson, and Hazel Gaudet. 1948. *The People's Choice: How the Voter Makes up His Mind in a Presidential Campaign*. 2nd ed. New York: Columbia University Press.

Levitsky, Steven, and Lucan Way. 2010. *Competitive Authoritarianism: Hybrid Regimes after the Cold War*. New York: Cambridge University Press.

Levitsky, Steven, and Daniel Ziblatt. 2018. *How Democracies Die*. London: Penguin Books.

Listhaug, Ola, Sabrina P. Ramet and Dragana Dulić, eds. 2011. *Civic and uncivic values: Serbia in thepost-Milošević era*. Budapest: CEU Press.

Louw, Eric. 2010. *The Media and Political Process*. 2nd ed. London: Sage.

Luhrmann, Anna, Valeriya Mechkova, Sirianne Dahlum, Laura Maxwell, Moa Olin, Constanza Sanhueza Petrarca, Rachel Sigman, Matthew C. Wilson, and Staffan I. Lindberg. 2018. "State of the World 2017: Autocratization and Exclusion?" *Democratization* 25 (8):1321–40. doi: 10.1080/13510347.2018.1479693.

Lührmann, Anna, and Staffan I. Lindberg. 2019. "A Third Wave of Autocratization is Here: What is New about It?" *Democratization* 26 (7):1095–113. doi: 10.1080/13510347.2019.1582029.

Малинова, Ольга Юрьевна. 2013. *Конструирование смыслов: Исследование символической политики в современной России*. Moscow: ИНИОН РАН.

Matić, Jovanka. 2007. *Televizija protiv birača: Televizijska prezentacija izbornih kampanja za parlamentarne izbore u srbiji 1990-2000*. Belgrade: Dobar naslov.

Milivojević, Anđela. 2020. "The Castle: How Serbia's Rulers Manipulate Minds and the People Pay." BalkanInsight, June 18, 2020. https://balkaninsight.com/2020/06/18/the-castle-how-serbias-rulers-manipulate-minds-and-the-people-pay/.

Minić, Zlatko, and Nemanja Nenadić. 2017. *Funkcionerska kampanja kao vid zloupotrebe javnih resursa – opis problema i moguća rešenja 2012-2017*. Beograd: Transparentnost Srbija.

Nedeljkov, Raša. 2020. "Election campaigning by state officials typical for Serbia, CRTA says." N1, May 27, 2020. http://rs.n1info.com/English/NEWS/a603956/Election-campaigning-by-officials-in-Serbia.html.

Ninković Slavnić, Danka. 2016. "Publika digitalnih medija: Informisanje na internetu." PhD diss., University of Belgrade.

O'Donnel, Guillermo. 1994. "Delegative Democracy." *Journal of Democracy* 5 (1):55–69.

OSCE/ODIHR. 2017. *Election Assessment Mission Report on Presidential Elections in the Republic of Serbia on 2 April 2017*. Warsaw: OSCE/ODIHR. http://www.osce.org/odihr/elections/serbia/322166?download=true.

Pavlović, Dušan. 2019. "The Political Economy behind the Gradual Demise of Democratic Institutions in Serbia." *Southeast European and Black Sea Studies* 20 (1):19–39. doi: 10.1080/14683857.2019.1672929.

Pérez-Liñán, Anibal, and David Altman. 2017. "Explaining the Erosion of Democracy: Can Economic Growth Hinder Democracy?" Varieties of Democracy (V-Dem) Institute Working Paper No. 42.

Richter, Solveig, and Natasha Wunsch. 2019. "Money, Power, Glory: The Linkages between EU Conditionality and State Capture in the Western Balkans." *Journal of European Public Policy* 27 (1):41–62. doi: 10.1080/13501763.2019.1578815.

Scammell, Margaret. 1995. *Designer Politics – How Elections are Won*. New York: St. Martin's.

Schedler, Andreas. 2002. "The Nested Game of Democratization by Elections." *International Political Science Review* 23 (1):103–22. doi: 10.1177/0192512102023001006.

Slavujević, Zoran. 2009. *Političko komuniciranje, politička propaganda, politički marketing*. Belgrade: Grafocard.

Slavujević, Zoran, and Siniša Atlagić. 2015. *Vreme neispunjenih obećanja: Teme u izbornim kampanjama u Srbiji 1990-2014*. Belgrade: Dobar naslov.

Slavujević, Zoran. 2017. *Pohodi na birače u ime države i naroda: Izborne kampanje u Srbiji od 1990 do 2016 godine*. Belgrade: Fakultet političkih nauka.

SNS. 2020. "Serbian Progressive Party election brochure." Accessed June 22, 2020. https://www.sns.org.rs/brosuraSrbija2025.pdf.

Strömbäck, Jesper. 2017. "News Seekers, News Avoiders, and the Mobilizing Effects of Election Campaigns: Comparing Election Campaigns for the National and the European Parliaments." *International Journal of Communication* 11:237–58.

Tomini, Luca, and Claudius Wagemann. 2018. "Varieties of Contemporary Democratic Breakdown and Regression: A Comparative Analysis." *European Journal of Political Research* 57 (3):687–716. doi: 10.1111/1475-6765.12244.

Uljarević, Marko. 2020. (Ipsos Strategic Marketing Serbia, public opinion polls director), in discussion with author. July 1 2020.

V-Dem. 2019. *Democracy Facing Global Challenges: V-Dem Annual Democracy Report 2019*. Gothenburg: V-Dem Institute.
Vladisavljević, Nebojša. 2016. "Competitive Authoritarianism and Popular Protest: Evidence from Serbia under Milošević." *International Political Science Review* 37 (1):36–50. doi: 10.1177/0192512114535450.
Vladisavljević, Nebojša. 2019a. "Media Discourse and the Quality of Democracy in Serbia after Milošević." *Europe-Asia Studies* 72 (1):8–32. doi: 10.1080/09668136.2019.1669534.
Vladisavljević, Nebojša. 2019b. *Uspon i Pad Demokratije Posle Petog Oktobra*. Belgrade: Arhipelag.
Vučićević, Dušan. 2010. "Demokratizacija Kroz Izbore: izborni Autoritarizam u Srbiji." *Politička Revija* 26 (4):1–28. doi: 10.22182/pr.2642010.1.
Vučićević, Dušan. 2020. "Reforma izbornog sistema Srbije: od „nema izmena u izbornoj godini" do „menjamo radi jačanja demokratije" u samo nekoliko meseci." Paper presented at the "Dialogue on 2020 Elections" Conference, Belgrade, June 12.
Vučićević, Dušan, and Nikola Jović. 2020. *Youth Emigration and Political Distrust in Serbia*. Belgrade: Westminster Foundation for Democracy. https://www.wfd.org/wp-content/uploads/2020/05/WFD-Serbia-Research-Survey-and-analysis-Youth-emigration-and-Political-Distrust-2020.pdf.
Waldner, David, and Ellen Lust. 2018. "Unwelcome Change: Coming to Terms with Democratic Backsliding." *Annual Review of Political Science* 21 (1):93–113. doi: 10.1146/annurev-polisci-050517-114628.

Index

Page numbers in **bold** refer to tables and those in *italic* refer to figures.

Alliance for Serbia (SzS) 99
Americanization 28
Armannsdottir, G. 13
audiovisual political advertising: 2015 and 2019 parliamentary elections **35**, *36*; exposure of leader in spots *37*; formal-symbolic and substantive dimensions 37; issues of **36**; strategic centralized personalization 35; strategic personalization 37

Baldini, Gianfranco 46, 54
Barišic, Branimir 49
Bruhn, Kathleen 61

campaign materials 1
campaign professionalization 9, 11
Carnell, S. 13
case of PAN in Mexico 60–2
celebritization 4
celebrity activists 45
celebrity diplomats 45
celebrity politicians 45–6, *47*
celebrity politics 45
celebrity populism 46–7, *47*; celebritization of politics 44; defined 43; methodology and research design 50–1
celebrity populists 44, 47
Central and Eastern Europe (CEE) 1; party communication under semi-authoritarian rule 5–6; political communication 4–5
Civic Platform 32, **34**
Communist Party of the Russian Federation (CPRF) 58–9, 62–3
competitive authoritarianism 94–7
consumption politics 8
convinced ideologists 4
Cooper, Andrew F. 47
coopted opposition, authoritarian regime 60
Corbett, Jack 46
Corner, John 45
Croatia: Croatian party system 48; HDZ and SDP 48; Živi zid 48; populist campaigning 48–50
Croatian Democratic Union 48

dealignment process 29
Democratic Left Alliance 32–3, **34**

digital media 49–50
digital technology 44–5
dominated cartel party system 63–4
door-to-door activities 17, 20
Driessens, Oliver 45, 46

Edelson, Laura 81
election campaign professionalization development: centralization, duration and professionals 14–18; informants 13–14; voting results 14
The 2015 Election in Irkutsk 65–6
electoral authoritarian regime 60
Enli, Gunn 46
European Commission-assisted Code of Practice on Online Disinformation (CoP) 77, 89
European Parliament (EP) election 75
European Regulators Group for Audiovisual Media Service (ERGA) 89
everyday celebrity politician 46
external professionalization 11

Facebook: ad spending **86**, *87*; advertiser pages, EP 2019 election **83**, *84*; data 82; force restructuring 79–80; formal/informal party affiliation *85*; individual politicians' political position *85*; normalization-equalization hypotheses 85; political leaning *84*; public expenditure *87*; stealth media 80–2; variables 82–3
face of a campaign 37
famed nonpoliticos 45
Farell, David M. 30
first-age campaigns 9–10
Flanagan, Tom 60
Flinders, Matthew 46
floating system 62
follower mentality 3
fourth-age professionalized campaigns **22**, 22–3
Frangonikolopoulos, Christos A. 52
Freedom House Economist Intelligence Unit 1
Freedom House Institute 95
functionary campaign/state marketing 99
"Future of Serbia", Vucic's campaign 98–9

Gapšys, V. 16
Giglioli, Matteo 46, 54

Gillingham, Paul 61
Grusell, Marie 10
Gudelis, D. 18

Hager, Anselm 75–6
Haggard, S. 1
Hart, Paul 't 47
Homeland Union—Lithuanian Christian Democrats 15, 20
Homolar, Alexandra 44
Huliaras, Asteris 52
Hungarian Plebiscitary Leader Democracy (PLD) 88
Hutcheson, Derek 63

individual-centered campaign 10
informants/politicians 13
internal professionalization 11
Ishiyama, John 60

Janda, Kenneth 60

Kara-Murza, Vladimir 66
Katz, Richard 63
Kaufman, R. 1
Kim, Young Mie 80, 81
Kiousis, Spiro 10
Kolakušic, Mislav 51–2
Körösényi, András 75, 78

Labor Party 20
Langston, Joy 58
Lapinskas, M. 16, 18
Law and Justice party's media strategy 32, **34**
leaflet distribution 17
Lees-Marshment, Jennifer 8
legacies 45
Levy, Daniel 61
Liberal and Center Union 20
liberation technology 79
Lilleker, Darren G. 8
Lithuanian election campaigns: budgets and political advertising 20–2, *21*, **21**; characteristics 12; fourth-age professionalized campaigns **22**, 22–3; individual-centered 10; marketing orientation, contemporary 18–20; methodology 13; modern political campaigns 10; parliamentary elections 12–13; postmodern/third-age campaign 10; premodern/first-age campaigns 9–10; styles of 9; *see also* election campaign professionalization development

Mair, Peter 63
Mancini, Paolo 10
March, Luke 63
Marland, Alex 60
Marshall, David 44–6
Marshall, Michael 60
Marsh, David 47
Matthew, Wood 46
Mazuronis, V. 17
Mazzoleni, Gianpietro 44

McAllister, Ian 63
mediatization 4
modernization 28
modern political campaigns 10
Morgenstern, Scott 58
municipal filter 65

National Action Party's (PAN) evolution 59
national politicians and mayoral candidates 80
Nord, Lars 10
Nozhikov, Yuri 66

oppositional actors 79
opposition candidates and parties 2
Orbán-regime 78
Order and Justice 20
Orman, John M. 45

Pagojus, A. 17
Panov, Petr 64
parties/electoral committees, parliamentary campaigns **33**
party branding 59–60
party communication 5–6
party system development 32
Pels, Dick 45
Pernar, Ivan (reality TV populist) 52
personal communication 19
personalization 4, 48
Pich, Christopher 13
Plebiscitary Leader Democracy (PLD) 75
Požela, J. 17
Poland 31–5
Polish People's Party 34
political actors 74
political advertising on Facebook 75–7
political agitation 17
political campaign organization 9–12
political celebrities 47
political communication 4–5
"political grey zone" category 94
political marketing: campaign professionalization 9; defined 8; *see also* Lithuanian election campaigns
political newsworthies 45
political outsiders 47
political pluralism 32
political propaganda 94
politician celebrities 45–6
Polity Project 1
pollsters and marketers 2–3
populism 44–5
populist campaigning 48–50
populist celebrities 44, 47
populist communication 44–5
post-socialist axiological gap 32
pro-Catholic politicians 61
professionalization 28, 29
pro-government actors 79
proportional electoral system 32
psychological coercion 94
public opinion polls 20

rebranding 59–60
regime and party system 62–5
Reuter, Ora J. 63
Ross, Cameron 60, 61, 64

Sakwa, Richard 63, 66
Scammell, Margaret 59
Schedler, Andreas 61, 69
Schneiker, Andrea 46
Scholz, Ronny 44
Seimas, unicameral parliament 12
Serbian 2020 General Election Campaign 100–2
Serbian Progressive Party (SNS) 95
Sharafutdinova, Gulnaz 66
Silva, Márcio 81
single mandate districts (SMD) 15
Škoro, Miroslav (people's president) 43, 48, 52–3
Social Democratic Party 15, 20, 48
Socialist Party of Serbia (SPS) 95
social media advertising 77–8
Solidarity Electoral Action 32
spot content analysis 42
State Audit Office 78
stealth media 80–2
strategic personalization 31
Street, John 45, 46
Strömbäck, Jesper 10, 29
superhero anti-politician celebrity 46

superstar celebrity politician 46
Swanson, David L. 10

tactical populist 3
techlash 74, 77, 80
't Hart, Paul 45
third-age campaigns 10
Tindall, Karen 45, 47
traditional politicians 3
Tsaliki, Liza 52
2018 Presidential Election 67
2018 Regional Elections, Khakassia and Primorskii Krai 67–9
2005 parliamentary elections 32

van Zoonen, Liesbet 51
V-Dem Institute 1, 95
Vukovic, Silvija 49
Vyšniauskas, A. 19

Waisboard, Silvio 46
Weberian Plebiscitary Leader Democracy (PLD) 78
West, Darrell M. 45
Wheeler, Mark 47
Wirz, Dominique S. 46

Zebadua, Emilio 61
Zelensky, Volodymyr 43